About the author

Sᴠᴇɴ Hᴀʀᴛᴇɴ holds a Ph.D. in Government from the London School of Economics. He has done extensive fieldwork in Bolivia, and currently works as Monitoring and Evaluation Officer for the World Bank–IFC in Lima, Peru.

The Rise of Evo Morales and the MAS

SVEN HARTEN

ZED BOOKS

London & New York

The Rise of Evo Morales and the MAS was first published in 2011
by Zed Books Ltd, 7 Cynthia Street, London N1 9JF, UK and
Room 400, 175 Fifth Avenue, New York, NY 10010, USA

www.zedbooks.co.uk

Copyright © Sven Harten 2011

The right of Sven Harten to be identified as the author
of this work has been asserted by him in accordance with
the Copyright, Designs and Patents Act, 1988

FSC
www.fsc.org
MIX
Paper from
responsible sources
FSC® C013604

Designed and typeset in Monotype Bulmer
by illuminati, Grosmont
Index by John Barker
Cover designed by www.alice-marwick.co.uk
Printed and bound in Great Britain by
CPI Antony Rowe, Chippenham and Eastbourne

Distributed in the USA exclusively by Palgrave Macmillan, a division of St
Martin's Press, LLC, 175 Fifth Avenue, New York, NY 10010, USA

A catalogue record for this book is available from the British Library
Library of Congress Cataloging in Publication Data available

ISBN 978 1 84813 523 9 hb
ISBN 978 1 84813 524 6 pb

Contents

Acknowledgements

I would like to thank above all my lovely wife Ellen Blommaert for making this book possible, not only by taking over so many things and allowing me to shut myself away to write, but more importantly as the person who introduced me to key contacts in Bolivia. Her charming way of asking the most difficult questions helped me out on many occasions, and her critical reading was essential to the completion of what I believe is an interesting and persuasive book. However, while working on this book, something much more important happened: you were born, Layra! Thank you for being there and I'm sorry for the many times I had to work instead of play with you. Perhaps one day you will read this and conclude that not all that time was wasted.

The research for this book would not have been possible without the collaboration of Oscar Coca Antezana, who was the perfect gatekeeper to introduce us to the coca producers' movement and to the Movimiento Al Socialismo. Thank you for the trust you had in us and in our work. I am thankful to Francisco Panizza for his support and stimulating observations. Many thanks to Ken Barlow for his patience, his careful reading and the useful comments that added so much to the manuscript, to Lucy Morton and to Robin Gable for great attention to detail and helpful suggestions. Many thanks go to my parents, parents-in-law and friends for always supporting me, and to Gill Lowther for reading the manuscript. I gratefully acknowledge the support of the Economic and Social Research Council (ESRC) for funding much of my research. Last but not least, I am grateful to lecturers and peers at the London School of Economics and the Essex Summer School in Discourse Analysis for intellectual stimulation and good advice. All opinions and arguments expressed in the book are entirely my own, and should not be taken to represent the official policy of the IFC or the World Bank.

To Oscar Panozo,
nuestro ahijado in San Isidro

and

To my mother,
who would have loved to have read this

A Journey

Dawn is breaking. Though it's still dark, we can see the sky clearing above the roofs on the other side of the little square. Cochabamba is awakening from its sleep. The air is crisp and clear, and it is freezing cold. Although I know the city, it is difficult to imagine that within a couple of hours it will be hot, the sun burning in the sky with that high-altitude intensity; the air will be full of dust and vehicle exhaust, and the city sprawling with life. But now, at 5.45 a.m., this all seems far away and I marvel at this almost surreal atmosphere. I am wondering whether it is worth getting out of bed so early without my vital morning coffee. Will Evo keep his promise or will he change his mind and give others priority?

My wife Ellen and I stand in front of the joint headquarters of the Six Federations of the Tropic of Cochabamba – the social movement of the coca growers. The *federaciónes* are the political and social home of Evo Morales; thanks to mutual support both have grown to national political prominence. Within a few weeks of this cold November morning in 2005, both will be in the international spotlight when more than 50 per cent of Bolivians will have given their vote to 'Evo Presidente' and the Movimiento Al Socialismo (MAS). Today is another important day in the campaign of Morales, because the *federaciónes* have planned an *Ampliado*, a large plenary meeting of the social movement. Yesterday, I interviewed Morales in the headquarters of the *federaciónes* and he promised to take us with him to the *Ampliado* in Lauca Eñe. 'We will leave at 6 a.m. *en punto*', he said. Given the six or seven important-looking people waiting patiently, his presence here today seems likely. But will he really take us with him? Will there be enough cars?

6 a.m. Still no Evo in sight and I feel that our chances are lessening as time goes by and more people arrive. Among them are two Americans, a photographer and a journalist – from the *New York Times* I later find out. Clearly, if Morales has to make a choice, we will not be able to compete with them. I cannot help but feel a little envy: after spending so much time in Bolivia, living among the coca growers and covering both the 2002 and 2005 campaigns of MAS, we may understand Morales and the Movimiento better but we cannot give him the publicity that an interview with the *New York Times* promises. I try some smalltalk with the journalists, but even after telling them that I am a researcher and also that I know what the plan is for the day, they remain more tight-lipped than might be expected expect for their profession.

6.30 a.m. It is light now, and around twenty people have assembled before the half-finished building – of the four floors, only the first two have windows, the upper two being still under construction. (In Bolivia, as in many developing countries, it is common to start building, stop when the money runs out, and then add additional floors once the extra resources are found.) Our conversations with the other bystanders were more successful. We learned that some were planning to accompany Morales to the Tropic of Cochabamba. Most of these were leaders of social movements, including the coca growers, but also from other parts of the country. Others hoped to talk briefly with Morales before his departure.

Finally three cars arrive, among them two Mitsubishi Pajero four-wheel drives: a new white four-door version and an older black two-door model. Both belong to Morales; the word being that the black one was his first car, bought with some of the money from an alternative peace prize awarded to him personally by European NGOs. It is said that Morales donated the rest of the money to the coca growers' movement.

At around 8 a.m., after what seemed an endless period of uncertainty, we finally leave for the *Trópico*. Morales had clearly remembered to whom he had promised the trip and to whom not. Emerging from the building, where he had been meeting two professors of Cochabamba's San Simon University who were advising him on his campaign, he nodded in a friendly manner to Ellen and me. We did not secure a place in his car – this honour was for the journalist – but sat rather in the back of his old Pajero, while the photographer travelled in the third car, a white Toyota Corolla sedan. We stopped for an early lunch break on the road at a trout farm/restaurant, to which all of us were invited by Morales. I suspect that Morales needn't have paid for the meal, as Morales was a loyal customer and the owner could reasonably expect to be rewarded in the case of his election. However, eschewing this practice, common in Bolivia, Morales personally paid for all of us; a bill that included six 2-litre bottles of Coca-Cola he had ordered, somewhat to the embarrassment of one of his advisers, which promptly found their way into one of the pictures taken by the *New York Times* photographer. To our surprise, we found ourselves in Morales's car for the second half of the trip: he was driving, the journalist beside him, and we, together with four advisers/aides, in the back of the car. Morales explained that he likes to drive but that he seldom had the opportunity to do so since much of his time went into travelling to meetings and interviews.

Far too soon we arrived in Lauca Eñe, a village in the Tropic of Cochabamba, between the large, semi-urbanized settlements of Shinahota and Chimoré, where the *federaciónes* built a half-open hall that serves to hold their *Ampliados* but that also functions as a football and basketball pitch. Here a crowd of several hundred people – all members of the local branches of the coca growers' movement, who had been attending the meeting since the morning

– eagerly awaited the arrival of Morales. The *Ampliados* are central both to the functioning of MAS and to its political communication. In the early days of the coca growers' political activism, the *Ampliados* were the place where the most important decisions of MAS (and its predecessor) were collectively taken. The *Ampliados* were also a stage on which political leaders emerged, and indeed a stage that turned leaders of social movements into leaders of a broader political movement. The *Ampliados* do not actually make the decisions of the MAS government, but act as a form of social ratification of policies, and as means of direct communication between Evo Morales and the grassroots. They thus cement the image of MAS as a very different political party, or better as a distinct political *movement* (the standing of political parties has fallen into disrepute in recent times, so now none of the major parties dares describe itself as such).

I have chosen to begin by retelling this episode, because it raises a number of issues that are central to this book. This brief narrative of a journey between the (provisional) MAS headquarters in Cochabamba and the meeting hall of the social movements in the rural Tropic of Cochabamba stands as an allegory for the bridge Morales was able to build between the extra-institutional, social movement politics on the streets and the official arena of political parties. It stands also for his strategy of maintaining close links with rural areas even as Bolivia's president, whose political life inevitably is played out for the most part in cities.

But fundamentally it prefigures a much bigger, and personal, journey: that of Morales from herdsman to social movement leader to president. My aim in the book is to help us understand the personality of Evo Morales, who like no other leader manages to stand with one foot inside official institutions and the other outside in the world of social movements. He has achieved this through, among other things, very hard work. The rhythm of the day described above, with the first meeting at 6 a.m. and the last past midnight, has been that of Morales's life for many years, before and since his election. It also shows that Morales seldom takes decisions entirely alone – he is usually surrounded by advisers whom he trusts, and he feels the pulse of his ideas among ordinary Bolivians as well as foreigners. For all his – at times – radical discourse, his actions are not always so: he is neither a hard-core anti-globalist nor a Marxist; he enjoys drinking Coca-Cola and driving his 4x4. This does not mean, however, that as an individual and as a leader he lacks coherence. Indeed I will show that there is a common logic in what he does and says, and that this logic deserves a more careful analysis than what is usually offered in descriptions of Morales as radical left-wing populist.

To understand Morales with a degree of empathy while maintaining a critical distance is hence the aim of this book. However, in contrast to, for instance, Hugo Chávez, Evo Morales cannot be understood without the social movement – the coca growers – within which he developed his political career. This book is therefore not a biography of Evo Morales. For such would not, in my opinion, be able to shed sufficient light on one of the most interesting political figures of the new millennium. Instead, it tells the story of Morales largely through the history of the social movement and of its *instrumento político* (political instrument), the Movimiento Al Socialismo – known as MAS. In this sense, the book recounts not only Morales's journey but also the closely linked journey of MAS from its role as the 'instrument' of a social movement to being Bolivia's largest political party, and indeed that of the country as a whole from a period of democratic consolidation, through a long and deep political crisis, into an epoch of dramatic political reforms initiated by the MAS government.

So, why a book about a president of a small, landlocked, poor Latin American country? One reason is that, in 2010, Bolivia is seen by some as an economic success story: low inflation, a growth rate among the highest in the region, large external reserves and an account surplus (IMF, 2010). Behind this, according to Finance Minister Luis Arce, is the new economic model of 'Andean Capitalism' or 'Evonomics', which is based upon a sound macroeconomic framework but nevertheless distinct from the recipes prescribed by the IMF. In a way, Bolivia has come full circle: from worst-case scenario with hyperinflation, to the best practitioner of orthodox structural adjustment, to the ostensible model for a third way to achieve economic growth. A similar trend can be observed in the political sphere: Bolivia was regarded in the 1990s as a success story of democratization after some twenty years of military dictatorship. Yet, after 2000 the country experienced several waves of popular protest, culminating in the resignation of two democratically elected presidents in 2003 and 2005. The widespread protests prompted commentators to warn against a downward spiral that could erase all democratic progress and ultimately bring about a new epoch of military rule. In addition, the Movimiento Al Socialismo, founded by the coca producers of the Tropic of Cochabamba (in the tradition of *sindicatos*[1]), became politically popular, with a discourse sharply critical of the status quo. With its radical left-wing rhetoric and its roots in an organization that defends the cultivation of coca – a crop that can be used for cocaine production, but that also carries an enormous cultural significance in Bolivia – the rise of MAS was frequently depicted as a threat to democracy: a particularly dangerous mixture of a Bolivian version of the FARC and Hugo Chávez's vision of Venezuela. This image of MAS became widespread in Bolivia's mass media between 2000 and 2005, partly due to the significant financial campaign resources of the mainstream political parties (especially the Movimiento Nacionalista Revolucionario, MNR, Bolivia's most influential party since the 1950s) devoted to blackening MAS's name.

Given these circumstances, MAS surprised even its own leaders by becoming Bolivia's second largest political party in the 2002 elections. Yet this was just a prelude to its historic victory, with 53.7 per cent of the vote, in 2005. The outcome was historic for two reasons: first, in a country plagued by political instability and weak political parties, none of which was able to garner more than a quarter of the votes, it was a big leap for MAS to obtain a majority, the first since Bolivia's return to democracy in 1982. This obviated the need for the much-criticized process of bargaining for the election of the president in Congress by a weak president in exchange for jobs in the public administration. Second, the 2005 elections established the historical precedent of an indigenous leader being elected as president of Bolivia, a country in which the indigenous majority had been marginalized politically since the Spanish conquest. For the first time, indigenous candidates were not mere adornments to bring in extra votes, but came into government with their own 'political instrument', MAS. Contrary to what is sometimes said, Morales is not the first indigenous president to be elected in Latin America; this honour went to Benito Juárez, five times Mexican president between 1858 and 1872. However, Morales is the first *modern* indigenous president. There are, of course, those who dispute that Morales is a *real* indigenous president, on the grounds that he is a mestizo and does not speak Aymara as a native. I consider this argument to be both misguided and wrong: whether or not Morales is a 'pure' Aymara is a delicate question. This question is ethnographically difficult to answer in a country such as Bolivia; but, above all, it is irrelevant because Morales is perceived by most of the population as indigenous. I would also argue that it is irrelevant whether or not his Aymara is fluent, because language is only one aspect of ethnicity, and not always the most important one. As I do not speak the language, I cannot judge how good Morales's Aymara is, although I was present on one of the rare occasions where he used it. In any case, he was brought up in an environment where indigenous people were stigmatized, so there were good reasons for the rising leader of a social movement to speak mainly Spanish. Furthermore, the rise of Evo Morales is much more than a story of personal success; it is also about a social movement establishing itself by means of its 'political instrument', one of Bolivia's most influential parties since the country's return to democracy.

By shedding new light on Morales and his party I provide an explanation of this historical outcome. Basically, I argue that the success of Morales is based on his creation of a new political identity, which positions 'the people' and 'the traditional parties' in two antagonistic camps. By calling for the defence of 'natural resources' and of 'national sovereignty', Morales has been able to unify the differing demands of social movements behind MAS in a general articulation of dissatisfaction with the status quo. In other words, the book will show just how the MAS took root among other sectors of the population, and how Morales managed to win electoral support at the expense of potential competitors. The argument proceeds by analysing how the political identity of 'the people' was constructed, how then a new imagined community of the 'nation of nations' or 'plurinational nation' was built, and finally how Morales has tried since his election to change Bolivia's political institutions and its economic system in order to accommodate this new identity and political community.

The analysis highlights the tension between the *inclusion* of such a diversity of interests and the *exclusion* of an antagonistic other. This tension is a vital impetus in Morales's discourse. It is central to an understanding of the challenges faced by the task of consolidating democratic institutions in Bolivia. Analysing Morales's discourse, and by extension that of MAS, reveals the existence of a populist logic of articulation. Yet this does not present a danger for democracy; rather, populism shows us what democracy in Bolivia is about and what it is lacking.

While one aim is to help develop an understanding of Evo Morales's government, the core of this book is the five-year period running up to his election as Bolivia's president. The reason for this is that during this time the ideological and organizational foundations for the MAS government were laid, and the most significant developments both for Morales and for MAS took place. It marks the culmination of the transition from purely extra-parliamentary opposition to an ambiguous stance that seeks to combine extra-institutional politics with governmental responsibility, a process that is ongoing. In other words, we cannot understand President Morales without understanding how he grew from being a single-issue leader of a social movement into a national political figure capable of attracting the support of a wide range of voters. This is not to underestimate the enormity of the change Bolivia underwent during the first five years of Morales's presidency. Rather, it is to register that, in their broad shape, these policies are the outcome of a history of struggle against exclusion and discrimination, and not the product of ad hoc populist decisions.

I will therefore seek to bring into focus a political process wherein various unmet demands became unified within an oppositional discourse that was powerful enough to challenge the status quo, thus creating a popular identity by establishing political frontiers between 'the people' and the elites. The incapacity of existing institutions to satisfy important demands was the precondition for overcoming the single-issue and regionalist characteristics of the country's popular discontent; Morales and MAS were able to unify the various demands in a general and national articulation of dissatisfaction with the status quo. It is necessary to see the way in which these diverse demands were combined, and how this resulted in the construction of a new political identity. In this analysis, I am influenced by the work on discourse theory by Laclau (2005), Howarth (2000) and Panizza (2005a). Following them, I argue that it is not helpful to define populism according to the characteristics of the leader, his organization or the politics pursued. Such definitions lead to an 'avalanche of exceptions', as Laclau points out. Nor is a simple appeal to 'the people' helpful – for then all democratic politicians would be populists. As I show in this book, if we regard populism as a discursive logic or as a particular pattern of articulating political ideas, it becomes a tool for analysing democracy, or 'a mirror for democracy' as Panizza puts it. By analysing the extent to which Morales's discourse is populist, I identify the tension between inclusion and exclusion not only as a key aspect of Morales's discourse, but in fact as *the* central issue of democracy in Bolivia.

Though this book will help us to understand who Evo Morales is, his story helps us construct a bigger picture of democracy in

Bolivia, since for several years he has been one of the country's central political figures. It explains why and how an indigenous coca grower – hence a political outcast – could become Bolivia's most powerful leader by taking advantage of the crisis of representation. He turned the stigma of his background into a marker for 'the common people' of which they could be proud. He promised that his government would bring an end to the marginalization of the majority of the population through a 'refounding' of the state. As symbol of 'the people', he united a diversity of demands against a common antagonist: the 'oligarchy' and the 'traditional politicians', who were held responsible for Bolivia's problems.

Morales's discourse reflects the tension between inclusion and exclusion that is the central challenge for democracy in Bolivia. Conflicts in 2005–07 over the new constitution and the autonomy of the regions were an expression of this tension. They raised the issue of how diverse interests can be accommodated under the same roof, and to what extent the general (the central state) can be excluded from the affairs of the particular (the regions).

The challenge for democracy in the years to come is how to unite the diversity of the Bolivian population and to overcome the crisis of representation. The key will be to define successfully what binds Bolivians together and what makes them different from the world at large, as opposed to concentrating on what divides them. Thus, what democracy in Bolivia needs is a renewed consensus on what unites Bolivians in their diversity. Although Morales remains bound by the logic of polarization that made him successful, he has at least tried to propose an answer to these questions. His government will not readily solve the troubles at the heart of Bolivia's democracy; the road ahead is rough and the risk of confrontation looms large. But Morales has set the country on a new course that is promising.

In order to begin to understand the significance of the rise of Evo Morales, we begin our journey with a brief look at Bolivia's political history.

PART I

CHAPTER 1

Bolivia's political history

Crisis of representation in Bolivia

What do we need to know about Bolivia's history in order to understand the rise of Evo Morales and the MAS? The most obvious answer is: everything! Only a holistic exploration into the depths of politics, economics, culture and foreign relations will give us the full picture. However, we do not have the time for such an academic exercise and so this section will concentrate on what is most relevant, namely the failure of political parties to represent more than just the interests of a tiny elite.

What are the functions political parties are assumed to fulfil? Put simply, they recruit political leaders, propose (alternative) policies, structure political competition and simplify electoral choices for voters (Dix, 1992). By looking at the functions parties perform, political scientists such as Dalton and Wattenberg (2000) classify them into three broad categories: first, 'parties in the electorate' reduce information costs, make complex political decisions easier, educate citizens by providing political information and mobilize them, at least for electoral purposes. Second, 'parties as organizations' recruit and train political leadership, and provide structured access to positions of government for elected representatives. By aggregating, articulating, and mediating the interests of the population, parties make the political spectrum more stable and predictable. Third, 'parties in government' create parliamentary majorities, implement policies and frame alternatives, organize the government as well as opposition to it, ensure that responsibility is taken for government actions, control government administration, and enhance stability in government.

However, this emphasis on functions has been criticized for rationalizing the patterns of behaviour of Western parties, and for using this generalization as a yardstick. Indeed, Bolivian political parties, aside from contesting elections and forming coalitions in Congress to elect the president, have historically fulfilled few of the functions theoretically attributed to them. The failure of most parties to develop stable roots in society (exceptions are the Movimiento Nacional Revolucionario, or MNR, and MAS) has meant that they have failed to structure political preferences over time, leading to somewhat erratic voting behaviour.

The disconnectedness of parties from society means that we have to look at their relation to the state in order to understand them. This observation, derived from advanced industrialized countries, helps us to see that parties are also a part of the state bureaucracy. Parties have their own interest in surviving and they use the state as a reliable structure of support. This does not necessarily mean that they are corrupt and misuse state resources. The relation can be harmless inasmuch as they support policies that are in their interest, and they would under normal conditions avoid anything that could threaten their existence (Katz and Mair, 1997). Indeed, it is useful to keep in mind that the main rationale for the existence of most political parties in Bolivia is not to represent certain interests but to obtain state resources in the form of public-sector jobs.

Despite some important advances, the return to democracy did not resolve this long-standing problem of the political elite treating the state as their private property while maintaining structural barriers, including more recently 'glass ceilings', to exclude especially the indigenous population. This resulted in citizens no longer believing that they were well represented by the existing political parties. In political science terms, there was a 'crisis of representation' (Main-waring et al., 2006). The main political parties were perceived as not acting in the interests of those they purported to represent, or for the common good, but rather for the exclusive benefit of a privileged few. This crisis manifested itself in the rise of political outsiders attacking the establishment, electoral volatility, declining confidence in political parties, and the inability of two democrati-cally elected presidents to finish their terms. In Bolivia the failure of the main parties to fulfil their representative functions was one of the reasons for the crisis of representation and the waves of popular protest since 2000.

From revolution to dictatorship to transition: 1952–78

In Bolivian history political parties play a paradoxical role. On the one hand, they are integral to a well-functioning democracy, an essential element of which is the provision of structured means for political participation through interest aggregation and representa-tion. On the other hand, parties have not fulfilled their potential and have sometimes even obstructed moves towards a more democratic political system. Since the beginning of Bolivia's history of party politics in the 1880s, political parties have functioned according to a 'patrimonial dynamic'. They have not represented a particular ideology or political project, but rather existed as vehicles to distrib-ute patronage for the middle class. Another good characterization, originally coined for African countries, is *politique du ventre* (Bayart, 1999), where control over the government meant principally the ability to distribute resources to followers. Not surprisingly, corrup-tion has been singled out by many authors as the main problem in Bolivia.[1] This was probably the major cause of popular disenchant-ment prior to 2005 and has been the only constant in the many different forms of government in Bolivia.

The 1952 revolution was one of the most important events in Bolivian history. It fundamentally altered how Bolivians saw the power relations in their country: that is, those whom they regarded as able to achieve political power and as suitable to hold high office. The reason for this was that under the bourgeois leadership of the Movimiento Nacionalista Revolucionario, an armed proletariat defeated the oligarchic state of the *Rosca* (clique) of the *Barones de Estaño* (tin barons). This was not so different to what happened in 2005, where in the popular imagination complete outsiders, previously depicted as unfit to govern, displaced the establishment. After the revolution, the MNR devised a *cogobierno* (co-government) with the national workers' union (Central Obrera Boliviana, COB), intending to mobilize and control the popular masses through corporatism. The 1952 revolution brought universal rights, and freed peasants from social bondage. To this end, the indigenous population of *indios* were rebaptized *campesinos* in the official discourse.[2] Although the significance of introducing political participation to the indigenous population through universal suffrage should not be underestimated, the revolution meant there would no longer be political competition. An electoral system based on party lists served quite effectively to control candidate selection and political participation, subordinating all candidates to the clientelistic logic of the MNR. This system remained until the 1990s a convenient means for all political parties to control entry to the official political arena. Another key factor was the Agrarian Reform (1953), which gave small plots to peasants in a relatively egalitarian fashion in the highlands. In the sparsely populated tropical zone in the East, the reform favoured landed elites, who did little more than simply rename their haciendas *empresas agropecuarias* (commercial farms). There was no plan to encourage development of indigenous communities, thereby prolonging the existing stark economic inequalities and limiting the participation of the poor. The 1952 revolution merely replaced outright discrimination against and exclusion of the indigenous and peasant population by more subtle forms.

The MNR was marked by internal contradictions. With its aim of forming an alliance of different classes and constructing a Bolivian nation-state, the MNR was able to attract a range of different, and at times incompatible, interests. Yet Bolivia's indigenous population has never identified itself with a particular 'class' and the idea of a class alliance remained more of a theory, while in practice the MNR had a bourgeois leadership. Furthermore, the MNR closed its eyes and ears to the *Weltanschauung* of its indigenous allies and was highly paternalistic with its goal of assimilating the *indios* into a Bolivian nation in order to liberate them and remove them as an obstacle to Bolivian development. The MNR nationalized the mines on the demand of the COB, but did not eliminate the influence of foreign capital; and indeed it arranged indemnification for larger companies (Mayorga and Gorman, 1978: 97–9). The MNR's state capitalist model[3] used state intervention in such a manner that the elites benefited disproportionately (Healy, 2001: 43). The clientelism that determined the selection of candidates increased conflict within the party and with the COB, which resisted the economic reforms and was subsequently excluded from power by the MNR. As a consequence of the open opposition of the workers to the government, policymaking became ineffectual and could be overcome only by the use of presidential decrees. Clientelistic, top-down practices let to increased factionalism within the MNR, which in turn hindered consistent voting behaviour in Congress and further contributed to decision-making by presidential decree.

The USA successfully adopted a policy of subtle influence and of exploiting the internal contradictions within the MNR. This steered the MNR to an increasingly orthodox, supply-oriented economic policy with austerity measures, which ultimately ended the fragile class alliance with the COB (Zunes, 2001). Bolivia's dependence on US aid came at the price of the 1956 stabilization and economic liberalization plan. The open opposition of the workers and internal party factionalism meant that effective policymaking was possible only through the use of presidential decrees. This in turn contributed to clientelistic, top-down practices and obstructed approval of government proposals in Congress. Hence we find that some problems of the contemporary style of politics emerged with the first post-1952 governments. This is hardly surprising given that revolutionary nationalism had been the dominant influence within Bolivian politics over the past fifty years.

Bolivian nationalism: a brief history

In order to understand contemporary politics, but especially everything that refers to the Bolivian nation or 'plurinationalism' of MAS, we have to examine first the nationalist ideas of the MNR (the so-called *modelo asimilacionalista*). The MNR was part of Latin America's 'national-popular' wave of the 1940s and 1950s, when populist movements raised the issues of social transformation and economic development in terms of the relationship between class dynamics and the nation. The articulation by the MNR of a 'national popular' political imaginary is a useful instance of the relationship between populism and nationalism, because it shows how a nationalist discourse can be articulated according to a populist logic.

Origins of Bolivian nationalism

The Chaco War with Paraguay (1932–35) created for the first time a sort of national consciousness with revolutionary characteristics. It destroyed the old feudal order, because it showed the 'poor organization of the country and the irresponsibility of its leaders, in a time when it was possible for Bolivians of different classes and regions to meet as brothers' (Rolón Anaya, 1999: 196). Unsettling as it was, the loss of the war provided the basis for the creation of a sense of a shared nationhood since it 'galvanized a process of rethinking and recreating new political projects concerned with nation-building' (Domingo, 2003: 368). It was articulated as an 'imagined community' (Anderson, 1983) of all ex-combatants and their relatives who had come into contact with others from similar rural-indigenous origins through the mobilization of the war. Furthermore, the war created a shared sense of despair, defeat and humiliation among the population.

This was the starting point for a collective recognition of being equal with a shared frustration at socio-economic marginalization and political subjugation. At the time, nationalism was the discourse of the leftist opposition, of mainly middle-class intellectuals, to what they described as the 'oligarchic' state of the *La Rosca* (clique) of *Barones del Estaño* (tin barons). However, the first nationalist governments of David Torro (1936–37) and German Busch (an ex-Chaco War combatant, 1937–39), who nationalized the Standard Oil Company, were rather short-lived.

The 1952 revolution and *nacionalismo revolucionario*[4]

The high tide of Bolivian nationalism was the period of the MNR governments between 1952 and 1964, although its legacy is still felt today. The MNR (founded in 1942) put into practice its *nacionalismo revolucionario* with the 1952 revolution, which was defined as the 'national, anti-feudal and anti-colonial' vehicle to transform national society. As Whitehead (2003: 41–2) argues, the 1952 revolution was a social 'dialectical process' that 'reordered Bolivia's collective understandings of relations of power' and 'expressed a clash of ideas about fundamental issue of national identity'. It developed a hold on the popular imagination, and elements of its discourse remain in evidence still. These include the construction of a basic antagonism between 'nationalism and colonialism' (Montenegro, 1990), also articulated as nationalists versus imperialists.

The title of the first manifesto of the MNR was unequivocal in its construction of an antagonism: *Nosotros frente a los traidores*, 'Us against the traitors' (in Arze Cuadros, 2002: Annex 3). Similarly, MNR co-founder Augusto Céspedes (1956) stated: there are 'two sides of the barricades' – the oligarchy and latifundistas (*La Rosca*) on one side, and the oppressed, popular classes on the other. The MNR wanted to liberate the 'oppressed majority' from 'slavery' that was sustained by a system of 'internal' and 'external colonialism' (*Bases y Principios del MNR*, 1942; in Arze Cuadros, 2002: 604–43). For MNR's founders such as Montenegro, Céspedes and Paz Estenssorro, the MNR tried to unite many different interests in a 'national front of oppressed classes' against the 'common enemy' of the 'anti-national', 'mining and latifundista oligarchy' (Céspedes, 1956) by constructing a 'multi-class alliance' (Paz Estenssorro, 1955).

Remarkably, the MNR articulated its aim as *recuperar la nación* ('refound the nation'), which is now a centrepiece of MAS's rhetoric, albeit directed against the nation constructed by the MNR. The parallels do not end here: both discourses endeavour to refound the nation in order to end a system of 'internal' and 'external' colonialism. Agents of internal colonialism are in either 'the oligarchy' or the 'oligarchic traditional parties' (*Bases y Principios del MNR*, 1942; in Arze Cuadros, 2002: 629) and both parties present themselves as broad movements of victims of internal colonialism. With respect to external actors, both discourses attack 'imperialism' and 'internal financial consortiums/institutions' (Victor Paz Estenssorro, cited in Rolón Anaya, 1999: 336). Again strikingly similar to MAS policy, the MNR proposed 'nationalizations' and greater state control over large companies and presented them as measures of democratic self-defence of the nation and explicitly not as communist policies.

The central idea around which the diverse demands united was the 'refounding of the nation', which was an effective rallying cry given the shame felt by these diverse interests due to the loss of the Chaco War. 'Refounding the nation' was forceful since it generated a sense of common destiny that had been lost. It made it possible to construct a common 'anti-national' or 'semi-colonial' enemy linking domestic, economic and political elites with foreign interests, and thus with the 'culprits of Bolivia's humiliation' (*Bases y Principios del MNR*, 1942; in Arze Cuadros, 2002: 627-9).

MNR's nationalism was thus a source of inspiration for the discourse of MAS, with the ironic twist that MAS identified the MNR itself with 'the oligarchy' and 'imperialism'. Whether MAS consciously adopted the discursive logic of the MNR is subject to speculation, but in my opinion a direct 'copy–paste' does not seem likely. Rather, having participated in governments for more than a quarter of a century, the MNR has shaped political culture in Bolivia like no other party; thus, as Rolón Anaya (1999) shows in his history of Bolivian political parties, the roots of most political parties are directly or indirectly linked to the MNR or the opposition to it.

Assimilationist nation

There is a significant difference between MAS and MNR inasmuch as revolutionary nationalism articulated a concept of the homogenous nation-state as the basis for the modernization of Bolivia. The basis of this modernization had to be a 'scientific study' to determine the 'adequate organization of the agrarian economy in order to obtain the maximum yield' (Arze Cuadros, 2002: 641). The core of the nation was the so-called *modelo asimilacionalista*, according to which the entire population was to be assimilated into a homogenous national culture promoted by a unitary national educational system redesigned to 'incorporate nationalist ideas'. The new *Código de la Educación Boliviana* (1955, reprinted in Sandoval Rodriguez, 1970: 221–2) specifies that education was aiming to 'form the new Bolivian Man', to 'integrate the country' and to shape a 'national consciousness' with a 'shared historical destiny'.

Modernizing Bolivia in nationalist terms meant creating one large unit with common mass communication in Spanish. The idea of this model was laid out in the *Bases y Principios del MNR*, which states that the aim of the MNR was to 'incorporate millions of campesinos into national life' and to liberate them from the chains of archaic traditions. According to Zambrana (2005), this 'liberation' entailed articulating the earlier *indio* identity as *campesino*[5] and supporting this with the spreading of education into rural areas, promoting Spanish over indigenous languages. The people were supposed to be unified within the same national culture, which was imagined as being based on objective, scientific facts as opposed to the 'superstition' of the uneducated rural population. As stated in the *Bases y Principios del MNR*, the end was to 'mould a Bolivian culture' and to construct a 'nation with true social justice'. In order to do this, the MNR introduced universal suffrage and provided land rights through its *Reforma Agraria* (1953). The idea was that all those who had been marginalized previously would become part of a new Bolivian nation by obtaining new rights and a better education, and by receiving a new identity as *campesinos*.

The noble ideas behind all this notwithstanding, the *revolutionary nationalism* of the MNR is problematic. The nation was constructed according to a Western image and was culturally anti-indigenous. The indigenous heritage was seen as an obstacle to successful development, and consequently indigenous people had to be assimilated into *mestizos*. In Healy's words, 'the MNR helped to emancipate the Indian peasants from many past abuses, political limitations, and abridged life chances, while it simultaneously replicated the same old, neo-colonial assimilationist patterns' (2001: 16).

Twenty years after the efforts to construct a Bolivian nation, Sandoval Rodriguez argued that Bolivia was still 'una Nación en formación' (1970: 262). The assimilationist nationalism failed to become hegemonic among those whom it sought to 'liberate' and to incorporate into the nation, because it did not take the perceptions and sentiments of the rural and indigenous population sufficiently into account. They continued to live in small rural communities and practise ancient customs and cultivate shared memories that maintained links to their ethnic past. Furthermore, the national culture was never inclusive enough to accept those individuals who wanted to integrate themselves, and rejected them on the basis of the colour of their skin. In a country with such profound inequalities, instituting some new rights – as fundamental as they are – was not enough to provide opportunities for social mobility, which is essential in order to produce a sense of a shared community inclusive of everyone regardless of their background.

In general, it can be argued that Bolivia has thus far continuously suffered problems of nationhood that the assimilationist nation of the MNR could not solve. Although there was a kind of popular identity of belonging to a sovereign 'people', local, regional, ethnic or class identities prevailed over a higher-level national identity. Problems of communication, literacy and transport were other obstacles to the creation of an 'imagined community'. Without infrastructure and transport connecting the different parts of the country,[6] standard-ized mass education and widespread literacy, it has been difficult for individuals to conceive of themselves as belonging to such an abstract community as the nation. A significant proportion of the population live in rural areas in relative isolation from the rest of the country with little formal education and does not speak Spanish well enough to participate in the common culture.

The legacy of 'revolutionary nationalism' implied the persistence of a political culture emphasizing the role of the state both as the exclusive realm for political activities and for economic development through support of the economic elites. For the majority of the popu-lation, politics was not much more than the top-down imposition of decisions, which moved their political activity outside the official institutions. The problems remained during the fourteen years of rule by military regimes (1964–78), which came to power with the promise of overcoming factionalism and ineffectual policymaking. The notorious regime of General Bánzer was sponsored by the USA and Brazil and was similar to other bureaucratic–authoritarian regimes in the Southern Cone that aimed to curtail the advance of communism. Like all his predecessors, Bánzer faced the problem of factionalism, which undermined his efforts to construct an in-stitutional base of support, and eventually forced him to rely on clientelism (Conaghan, 1992).

The rise of democratic institutions without democratic politics

Bolivia's transition to democracy (1978–82) came about largely through splits within the military, the regime's disastrous eco-nomic performance, the withdrawal of US support, and national protests, including a hunger strike of 1,300 middle-class activists.

Nevertheless, the transition turned out to be more protracted than in most other Latin American cases, including no fewer than seven (military and civilian) governments, outbreaks of violence and signs of state disintegration. The main reason was that the political culture of the elites stood in the way of a smooth transition, because politics was not conceived of as a participatory activity in which various groups express their interests. From 1985 onwards, revolutionary nationalism entered a period of crisis. It was actively contested and deconstructed by the MNR/ADN governments with their neoliberal ideology, as exemplified by the (in)famous *Decreto Supremo* 21060. The elites tried to use democracy as a means to maintain their power and to curb the influence of civil society. The Bolivian case shows that authoritarian regression was less a threat to democracy than the installation of a hybrid system that combined democratic elections with an authoritarian political culture run by the elites.

The first democratic government, Hernán Siles Zuazo's Union Democratica Popular (UDP), had to cope with the legacy of previous regimes (especially economic crisis and undemocratic actors inhabiting power niches). The unyielding MNR/ADN opposition and weak governmental institutions made it impossible for the UDP to address Bolivia's urgent economic problems successfully. The COB, and within it the mineworkers union, FSTMB, emerged from the period of military rule exceptionally strong in relation to a weak democratic government. In the face of imminent economic collapse,[7] and despite being aware of the detrimental effect of their demands, the union leaders were obliged by their internal organizational dynamics to continue their confrontational line. As a result of internal manoeuvring, the COB rejected compromise as a betrayal of its historical objectives (Ibáñez Rojo, 2000). While the political class developed a capacity for (self-interested) coalition-building after the transition, there was no break with the clientelist logic of relationships with civil society. When the government was unable to get its way by co-opting civil society, the only alternative it saw was to use force to implement policies. 'The UDP government [and the MNR/ADN opposition] recognized only representative democracy, with parties as the sole means for representing interests. It lived in an imaginary that was blind to the fundamental cleavage between leftist parties and social movements' (Mayorga, 1987: 32). In sum, although some new institutions were established and explicitly anti-democratic leaders were removed, the transition to democracy brought little in the way of further participation by citizens in political decisions, with the exception of periodic elections. At that time, it appeared as if democratic shortcomings were not a priority for the majority of citizens, who wanted above all a government that was able to overcome the economic crisis. Since the 1970s there has been one important means by which poor Bolivian peasants can achieve a degree of economic security, and during the economic crises of the 1980s this became even more attractive: the production of coca.

Coca: a cursed holy plant

Coca is one of the key factors in understanding Bolivia. There is no other crop that is so significant and at the same time so controversial as the 'sacred leaf'.[8] Coca has been part of daily life in the Andean region for about 7,000 years, and has been cultivated domestically for around 1,000 years. Today, approximately 8 million people in the region consume coca leaves on a daily basis. This alone makes it a notable economic factor, even if we ignore for a moment the economic consequences of coca sold for drug production. Its significance is further enhanced by the plant's nourishing, medical and ceremonial functions (Oomen, 2003). Coca can claim better average nutritional values than milk, meat or potatoes, as a Harvard study by Duke et al. (1976; cited in Oomen, 2003: 6) has found; it contains roughly the same amount of protein as meat, and provides more fibre, calcium, phosphorus, iron and vitamins (A, B1, B2, B6, C) than all three basic foodstuffs. Recently, flour made from coca has been proposed as a solution for malnutrition and rising food prices in the Andes.[9] Urrunaga (in Oomen, 2003: 7) has found that the leaf can be used as a natural antibiotic against infections or diarrhoea, and as a means to regulate blood pressure. A well-known property of coca tea is to increase the oxygen absorption of the blood, and hence many tourists consume it to combat altitude sickness. Such qualities have inspired the development of a number of alternative coca products to the stage that they could be commercialized; these include homeopathic treatments, sweets, toothpaste, soap and shampoo.

On the symbolic level, the leaf functions to confirm social bonds and to build a sense of community. Coca is used in various ceremonies, such as predicting the future, communicating with the dead, and soliciting a benevolent future through an offer to *Pachamama* (Mother Earth).

Unfortunately, coca is commonly associated with the production of cocaine. The complex chemical production process necessary to turn coca into the drug is conveniently ignored. The prohibition of coca by equating it with cocaine production is based on a scientifically unsound research project of 1961 (Painter, 1994: 23). Nevertheless, coca was included in the United Nation's list of illegal substances. Domestically, small-scale coca production was allowed in parts of the Yungas (Department La Paz) and the area of Vandiola.[10] In 2005, MAS and the Mesa administration reached an agreement that would allow every household in the Tropic and the Yungas to have its own *cato* (160m²) of coca. Coca became defined as 'cultural patrimony' and a 'renewable natural resource' in the new constitution, but nothing concrete was set down except that its production, revalorization and industrialization would be regulated by law. Since MAS came to power in January 2006, it has searched for ways to extend the legal production of coca without an increase in the supply of coca leaves destined for the narcotics trade, which would mean increasing the production and sale of alternative products such as tea or toothpaste. However, the prohibition against the export of such products limits the commercial possibilities, and

US opposition makes it unlikely that the ban will be lifted in the near future. What is remarkable is that the coca producers seem to have kept their promise not to augment their yield until legal alternatives to drug production are in place.[11] The politics of coca remains difficult even for a government broadly in favour of using coca for non-narcotic purposes. For instance, the Bolivian office of the United Nations Office on Drugs and Crime (UNODC), which was responsible for producing a yearly report on the state of coca production, was closed in 2009, allegedly due to lack of funding. Despite the offer of international donors to cover the costs of keeping the office in the country, this did not happen. One possible explanation is that there was political pressure on UNODC to close the office in order not to contribute indirectly to Morales's drug policy. On the Bolivian side, the promise of a comprehensive study of the legal use of coca has not materialized (yet), despite funding from the European Commission. The results from such a study will be highly political and sensitive, of course, since they will have to show the volume of coca consumed legally, which would then serve as the yardstick to determine how much coca may be produced (possibly also in volumes and moving away from the less precise prescription in hectares).

Whatever the actual policy regarding cultivation, coca as a cash crop is for many peasants the only way of sustaining their livelihood. Whereas prices of nearly all crops have fallen steadily, revenues generated by coca production have increased 11 per cent per year on average since the mid-1980s (Painter, 1994: 39). One coca plant can be harvested three to four times a year for a period of eleven years. Coca leaves are frequently the only agricultural produce that peasants from remote places can transport to the nearest market. Coca is very labour-intensive, especially during harvest, which needs to be done manually. Overall, no other crop is able to compete with coca in terms of the relation between revenues, labour and infrastructure, as several studies have shown (Sanabria, 1993; Painter, 1994; Blommaert, 2003).

At this point it should be emphasized that the coca-growing peasants should not be linked automatically to the circuit of cocaine producers and drug traffickers. It is a common misconception to link coca in Bolivia directly with cocaine production and organized crime, a relation that probably holds true in the Colombian case.[12] The coca produced in Bolivia is not automatically destined for cocaine production; indeed only a fraction of all cocaine produced stems from Bolivia. In contrast to parts of the military and some politicians, 'there is no evidence that the peasant producers are involved in organized crime' (Assies and Salman, 2003: 36). Some defenders of coca go even further, arguing that 'coca farmers should be regarded as nothing more than farmers who have adopted the strategy to produce a particular [traditional] crop' (Red Andina de Información, 2001). Coca producers could perhaps be compared to farmers producing the barley from which was made the malt destined for whiskey during Prohibition in the USA. Cocaine and whiskey both involve complex production processes requiring technical knowledge and equipment. Cultivating a particular crop and selling it on the open market, so the argument runs, does not make the growers accomplices to the subsequent illegal use of the crop, provided that there are other potential uses for which the buyer could purchase it. Concerning the potential harm of coca derivatives, there are many examples, especially in the USA (e.g. small firearms), where the potential harmfulness does not lead to a ban of the product. The logic behind coca eradication would imply similarly eradicating the plants of American tobacco farmers since these are the basis for a product that is responsible for the death of millions of people annually.

Bolivian coca, then, is not destined to be the basis for harmful products. It is estimated that some two-thirds of production is used to satisfy the substantial domestic demand for coca as leaves for chewing or as tea. Carter and Mamani (1986) reported (in a USAID commissioned study) that in the late 1970s at least 60 per cent of the rural population used coca for legal traditional consumption (*acullico* or chewing). Laserna (1996), who updated their study, conservatively estimates the number of traditional coca consumers in rural areas alone to amount to some 1.5 million people, or 1.9 million if consumers of coca tea are added. Depending on the estimate used for daily consumption, the absolute minimum amount of coca chewed equalled 12,000 tons in 1992.

The most interesting aspect of Laserna's study is, however, that if one accepts the (higher) daily estimate given in the official strategy paper for the eradication of coca (the *Plan Integral de Desarollo y Sustitución de Cultivos*), the total amount of coca consumed traditionally rises to 19,000 tons per year.[13] To this figure needs to be added an estimate of the total number of urban and foreign (especially Argentinean) *acullicadores*, coca-tea consumers, as well as the small amount of coca leaves exported legally for medical use. Laserna (1996: 53) concludes that a conservative estimate of legal consumption would be around 26,000 tons per year (without accounting for the increasing demand for *mate de coca* [tea] in Argentina). Although this represents only 37 per cent of production in 1996, when 48,600 hectares yielded approximately 70,000 tons, legal consumption accounted for roughly 70 per cent of total production when the surface area had decreased to 24,400 hectares (UNODC, 2002). Moreover, if coca tea were legalized, today's total production would not be sufficient to satisfy the potential international demand. For instance, in 2002 the Chinese embassy proposed opening a factory for coca tea in Bolivia in order to supply 10 per cent of its population with one teabag per day. This would amount to 36,500 tons of coca leaves per year, or the harvest of 25,000 hectares (Oomen, 2003: 33).[14] An EU-subsidized workgroup cited an international research project which concluded that if coca tea achieved a share of 2 per cent in the global market for tea, the entire Bolivian production (then 50,000 hectares) would be insufficient to meet the demand (Janssen, et al., 1993: 51).

The legalization of coca in Bolivia will not necessarily lead to a substantial increase in the production of cocaine. This has been

confirmed by the most recent UNODC report (2010), which states
that cocaine production increased by only 1 per cent – significantly
less than in Peru, where Coca is illegal.[15] Managed correctly, the
entire present production of coca could be used for legal derivatives
and thus sustain the livelihood of those peasants depending on
coca as their only cash crop. This would be a more viable source of
income than the 'alternative development' projects, which have been
a failure (Blommaert, 2003; Coca Antezana et al., 1999).

For the individual peasant, there is actually not much difference
whether his coca is used for traditional consumption or exported to
cocaine laboratories. The price of coca remains the same, since all
coca is sold to specialized local markets, being bought by middlemen
who keep the destination and purpose secret. For the middlemen,
however, the destination of coca does make a financial difference.
Having said that, the fact that some coca goes to drug production
probably keeps the price up, which means that all producers benefit
indirectly from the link with the narcotics business through higher
prices.[16] However, there are enormous fluctuations in price, not
infrequently a more than 100 per cent increase or decrease within
a few months (Sanabria, 1993: 46). Small producers of coca, who
often need money in hand to pay school fees, for instance, are not
able to benefit from the fluctuations as middlemen can, who stock
the coca or turn it into paste and sell it when it is most profitable.
One could argue that the link to the price of cocaine is more likely
to have a negative effect for the coca producers since – in contrast
to the relatively stable prices achieved by legal derivatives – the
influence of the drug business causes significant price fluctuations
that make stable, long-term investment impossible.

Although it is possible to earn more from a harvest of coca
than from any other crop (though the revenue from cacao was
for some time not much less; see Janssen et al., 1993), unstable
prices combined with the extra-legal situation of its production
have caused the coca-producing areas to fall back, according to
scales measuring poverty used by Rolando Morales (1984, 1990).[17]

On the Human Development Index (Laserna et al., 1995, in Laserna, 1996: 109–10), areas where coca is grown rank below the departmental and national average. Concluding his analysis of the socio-economic indices, Laserna (1996: 110) argues that the increased demand for cocaine has not resulted in a better standard of living for those growing coca. This means that even if the price of coca is higher due to its link with cocaine production, this does not make the individual coca producer any better off than peasants in many other regions.

Yet there is without doubt a link, albeit indirect, between coca producers and the drug business, which only the full legalization of coca has the potential to break. It must be pointed out that the actual profit generated by cocaine production does not trickle down to those who sell coca for such 'other purposes', as the peasants euphemistically refer to it. In fact, evaluating data from USAID and an independent Bolivian research group (Muller Associates), Painter (1994: 40–51) concludes that coca producers receive only between 0.65 per cent and 2.1 per cent of the final value. Janssen et al. (1993: 75) come up with an even bigger difference: a coca producer in Bolivia receives only US$0.35 for the leaves necessary to produce 2 grams of cocaine (50 per cent purity) with a European street market value of around US$140.

The willingness of the coca producers' organizations to self-limit production to one *cato* per family seems to indicate their willingness to combat the use of coca for drug production, as they have always emphasized. With only one *cato* per family the quantity produced would not exceed the legal demand according to the calculations of MAS.[18]

War on drugs

Nothing of the alternative potential of coca has been realized thus far; indeed, until the presidency of Evo Morales the main aim of the government was to eradicate coca – if necessary by force. This has meant that whereas a certain democratic deficit has been the common grievance that fuelled social mobilization in Latin America, Bolivia faced the particular consequences of the 'war on drugs'.[19]

Despite the vast resources committed to the 'war on drugs' in the region – more than US$30 billion was spent in the period 1980–2000, including US$5 billion in Colombia alone between 1999 and the end of the millennium (*The Economist*, 3 May 2007: 61) – it proved impossible to reduce drug production or make a dent in the US market.[20] Vast areas were militarized, resulting in a loss of state sovereignty, since the Bolivian military responded more to the USA than to Bolivian governments (Ramos Cachi, 2001: 125–36). The failure results from the misguided adoption of an anti-supply approach (i.e. the eradication of crops) to solve an inherently demand-driven problem (the drugs trade). 'The "drugs war" has had the effect of shifting the trade from place to place, rather than halting it' (*The Economist*, 3 May 2007: 61). Furthermore, the armed forces in the area have behaved like paramilitary organizations. They have exerted great pressure upon social movements because they were not subject to civilian control and make ample use of their impunity, which led to 'serious human rights violations' between 1993 and 2003 (Amnesty International, 2004: 3). The human rights of *cocaleros* were virtually non-existent in this period (Pettersson and MacKay, 1993; Red Andina de Información, 2007b; Rensselaer, 2001).[21] This situation later worsened due to the post-9/11 US security doctrine that defines coca producers as drug traffickers and links all drug traffic with terrorism (*La Razón*, 31 January 2003). This is the context in which Evo Morales came of age politically and which, to a large extent, influenced his political views.

CHAPTER 2

Evo's youth and upbringing

I keep wondering how he does this. I have already been listening for a couple of hours to these speeches, and since I am hidden in the back of the assembly I can sometimes sneak out to get something to drink or eat from the women selling home-made food and juice. Chewing the harmless coca leaves, like all those present, also provides a distraction; their only effect is like that of having a cup of coffee, which is more than welcome. Still, I find it hard to concentrate, not to yawn, and to understand what some of the contributions have to do with the topic. But that is of course not the point, which is the notion that everybody can make his or her voice heard, and that through a slow process a common understanding will emerge. Nevertheless, it is a long day: the meeting started at 6 a.m.; now it is 2 p.m. and it will probably go on without a break until 5 p.m. But Evo – or 'Iwu' as it sounds pronounced with a Quetchua accent – seems actually to listen attentively, at times signalling agreement or looking sceptical. He is clearly used to this and I cannot detect any sign that he is tired.

Morales shows appreciation for the speakers, thanking them for their contribution, at times summarising their key points. And, apart from these thanks and some introductory remarks, he has not yet spoken. He will wait until nobody else in the assembly of about 200 leaders of the coca growers' movement wants to speak. Then Morales will give a seemingly improvised speech, where he manages to connect points raised by various speakers and thus guide the discussion in the direction he wishes but without imposing his views directly. After he has finished, the discussion will start again, with some agreeing with and others opposing Morales, while some will seek to indicate overlaps. Through a reiterative process where Morales intervenes several times, at the end of such sessions a decision is reached that carries a broad consensus. There is no need for voting because it is clear that this is the outcome closest to unanimity.

I confess that I am impressed by Morales's patience and how at the meeting he managed to indirectly steer the at time emotional and sharp debate towards a result that seems acceptable to everybody and that is still broadly in line with what he said in his opening remarks. I don't feel he has manipulated these leaders; from working with them I know that they are well-informed and hold strong opinions. The only hint of orchestration is the tactic of letting them talk to release their anger and once the mood has calmed down directing them towards more moderate positions. On the other hand, outcomes are not always straightforwardly what Morales wants: he also has to give on certain points. Guiding the discussions of the coca growers' movement to reach a consensus is a considerable art. Participating in meetings of several *sindicatos* helped me to understand this, and to realize that many leaders fail. Many have mastered the art, however, and Evo Morales is one of them. However, whereas he is probably the most able, he is perhaps best thought of as *primus inter pares* rather than as a fundamental exception.

So, how did Morales become a leader of the coca growers' movement and what does this tell us about his leadership style and his political vision? Let me start by telling the story of how he came to the coca growing area of the Tropic of Cochabamba.

Early life

Juan Evo Morales Aima was born one of seven children (four of whom died in their infancy) in the poor Aymara village of Isallawi, in the canton Orinoca, close to Oruro's Lago Poopó on the Altiplano. His family home was a single-room house built of mud bricks. The village had no doctors or midwives, and his mother, aged 39, almost died from a postpartum haemorrhage after giving birth to Evo on 26 October 1959. The somewhat peculiar name Evo seems to stem from Evaristus (or Evaristo in Spanish), who was the fifth pope and was declared a saint. Evo's parents probably chose this name following an ancient requirement by the missionaries to use the name of the saint whose feast day coincides with the day of birth. Following Aymara custom, however, the father buried the placenta – considered sacred – in a location specially chosen for this purpose. As a child, Evo took care of the family's most valued possession, a herd of llamas and sheep, but always took a self-made football with him so as not to become bored.[1] Evo contributed as any other child in the Altiplano to the chores of rural life, such as helping with the subsistence farming, for example planting and harvesting. During harvest, Evo's parents deemed it more important for him to help them than go to school. Morales still lives to the rhythms of daily life in the countryside: he gets up between four and five in the morning and has his first meeting an hour later. For instance, following the elections in 2009, he scheduled a meeting with the EU Electoral Observation Mission and representatives from the European Commission at 6 a.m.

K'alawillka, as Isallawi is also known, is a community of some thirty houses scattered across an area of 4 square kilometres. It belongs to the *Ayllu Sullka* that unites six communities. *Ayllu* is an ancient indigenous concept of a discontinuous social space, which cannot be mapped with clearly defined boundaries. Rather, it consists of territorial journeys, a social space that moves together with the population, 'materially spreading cultural immanence' (Prada Alcoreza, 2002: 90) with its rituals, festivities, collective imaginaries, and so on. Through this network of relationships, *Sullka* is connected with the Valle Alto of Cochabamba and with the Tropic of Cochabamba. Summarizing this perception, Prada Alcoreza (2002: 90) calls the *ayllu* 'a living territory' or the principle of 'bio-territoriality'. An *ayllu* typically includes communal land that is used by all inhabitants to graze their llamas and sheep. There are also different communally owned but privately used plots set aside for agricultural production, primarily *yuca* (similar to manioc) and cereals, which are grown rotationally to allow for the regeneration of the soil. Though private usage meant that a family was primarily responsible for the plot and harvested its yield, frequently the actual work was done through the reciprocal *ayni* system whereby families work together on their respective plots. The community in which Morales was born was poor in terms of material possessions and meagre agricultural yields. But, in common with many other Altiplano communities, it was spiritually and culturally rich in that an elaborate web of *usos y costumbres* (norms and customs) made up the Aymara *cosmovision* or *Weltanschauung*. Morales learned from his father the most important Aymara rituals, such as the sacrifice of a llama, or *wilancha*, in the week before carnival as a form of ritualistic purification of the soil with the blood of the animal.

At the age of 5, Evo entered primary school in his village after a short period in the preparatory school in Orinoca. The school, typical for small villages, had a single classroom for all pupils. When Morales was 6 years old, he went with his father and sister for six months to the North of Argentina, where his father worked in the harvesting of sugar cane and Evo sold ice cream. He briefly attended school there, but speaking primarily Aymara he could not follow lessons and had to leave. Young Evo also walked regularly with his father and their llamas to Arani province in the department of Cochabamba, which constitutes the gate to the Tropic. The journey could last up to two weeks, during which they walked for long hours, starting as early as 4.30 a.m. and sleeping outside together with their animals. They brought salt and potatoes from the Altiplano, which they exchanged for maize and coca. Morales recounts that they heard on the radio the news about the coup of General Bánzer on 21 August 1971. When they crossed the large Cochabamba–Oruro road he saw the *flotas* (long-distance passenger buses). Thereafter, as a boy, he would dream about travelling one day on one of these buses.[2] After about a month in the area of Arani, they began their journey home. In all they could easily be away from home for two months.

Despite these interruptions to his schooling, Evo finished primary school and went to the Agrarian Humanistic Technical Institute of Orinoca (ITAHO), the secondary school, where he completed all except the final year. His parents then decided that he should study for his degree in Oruro, probably because it was thought a degree from a 'national' school in a major city promised better opportunities. Although Morales was able to finish all courses and exams by 1977 while working in parallel as a brick-maker and day labourer, he never collected his degree certificate. He most likely lacked the necessary financial means to fund the expensive procedure this entailed. Obtaining a certificate for completed studies, or even the proof of having fulfilled military service, remains to the present day a very costly and time-consuming affair in Bolivia. Morales has said that he would have liked to study journalism, but his parents were not able to finance university studies for their son.

In 1978 and 1979, Morales was a conscript in the Bolivian army. He had presented himself at the Centre for Instruction of Special Troops (CITE) in Cochabamba, but was sent to the army headquarters in La Paz for his military service. This coincided with the beginning of one of Bolivia's politically most unstable periods, which saw five presidents in two years. During Morales's service, there were two military coups, led by General Pereda Asbun and by General Padilla Arancibia. During the short-lived government of the latter, Morales became a guard of the Presidential Palace – or

Palacio Quemado as it is commonly known. It has also been said that Morales was sent on one occasion to the Yungas of La Paz, where the military was used against protests by the coca growers.[3]

Having completed his military service and found the money to obtain the corresponding certificate, among other things by playing the trumpet in the *Banda Imperial* of Oruro, Morales returned to Isallawi. However, in 1980, the phenomenon of *El Niño* hit the Altiplano of Bolivia, bringing long droughts and drastic, unexpected temperature drops, which destroyed 70 per cent of the harvest and killed half the animals. This latest setback compounded the existing hardship experienced by Morales's parents, causing them to decide to leave the Altiplano. So they undertook several journeys to the Yungas of La Paz. Finding that the *chacos* (plots) were too expensive, they therefore decided to move to the Tropic of Cochabamba. Since they had no place to stay in the area and were not sure where to settle, they stayed some time with maternal relatives in the poor Cerro Verde neighbourhood of Cochabamba. There they met their future neighbours, who informed them that they could obtain a *chaco* of 20 hectares, which constitutes a sizeable piece of land in the area, in the Sindicato 2 Agosto, which belongs to Puerto San Francisco. The Tropic attracted them, like many other peasants from the Altiplano, because of the more fertile soil and, in particular, the possibility of growing coca and thereby having a more stable livelihood.

Although leaving their ancestral home, which had seen at least four generations, might seem a drastic step for the Morales family, it fits the notion of the *ayllu* as discontinuous territory that connects different *pisos ecológicos* such as the Altiplano, the valleys (Valle Alto) and the tropical zones of the Yungas and the department of Cochabamba. Since the time of the Inca empire, people have moved back and forth between these different climatic zones in order to diversify their livelihoods. Hence the decision by Morales's father to move to the Tropic was inscribed within an ancient cultural logic that implied that the migration was not perceived as permanent and that there would always be close links with the Altiplano. However, for Evo, and to some extent for his brother Hugo (who would return to live in the Altiplano after the death of the parents in 1993), this was different: although they stayed in contact with Isallawi, the family's gravitational centre became the Tropic of Cochabamba. They started by clearing their plot in the semi-tropical forest, which was the common practice for settlers, causing large deforestation with all the associated problems such as erosion and rapidly degrading soil quality. They then began cultivating rice, bananas, citrus fruits and, somewhat later, coca. Morales remembers: 'beyond my dreams, I had plantations of oranges, grapefruit, papaya, banana and coca'.[4] It should be said that it was the location and size of the plot that made the range of crops an option, whereas in many other areas of the Tropic, especially those that were inhabited later, the plots are too small and too poorly situated to produce anything but coca.[5]

Life in the Tropic of Cochabamba has been and still is the most important influence on Evo Morales. Often this is reduced to his defence of the coca leaf and anti-imperialist rhetoric, but other factors are also important. Though as president he has steered clear of the sort of territorial favouritism that you might expect from a leader of a regionally based social movement, his experience in the fertile yet commercially underexploited Tropic nevertheless comes to the surface in his economic policy when he talks about the ability of small-scale farmers to make Bolivia self-sufficient in food. The decision of his government to reduce state support for large-scale commercial farming and to concentrate instead on helping peasants and co-operatives flows directly from a widely held view in the Tropic that with the right kind of support they could produce a greatly increased food crop for the domestic market. Morales, who appreciates the quality of local produce, still stops whenever he can at one of three locally renowned fish restaurants for a plate of *surubí*.

Morales has repeatedly stated that activism within the social movement of the coca growers was his university. This does not mean, however, that he fails to value academic knowledge. Indeed, he is an autodidact curious to learn from others, and frequently cites academic work approvingly and in a way that lends major weight or credibility to his own statements. On the other hand, he maintains a critical distance and usually trusts his instincts more than elaborate academic arguments.

Evo Morales's political ideas are based mainly on his own experience, complemented here and there with theoretical works he has read, such as *La Revolución India* by Fausto Reinaga, and with articles from the Centro de Documentación e Información Boliviana (CEDIB).[6] Morales also seems to be good at picking up ideas from conversations with others, and is known to have used his interviews to this end. He likes to impress his audience (with considerable success in the case of many social movement activists) by citing 'scientific' facts or by referring to 'scientists' who agree with his point of view. On the one hand, we see deployed here a common rhetorical device: *argumentum ad verecundiam*, the use of an authority as proof of an argument. On the other hand, it shows that Morales absorbs these various ideas and uses them to inform his decisions. One of Morales's first political influences was his elder cousin Marcial Morales Aima, a socialist and Marxist, who when the 15-year-old Morales first encountered him had long been active in miners' and peasant unions. This may have motivated Morales to go into social movement activism, but it has not made him a socialist. Although he sometimes comes up with socialist notions, his ideology is more eclectic and he deals in ideas from various ideological currents.

In the more practical realm, Morales's love of football led him to start organizing football games in his home community, and he became the captain of the high-school team. Although it wouldn't do to overstate this, through football Morales has acquired experience relevant to his later career. Indeed, he himself has compared politics to managing a football team, where he has to look for the best players for the team, motivate individuals, choose tactics, as well as organize practical aspects such as travel, negotiating suitable dates and handling a budget.

Evo's university: looking for another form of democracy

Morales learned most of his political skills and honed his convictions through his engagement in defending the cause of the coca growers. Morales and the movement have evolved together, from defending a rather narrow issue expressed in economic terms to criticizing the very fundamentals on which the modern Bolivian state is built. Whilst Morales became a national political figure that represented a broad anti-status quo coalition, the actions of the *sindicatos* came to be seen by many as normatively oriented to demonstrate the possibility of an ideal form of democracy, one that is more deliberative and participatory. As a communicative space, the assemblies are presented as a forum where 'true' democracy can be observed. That is, conceptions and practices of democracy are elaborated 'from below' and implemented within the internal organization of the social movement. Underlying this discourse of the internal practice of the movement is the aim, not least by Morales, of redefining citizenship. He regards the system prior to the new constitution as having excluded him and all indigenous peoples as full citizens. Morales perceives it his role as citizen to practise, together with his fellow coca growers and their allies, 'true' democracy in order to show that there is an alternative to the status quo that has denied them their legitimate place in the polis.

Morales's discourse about the participativeness of the *sindicatos* has some ambiguous consequences: on the one hand it constructs a frame of meaning for the grassroots members to make sense of the functioning of their organization. Participation, deliberation and consensus are regarded as the main factors behind the voluntary support of the grassroots, because decisions are the result of a social process through which people become 'owners' of the organizations. Voluntary support functions in the discourse of the movement as a foundational myth. Its distinctiveness and ability to function are related to the voluntary engagement and cooperation of its members.[7]

On the other hand, however, the construction of the organization as participatory can also be a way for the leaders to contain the members and maintain control over the decision-making procedure. Decisions are assumed to have been taken by consensus and unanimity. Since this is in practice very difficult to attain, such a discourse can be a way of controlling dissident opinions. The mechanism of controlling internal opposition shows the functioning of Aboy Carlés's (2005b) logic of 'hegemonism', which refers to the radical claim to include all political differences within a community so that the space for differences is closed.[8] Similarly, the discourse of grassroots participation and decision-making arranges all the differing demands of the members of the *sindicatos* into one 'chain of equivalence' (Laclau, 2005),[9] whereby they lose some of their particularity in the cause of stressing what they have in common. This has been a very effective way of unifying the movement and strengthening it by concentrating on common demands.

Yet the discourse has also had a disciplining effect that has made articulating fundamentally different views very difficult. This risks becoming associated with the antagonistic other against which the chain of equivalence is constructed. This points to the presence of an element of force within the concept of hegemony. For example, during my fieldwork I talked to one member of a *sindicato* who was convinced of the benefits of cultivating crops proposed by 'alternative development' projects.[10] He mentioned in private that there was no space within the movement for such a deviant opinion. Anyone actively defending 'alternative development' ran the risk of being seen by the movement as allied to efforts to eradicate coca – that is, supporting the enemies of the movement.[11] In summary, the discourse regarding the participatory nature of the organizations is largely empowering, and stimulates members to express their opinions and to participate in the organization. However, there is also an element of controlling dissident opinions and of giving leaders the opportunity to get their way under the cover of unanimity.

School of democracy

> In the *sindicatos* we practise true democracy. We meet, all express their opinions and we agree consensually, by deliberation, not by imposition. (Doña Flora)

One of the most remarkable characteristics of *sindicato* leaders, epitomized by Evo Morales, is their ability to give long improvised speeches that seem to touch the nerve of many of Bolivia's (rural) inhabitants. This capacity is developed during the assemblies, where people learn at a relatively young age to stand up and make their case in front of a critical audience.[12]

My informants pointed out that prior to a good debate, information needs to be disseminated to those participating in it. For them, the foundation of the political role of the *sindicatos* is the organizational structure that facilitates the flow of information down to the local level and even to the most remote *sindicatos*.

> Watch out, *compañeros y compañeras*, that it does not happen that you decide not to go to vote when it rains. Our votes are at this moment, as somebody has said, a coin of gold! (Evo Morales)

> It must be remembered that this time we have three votes: President, MP and Prefect. There was a small problem, but not really: in 2002 the vote for Evo as President was 87 per cent in the Tropic, the vote for Evo as MP was 84 per cent; there was a difference of 3 per cent.... Let us see, for sure some *compañeros* or maybe many *compañeros* have voted once: Evo for President, nothing else; from this resulted the difference of 3 per cent. This is not about crossed votes, there were no crossed votes.
>
> So, we must not forget the difference between President, MP and Prefect. We have to vote three times! We do not let them fool us. (Evo Morales)

It is from the *sindicatos* that Morales obtained much of his early knowledge about political issues; as is the fact that the rural population of the Tropic has a reasonable knowledge about their political rights and the functioning of the political system. For instance, practically all my informants could explain to me the main elements of Bolivia's complicated electoral system. Furthermore, the social movement is a platform for learning about wider political issues, including about Bolivia's foreign affairs and key global political matters. A recurrent theme in *sindicato* meetings, as reported by Morales and other leaders, was the struggle of poor countries against free-trade agreements to gain control over their natural resources or to sell them under better terms for Bolivia. The World Social Forum has been particularly influential on Evo Morales and other *sindicato* leaders. There they met people from other social movements, such as the Zapatistas from Chiapas, Mexico, and learned how to combine local demands with a global perspective. With this inspiration, it was not such a big step for Morales to link debates and demands to wider issues. From a relatively early phase of the development of the *sindicatos* as a political movement (in the early 1980s), Morales protested against the presence of US troops in Bolivia. This developed into the raising of issues such as the 'imperialism' of the USA and the violation of the national sovereignty of poor countries. Hence participation in social forums broadened Morales's horizon, and helped him to transcend local boundaries by reaching out to other social movements in Bolivia.

The understanding that local demands had elements in common with other social movements helped lead Morales to the view that a united Bolivian movement could function as a school for democracy. More importantly, perhaps, the fact that the movement was a forum where people felt as though they were equals and were being listened to helped to sustain collective action in support of their 'political instrument'. The idea of a group of equals also made possible the broadening of the discourse to include the demands of other social sectors. In short, under Morales the movement could broaden its appeal to other, previously isolated, social interests by understanding and articulating the sinficant connections between them. Thus Morales's main achievement is not so much the developing of his own ideology or set of demands, but rather the wisdom and capacity to take up demands from other groups and make their ideology his own.

The origins of Evo Morales's notion of the nation

The roots of Morales's understanding of the Bolivian nation lie within the 'revolutionary nationalism' of the MNR, but the actual content of the nation was influenced by the *Kataristas*[13] and the Lowlands (*Tierras Bajas*) indigenous movement. *Katarismo* emerged in the Aymara Altiplano around La Paz in the late 1960s among a small group of indigenous intellectuals and students who believed – based on their experience in La Paz – that the indigenous culture in the Altiplano was under threat of dilution by *mestizo* culture.[14]

Their ethnic Aymara nationalism aimed to revive traditional culture and to resist assimilation and homogenization. *Katarismo* described Bolivia as a mosaic of cultures and identities, an idea that was subsequently adopted by Morales and the MAS. *Katarismo* became a rather elaborate ideology consisting of a blend of class appeal and ethnic claims. It constructed a view of the state and the nation on the basis of ethnic criteria, but also included aspects of Western and indigenous forms of government. The most important legacy of *Katarismo* is the description of the nation as a 'pluri-national' mosaic. But other ethnic elements were also taken up by MAS, such as the use of the symbolic location of the Tihuanacu ruins. The nationalism of MAS has yet to achieve such sophistica-tion, though it seems this is the intention of its leaders, who do not wish the movement to become particularistic like the *Kataristas*, who signally failed to reach out to non-Aymaras.[15]

Another influence on MAS's notion of the nation were the indigenous movements of the eastern lowlands, including the Confederación de Pueblos Indígenas de Bolivia (CIDOB) and the Coordinadora de Pueblos Étnicos de Santa Cruz (CPESC). These movements were formed in the early 1980s by the smaller and more isolated indigenous peoples (e.g. Chiquitanos, Chimanes, Guaranís, Mojeños, Moxos). In 1990, 1996, 2000 and 2002, these movements organized marches to La Paz demanding official recognition of their communal territories, and of their communal forms of government, and the installation of a constituent assembly to rewrite the constitution. MAS took from them not only the notion of the *pueblos originarios* ('first peoples') or *naciones originarias*, a name they started to use around 1991, as the only identity not imposed by others and without a negative connotation. The use of these two concepts resulted in an understanding of the Bolivian state as the host of various nations – that is, a 'plurinational' state.

In sum, the key concepts employed by Morales concerning the nation have their origins in *Katarism* and the indigenous movements in the east. This does not mean, however, that Evo Morales simply took over convenient concepts from others without having been involved in the process of their development. It is true that the motivation for developing these concepts was outside MAS and its predecessors; nevertheless Evo Morales and other leaders were involved at the grassroots in the shaping of these ideas. For instance, one of the founders of *Katarismo*, Jenaro Flores, later became the leader of the national peasant confederation (CSUTCB), in which the coca producers participated. An important link with *Katarismo* is, of course, Vice President Garcia Linera, who participated in the leadership of the *Katarista*-guerrilla organization Ejército Guerrillero Túpac Katari (EGTK). There has been a similar interaction, at both grassroots and leadership levels, between MAS and the indigenous movement in the lowlands. Evo Morales, as leader of the *sindicatos* of the coca producers, participated in the marches organized by this movement. An indication of the connection with the lowland movement is that Morales invited it to select its own candidates for MAS's electoral list, though it should be noted that much of the movement retained a critical but empathetic distance from MAS. Hence *Katarismo* and the lowlands indigenous movement have influenced Morales's and MAS's understanding of the nation, though they were involved in the ideological development of the two earlier movements. Although the coca producers' movement was not in the ideological vanguard, it nevertheless became the most influential civil society actor after the demise of organized labour.

CHAPTER 3

The rise of the coca growers, mid-1980s to early 1990s

History of the coca growers' movement

The area to which the Morales family migrated in the 1980s is commonly known as *El Chapare*, but the actual name is Trópico de Cochabamba, which includes the regions Tiraque Tropical, Carrasco and Chapare. The Tropic of Cochabamba is one of the two main regions of coca production in Bolivia, the other being the Yungas in the department of La Paz.

After the *Reforma Agraria* in 1953, the Tropic of Cochabamba became a reception area for migration (Blanes and Flores, 1984). People migrated to the largely uninhabited Tropic to escape the poverty of the infertile Altiplano highlands.[1] Migration was organized partly by the state, with land titles issued through the Agricultural Reform, and partly spontaneous – that is, people moved onto vacant land without legal title (Blanes, 1983; Yañez, 2002). Some 85 per cent of all families in the Tropic are members of a *sindicato* (Rivera Pizarro, 1991). Every owner of a *chaco* (plot of land) has to be a member of a *sindicato*, because the *sindicato* has the power of distributing the land. That is, although legal land titles have been introduced by the state and land can be bought and sold, nothing happens without the approval of the *sindicatos*. So, membership is automatic in the majority of the cases of new land ownership. In any case it is virtually impossible for an individual to own a plot of land against the will of the *sindicato* in the area. Evo Morales therefore automatically became a member of the *sindicato* to which his plot belonged; though initially he took no particular interest in the organization.

Two main factors prompted the founding of the movement: one, the requirements of the environment (i.e. the need to administer land distribution and the challenges of survival in a sparsely populated area), and, two, the previous experience of leaders of civil society organizations prior to their migrating. Interestingly, the history of the *sindicatos* confirms the nowadays less fashionable argument of Olson (1992: 16–22) that 'selective benefits' and sanctions are important for motivating people to join and participate in social organizations. The *sindicatos* achieve a high rate of active participation by offering the selective benefit of land use, and by sanctioning non-participation by taking away the land. As I will argue below, this also shows that, as argued by Gramsci (1971), hegemony contains an element of coercion.

The movement began in the 1950s as an instrument of solidarity to help others out by meeting together on a regular basis. The most common way of founding a *sindicato* was for a number of individuals living in relative proximity to come together as neighbours, and then to set up the organization, which would regulate land occupation by new migrants. Sometimes *sindicatos* were also established by individuals who had occupied a large plot of land and sold it to new migrants.

> Before I came to live in the *Chapare*, I had lived in a village near Colomi. I ... came then in 1953 to the *Chapare*. At this time, there were only two settlements in this area here and these belonged to Torota.[2] Where I settled, there were only eight people living.
>
> A year later, we got organized and joined Sindicato Torota. The people from Torota obliged us to help in the construction of their roads.... In those days, it was not like today with authorities, leaders, *corregidores*: there was nobody....

Our own roads were a disaster where the horses fell down. That's why we organized ourselves; and the *dirigente*, who was in Torota, informed us that we could work for two days to truly open our roads and a lot of people worked. (Don Ebrahimo)[3]

Evo Morales, along with some of the older people in the Tropic, recalls that their life as migrants was harsh and that his hands were bloody from working with the machete to clear his land. However, building close-knit communities, in which information was passed quickly, helped him and the other newcomers to survive and to become more successful with their crops. For instance, Morales initially had no idea, of course, how to grow tropical fruits such as banana; neither did he have experience of growing coca. Furthermore, the area was almost inaccessible and therefore the organizations assumed a key role in the development and maintenance of basic infrastructure, and later in income-generating activities.

I came here in 1953; there were only three or four families in Matanzas and it was full of mosquitoes; there were also tigers, lions.... Life was very difficult, there were no roads, we had to bring everything by foot from Torota. But we helped each other. To get land, we had to become members of the Sindicato Torota. More and more people came to live in Matanzas and so Torota became too big and we decided to set up our own *sindicato* to solve our own problems. (Doña Maria)

We needed our *sindicato* to be organized in these difficult times. Young people today do not understand how difficult it was.... Our *sindicato* helped us also to get titles for our land, because we collected money, contracted an engineer, who made a map with the measurement of our land, and with this we sent our *dirigente* to a lawyer, who helped to give us land titles.... You see, the tasks at that time were different from today: apart from defending coca, now we also discuss development projects and all is more political. (Don Santiago)

A minimum of twenty members per *sindicato* were required and the founding was done in the office of the Federation.... I already had experience in a union in the place I came from and I used this

experience here to start our *sindicato* and to be a good *dirigente*.
(Don Marcelo)

The first *sindicatos* were instrumental mainly in regulating the
stream of new migrants. With a growing population, new *sindicatos*
were established in places that had no organization, or they were
founded by splitting from existing ones.

With the boom of cocaine consumption in Western countries in
the 1970s, and following the neoliberal reforms in the mid-1980s,
two waves of immigrants migrated to the Tropic, among them
many former mineworkers, looking for new work after the mines
were closed down. The population of the area increased from a few
tens of thousands before the agrarian reform to well over 300,000
today. Until the mid-1990s, state institutions were either entirely
absent or only present in the form of repression. The problems
of survival for the migrants were compounded by insufficient
knowledge about their new environment, necessitating cooperation and association. Collective organization was needed for the
following tasks: the occupation of land and its regularization; the
organization of a form of agriculture different to that in the valleys
and Altiplano, including new technical knowledge; the solving of
problems related to housing, infrastructure, education and health
care. In consequence, the migrants founded local *sindicatos* using
their previous experience in urban and rural unions, which meant
they were modelled after the *sindicatos mineros* and *campesinos* of
the Altiplano.

When the population in the Tropic grew, an average of ten *sindicatos* formed a *central*, which synthesizes the interests, priorities
and demands of the members of its *sindicatos* and resolves conflicts
between individual organizations. The *central* is frequently the body
that interacts with the local authorities (e.g. to elaborate the five-year
plans of municipal investment) and non-governmental organizations
(NGOs). The *central* decides about development projects in the
area, and articulates the views of its affiliated *sindicatos* at the higher

level of the *federación* as well as informing the grassroots about discussions in the *federaciónes*.

At least three *centrales* are needed for a *federación,* which functions, in effect, at the provincial level. The *federaciónes* primarily link their members with the rest of the popular sector and with the state. *Federaciónes* coordinate collective actions (e.g. *marchas,*[4] demonstrations and road blockades), channel political participation, help shape the political proposals of MAS and participate in negotiations with the authorities. Since the members of the *sindicatos* decided in 1993 to become involved in politics, the five, and subsequently six, *federaciónes* have constituted a pool of candidates of the movement for local and national elections.[5] The *federaciónes* hold elected candidates accountable, at monthly assemblies, by requiring them to justify their actions. In the Tropic all elected officials in the municipalities, as well as the majority of the administrative staff, have formerly been in leading positions in the *federaciónes*, which hold primary elections to decide who will be the candidates for MAS.

Since 1996, the *federaciónes* have cooperated under the umbrella organization of the Comité de la Coordinación de las Seis Federaciónes (CCSF, Coordination Committee of the Six Federations), the highest tier of the social movement and member of the Central Obrera Boliviana (COB, National Workers Union). With Morales as its leader, the CCSF tried coordinating activities and promoting unity behind an alternative political project of all those disillusioned with traditional parties. In 2007 there was a total of about 590 *sindicatos* with an average of 53 members, 60 *centrales* and 6 *federaciónes*. Each organization has an elected executive committee of leaders, with up to twelve leadership positions. This means that between 3,000 and 4,000 people are part of the leadership of the coca producers' movement.

The growth of the movement proceeded in a bottom-up and decentralized manner. It was basically defined by migration: in areas where people arrived, new organizations were established, and as *sindicatos* grew larger they began to divide themselves and to cooperate within a *central*. This means that a patchwork of organizations spread over the Tropic, starting with the grassroots *sindicatos* and subsequently forming overarching organizations. Growth proceeded without any central control or planning and resulted in various *sindicatos* coexisting in very close proximity in some areas, while other *sindicatos* have much larger territories, and no immediate neighbour.

Structuring force of society

The absence of the state or any other institution until the mid-1980s gave the *sindicatos* the unique opportunity to establish themselves as a de facto sovereign power over a given territory. They structured local social relations and functioned as quasi-government, which challenges conventional views on social movements that see them as distinct from state institutions. The *sindicato* is the institution exclusively able to give social and legal legitimacy to new settlers:

> Here exist only the laws of the *sindicatos*. There is no state, no police, and no lawyers who can tell us what to do or how to resolve our conflicts.... The *sindicato* determines if somebody is a legitimate inhabitant or not. (Don Maximo)

> *Sindicatos* claim to have sovereignty over a local area, which means setting the rules of the game, including determining when the right to use a plot can be abrogated. The power to distribute land implies a powerful incentive for people to join the organization and to keep participating in it (Olson, 1992).

The *sindicatos* can influence the composition of the social structure in a given locality, since it is virtually impossible to live there without the permission of the *sindicato*. In addition, *sindicatos* fulfil some tasks of the state: they develop the infrastructure or build schools:

> Before we used to live in the mountains and it was very hard to bring our products to market, to bring supplies to our houses or for our

children to go to school. Therefore we decided in the *sindicato* to collect money and to buy half a hectare from Matanzas.... We have built a road, a football ground, and water and electricity connections. (Don Ernesto)

About the construction of our school: we came together and discussed everything. All eight families agreed to collect money, to build our own school and to pay a teacher. (Don Ebrahimo)

This means that when the young Morales moved to the area, he arrived in a complex and potent social structure that would greatly facilitate his rise to political power. That is to say, although the coca growers' movement benefited from his rise to the presidency in the sense that *controlled* and *limited* coca production for traditional use is now possible, it is Morales who is the product of the *sindicatos*, and not the reverse. The reason is that through the development of settlements with communal facilities the *sindicatos* turned individual migrants into communities. The *sindicatos* functioned also as an expression of collective interest in bureaucratic procedures, such as applications for land titles. They collected money to supplement the salaries of the teachers, who would otherwise not have stayed to teach in the Tropic. This range of tasks developed in a gradual process, which required an institution to structure social relations.

Stimulated by growing settlements and changing living conditions, the organizations developed a multilayered structure (*sindicatos*, *centrales* and *federaciónes*), and adapted their functions to the needs of members. They organized social life with, for instance, football tournaments between different *sindicatos* – which was one of Morales's first tasks. Nowadays, they also serve as vehicles for political participation in defence of common interests. That is, they have developed an increasingly important representative function, which was initially limited to presenting basic infrastructural and economic demands to the authorities. Due to the war on drugs the demands developed into a general political challenge to the status quo. In short, hardly any aspect of life in the Tropic was left untouched by the *sindicatos*: they are the single most significant social institution beyond the immediate family.

The *sindicatos* are a very interesting form of social movement, since they have developed 'quasi-state' characteristics, and therefore do not fit the conventional notion that state and social movements are by definition distinct. Since the introduction of directly elected mayors, the *sindicatos* have also become involved in local politics – albeit after initial resistance to political decentralization. The *sindicatos* are directly linked to local government, since all elected local positions are filled with (former) *sindicato* leaders. They became candidates through 'primaries' held by the movement. This is how, for instance, MAS minister Felipe Cáceres became major of Villa Tunari, where he gained his first experience in managing a public entity, albeit a small one. At the same time, the *sindicatos* are the most important civil society opposition group in the area. The fact that those elected belong to the same organizations does not mean that they are immune from criticism. On the contrary, they have to defend their decisions both within official institutional channels and within the social movement itself. According to Evo Morales and to most inhabitants of the Tropic, this has helped reduce corruption and increase the accountability of local municipal administrations. The *sindicatos* thus provided the model for Morales and MAS to remain with one foot outside the political institutions.

Internal functioning

The above sketched history of the *sindicatos* is intended to stress the complexity of the organization and to avoid the impression that the movement was somehow founded by Morales. This section will discuss the internal functioning of the *sindicatos* in order to show how the leader, Evo Morales, was formed. The functioning of the *sindicatos* is characterized by numerous meetings, committees and a large number of leadership positions, which give ordinary members the opportunity to discuss at length matters of concern, and allow (even force) them to take positions of responsibility in the organization.

Morales's initial lack of interest in the social movement changed, according to him, dramatically in 1981 when he witnessed soldiers of García Meza's drug-funded regime burn a peasant alive in front of his family (Contreras Baspineiro, 2005: 10). After this experience, Morales felt that he had also to defend human rights and the cultivation of coca. But only two years later, owing to his passion for playing football and his drive to organize games whenever he had a chance, Morales accepted the post of *secretario* of sports in his *sindicato*. Here he learned to speak in public, and through the meetings that informed its members about political and economic issues he became more politically aware. Given his talent for organization and his relatively high level of education compared to some older inhabitants, he was elected leader of his *sindicato* in 1985. Three years later, aged 29, he became the leader of the Federación Especial de Trabajadores Campesinos del Trópico de Cochabamba (FETCTC), one of the highest positions in the movement's structure. He had already stood for election two years earlier, but was considered too young and inexperienced and was defeated. How did the movement's structure influence the young Morales?

Formalized organizational structure

The *sindicatos* are characterized by a broad array of leadership positions, which give many members of the community the opportunity to participate; indeed many see this as a duty. The example of Morales shows how this low threshold for becoming involved helps create future leaders for the movement. What is interesting is that these are actually rather formalized organizations with (nowadays) detailed statutes that play an important role in their daily functioning and that can be quoted by many members. The statutes emphasize as 'general principles' of the movement: mutual respect, accountability of the leaders, communication, participation and decision-making by consensus. In most cases, statutes were approved unanimously by the general assembly of a *sindicato*. The bases decide on the monthly dues of the members, and elect the executive committee of the organization, which is (maximally) composed of the following positions:

1. Secretary General or *Dirigente*
2. Secretary of Relations
3. Secretary of *Actas* (Documents and Minutes)
4. Secretary of *Hacienda* (Finances)
5. Secretary of Organization
6. Secretary of Press and Propaganda
7. Secretary of Education
8. Secretary of Sports
9. Secretary of Conflicts
10. Secretary of Roads Administration
11. Secretary of *Salubridad* (Health)
12. Secretary of *Control Campesino* (Peasant Control)
13. *Vocal* (Responsible for convening meetings)

Even small *sindicatos* have most of the above-mentioned secretarial posts. Obviously, the position of *dirigente* carries the most prestige. But, given Morales's beginning as Secretary of Sports, this position grants a degree of prestige too. I encountered many young men in the same position who said that one day they will be 'like Evo'. The many formal positions may mean that around half the members have a leadership role in the organization. The aim of this structure is, according to the statutes, 'to facilitate the participation and deliberation' of a *sindicato*'s members, as well as ensure the 'accountability of its leadership'. It is paramount that all members are able to express their opinions without restriction and that they take part in the decision-making process.

The assemblies

The core of the movement is the various assemblies: they make possible the processes of communication and participation that Morales's discourse about the movement so cherishes. Assemblies provide the opportunity for every individual to exercise the right to communicate his/her views (without a time limit on speeches). The foundation for deliberations during the meetings is assumed to be the right to communicate. Assemblies can take up to three days, with eighteen hours of meetings a day, marked by long speeches and exchanges of opinions, until a consensus is reached on the issues at stake. They play a significant role in reinforcing the collective identity of the coca producers, as they are a forum for everyday encounters, where people begin to 'share and mould the distinctive and prosaic elements of identity' (Scully and Creed, 2005, cited in Davis, 2005: 251).

Type and sequence of meetings

The highest governing organ of the organizations of the coca producers is, interestingly, not the committee of the leaders (*Comité Ejecutivo*), but the plenary meetings: *Congreso* (yearly), *Ampliado* (roughly quarterly) and *Asamblea* (monthly). The various meetings can be ordered in importance. First comes the biannual Congress, attended by all leaders and a (simple) majority of members. This is a general meeting that discusses all broad issues concerning the organization. For instance, its remit includes the political situation and collective action, and it can alter the organizational statutes. Next comes the *Ampliado*, which deals with pressing or temporary matters; for example, an urgent border involving other *sindicatos*. Third, all organizations hold a regular monthly assembly; these are coordinated so that the assemblies of the higher-level organizations come before the more local ones.

This structure stands somewhat in tension with the discourse of Morales and other leaders, which insists that the grassroots decide and the higher level organizations follow; for, were this the case, then the authority of the assemblies would emanate from the local level. The fact that the meeting of the highest level comes first indicates that decisions are, on the contrary, communicated towards the local level. Confronted with this tension, Morales argues that it is actually a circular process, whereby information is first sent to the local level, at which the members decide and communicate the consensus back to the higher levels. While I cannot refute the general thrust of this claim, it would seem that – at least in matters of urgency – there is not enough time available for this process of consultation and consensus-seeking.

The meetings start gradually with a slow influx of people that can take up to three hours. At some point, there seems to be a spontaneous consensus that enough people are present, and the meeting suddenly takes off. Within a very short time the room is filled with even more people. The meetings proceed according to a fixed order, where first the attendance is documented. The *dirigente* proposes the agenda for the meeting and, after its approval, reads out the minutes of the previous session and submits them for discussion and approval. The main items on the agenda might then go (in roughly hierarchical order) something like this. First, there is discussion about the general economic situation of the members and how to improve it. This may include instances of failure to pay membership dues, or the issue of financial compensation for those members who participate in the campaign of MAS.[6] Second, internal organizational issues are discussed, concerning especially the activities of the *dirigentes*. On occasion members will 'quarrel' (*pelearse*) extensively with the leaders, sometimes to such a degree that one wonders whether they will remain in office. Obviously, at such moments shrewd leaders will try to strike a balance between showing they take the criticism seriously, defending themselves, and presenting an appeasing future perspective. Third is the issue of the *Instrumento Político*, the importance of which has grown since 1997. Here issues concerning MAS are discussed, including what the latest proposals are, how candidates have performed, and what needs to be done to support its campaign. Speeches of Morales are frequently quoted. In addition to relatively in-depth debates over policy proposals, one can hear a lot of 'pep-talks' generating (rather inflated) hopes about what their 'political instrument' will achieve.

The fourth item, 'Coca and Territory', includes offerings about the importance of coca for the individual grower and as a symbol of national sovereignty, Bolivian culture and as a holy plant.[7] In addition, information is given regarding sites of eradication, and the danger of this happening in their *sindicato* is weighed up. When there is a significant threat of eradication, members agree to set up *comités de autodefensa* (self-defence committees) to patrol the paths leading to the *chacos* (plots) where coca is planted.

These meetings exemplify Morales's view of direct democracy at work. Their main aims are the facilitation of communication between leaders and the grassroots, the sharing of information, and consensual decision-making by the bases after extensive discussion. In the same way Morales tries as president to visit grassroots organizations weekly, communication between leaders and the grassroots is considered in the *sindicatos* an essential prerequisite of making informed decisions. As indicated at the beginning of this chapter, every member may participate in the discussions, and has the opportunity to express his or her point of view on all topics for as long as he or she wishes. It is therefore not unusual to hear spontaneous speeches of thirty minutes or more. This forum provided important training for Morales in two aspects: he learned, through extensive practice, to speak well in public; and he mastered the art of persuading a sceptical audience.

Although Morales has had formal speeches prepared for important occasions, such as for his inauguration and addresses to the UN General Assembly, he nevertheless has tended to deliver them from memory, deviating somewhat but never fundamentally from his script. This ability to make a reasonably good speech spontaneously has impressed some Western diplomats, as I learned in private conversation. When speaking to a Bolivian audience, Morales still concludes his speeches with the typical *'Está bien, Compañeros?'*, which is used in the *sindicatos* to ask whether or not the others agree with what was said. In the *sindicatos* this tends to provoke other speeches, slowly narrowing the range of opinion until a consensus emerges. At no point is the discussion cut short by a demand for a vote on an issue, which means that the meeting can easily take twelve hours. However, as Morales and others members of the *sindicatos* told me, the point is not to put the stress on efficiency; what counts is the process of arriving at a consensus through the expression of all members' opinions.

This emphasis on communication and information-sharing renders the assemblies an important social space that synthesizes everyday social relations and generates a common discourse, which in turn has shaped Morales's way of expressing himself. This common discourse is the foundation for a shared identity on the part of the community of coca producers, who sometimes live in remote areas far from each other. The meetings constitute central nodes of the network of coca producers. If Morales and MAS need resources, for instance for a campaign, this network can be activated to mobilize people: Morales and other leaders attend the meetings, discuss their plans and the grassroots decide how to support the party, usually by making volunteers available.

Leadership

According to the discourse of the movement, two features testify to the fact that a 'true democracy' (Evo Morales) is practised internally. One is the movement's internal structure, discussed above. The other is its leadership, the most important task of which is to enable unimpeded internal communication and to disseminate information as the basis of movement democracy. Leaders are judged by how well they succeed in this; how well they generate consensus, articulate the views of the grassroots at other levels, and facilitate communication with other organizations.

As in the case of Morales, leaders of the movement are elected, usually for two years, by consensus during the annual Congress. If the members of the Congress are unable to reach a consensus, there will be a secret ballot, the candidate with the majority of votes being declared the winner. The *sindicatos* are not professionalized in the sense of having full-time, paid leaders. Thus far, then, being a *sindicato* leader is not a career that one can choose. This is owing to the principle of rotational leadership, which means that a leader is not supposed to be re-elected. Immediate re-election is considered undesirable, the continuity even of experienced and successful leaders not important. Nevertheless, as the movement has so many leadership positions, a *dirigente* can move to take another position and support the new leader with his or her experience indirectly. Every member of the community is expected to assume a leadership position at least once. It is, therefore, rare to find a male[8] inhabitant of the Tropic who has never been in a leadership position.

However, exceptions to the rule of rotation do occur. Most notably, Evo Morales was re-elected over and over again when he was still a junior leader among more experienced colleagues. I would go so far as to argue that this runs contrary to the entire logic of rotational leadership within the movement, which remains the most common practice at all the levels of the movement – except the very top. Leaving Morales at the top was certainly important for the success of the movement and of MAS, so the decision to override the principle of rotation has been defended by some leaders as necessary on pragmatic and strategic grounds. It should be observed that the rotational leadership system continues to operate at the grassroots, with the potential to produce an able successor to Morales as the leader of MAS. Julio Salazar, who finally replaced Morales as head of the Comité de Coordinación, might become one possible candidate. Thus, even though the continuation of Morales as top leader contradicts the ideal of a perfectly functioning democracy inside the movement, the system at least has the potential to ensure a successful generational change in leadership. Although it is too early to say, the mere existence of a principle intended to refresh the leadership ranks testifies to the movement's democratic credentials in comparison to the internal functioning of all the other major parties.

Another contentious issue, which constitutes a parallel concern in the *sindicatos* and the Morales administration, is that of hegemony and consensus. Don Julian's story below is similar to that of Evo Morales, because both were part of the first wave of a new generation of leaders, who were elected when daily problems of survival became less pressing. The focus subsequently switched from survival to the internal functioning of the movement and then to interaction with the authorities, both of which demanded different leadership skills.

> I became a *dirigente* when only 21 years old. At 23 or 24, I was elected *Central*. In general – I would say most importantly – leaders have to communicate well to inform the bases. Everybody will be a leader once, but the issue becomes whether the bases want you to become a leader again or to take on other tasks.... In the beginning, it was not easy for me, I was still young and there were many things to do. Sometimes members did not pay their dues and nobody had bothered about it. At this time [in the late 1970s], the leaders were mainly the elders, owing to their long experience here. But they were afraid to ask for outstanding dues and to issue fines. I changed the system of collecting dues; we still try for a long time to talk to them and to convince them, but sometimes this is not enough. Before, a group went to these members and tried to get the money; if unsuccessful, they would physically castigate the person. Now we go there and seize valuable property belonging to the member, which he will only get back when he has made payment. (Don Julian, ex-Central of Matanzas, MAS member of the municipal council)

As this quotation shows, the *sindicatos* have a hegemonic status in the area, but we see that this hegemony rests not only on the generation of consensus but also on force. Similarly, MAS is clearly the hegemonic expression of a number of social interests, but this does not mean that there always exists a broad consensus on everything MAS does, as is sometimes suggested in Morales's discourse. Indeed, while MAS does not use the physical force which can sometimes be applied by grassroots organizations, there is nevertheless an element of force in the imposition of certain candidates or of certain decisions taken by Morales that are only ratified by the grassroots. This fits Gramsci's conceptualization of hegemony as

the combination of force and consent, which balance each other
reciprocally without force predominating excessively over consent.
Indeed, the attempt is always to ensure that force would appear to be
based on the consent of the majority. (1971: 80)

In the *sindicatos*, the element of force can be the threat of taking
away land or even physical force to coerce people to follow the
rules of the movement. However, great emphasis is put on the fact
that the use of force against individual members is always based
on a consensual decision by all members (excepting the individual
member in question). This exercise of hegemony is partly the reason
for the survival of the *sindicatos* in a repressive environment, since it
has made them a unitary bloc. It also removes pressure and responsibility from the shoulders of the leaders, as they are able to take
refuge behind the principle that decisions are made by consensus.
To a certain extent, Morales has carried this logic over into MAS,
where sometimes decisions taken by a small group of people are sold
as a consensus reached by all social movements in Bolivia. Similarly,
there is a clear limit as to how far dissenting opinions can be raised,
at least in public. The most dramatic case in point was certainly the
expulsion of Filemón Escóbar, one of Bolivia's best-known trade
unionists, co-founder of MAS and mentor of Morales, after he had
disagreed publicly several times with Morales. But there are also a
number of lesser-known cases, especially of MPs unhappy that they
had not gained a place on the electoral lists of MAS again, despite
having the support of their local organization. Wishing to remain
anonymous, three former MPs suggested that this was due to their
internal criticism of certain decisions. It is impossible to judge how
serious a threat this exercise of discipline is for the rank-and-file
MPs of MAS. A certain degree of party discipline exists in every
democracy. Given the polarized situation in Bolivia, it is hard for
dissenters not to appear to be supporting the opposition. What these
examples show, above all else, is that the notion that everything is
done by consensus is an ideal constructed by Morales's discourse.
As I will argue throughout this book, there exists a tension between

the requirement to include the broadest possible range of views or demands and the impulse to exclude the external other.

While we should be aware of the potential exclusionary down-side of attempting hegemonically to include a range of people, it should also be noted that leadership is quite demanding on the individual. Being a leader both in the social movement in MAS is a very time-consuming task, which sometimes requires personal and economic 'sacrifice for the community' (Evo Morales). During their incumbency, *sindicato* leaders have no time to work on their fields. Although they are entitled to get help on their *chacos*, the fields cannot be cultivated as intensively as the owner would normally do. Only the leaders of the *federaciónes* receive a small reimbursement for their expenses, paid by the *sindicatos*. MPs, on the other hand, are expected to contribute part of their salary to support their grassroots organizations. Apart from the prestige and recognition of the position, being a leader is not something one would do out of material interest. In any case, nobody can refuse the position:

> Being *dirigente* is an obligation on everyone when the bases demand it. In this way my bases have carried me to the position of a *central* and later the *ejecutivo* of the *federación*, because they thought I was capable of communicating and organizing. (Fernando Grosso, former *ejecutivo* of a *federación*)

> To be a leader is a lot of work and it's difficult. It is a sacrifice. Sometimes we do not eat, we only chew coca. When we do not travel, we do not receive any money.[9] (Don Carlos, *ejecutivo* of a *federación*)

Morales has frequently stated what leadership, including being president, means to him: it is a service to the community. Arguments over internal democracy notwithstanding, this notion is obviously dear to him and expresses how he perceives his task. The decision to reduce his salary by more than 50 per cent to 15,000 bolivianos (about $2,150 per month, at 2006 exchange rate) was therefore not merely a populist move, though he allowed himself a 25 per cent increase in early 2011. In any case, Morales's long stint as leader of the movement has hardened him to long days of meetings. *Sindicato* leaders not only have to attend many long meetings within the social movement, in other movements and with the authorities; they also have paperwork to do for the members, and must maintain close personal contact with the base. This may involve long journeys to remote houses of members. Whilst it is possible that the sacrifices of incumbency are somewhat exaggerated by leaders, it is noteworthy that the discourse about leadership stresses responsibility towards the community. It is certainly the case that the leaders were the ones targeted first by the authorities when strikes, road blocks or simple demonstrations had been organized. For example, Morales was arrested several times for organizing protests, and was even expelled from parliament on one occasion, though he has never been convicted of any criminal activity or drug-trafficking offence. (Prior to the election of Morales, the authorities' strategy of suppressing social protests by arresting or intimidating leaders had changed little since the era of military dictatorships. Though it became more covert and concentrated on certain groups such as the miners and the coca growers. A well-known story tells how Morales was arrested and severely mistreated by several soldiers on 28 June 1989 after having organized a march to remember the fifteen coca growers killed by the army in the so-called 'Massacre of Villa Tunari' a year earlier.)

The guiding notion of leadership as responsibility means – in conjunction with the practice of rotational leadership – that there is no overt campaigning for positions. The *sindicatos* do not elect those who most convince others that they will do a good job.

> Concerning the election of leaders in rural areas, they are not elected because they want to be a leader ... and make propaganda, and convince the people. Rather, it is a responsibility to become the leader of the community. And it will always be somebody else's turn to lead for some time. This is the rotational system that is practised. (Don Humberto, member of the board of leaders of a *federación*)

This absence of campaigning has long been an important idio-syncratic characteristic of the movement. When I talked in 2002 to possible candidates shortly before the elections of new leaders, there was a noticeable silence regarding why they would be good leaders. It does not mean, however, that during meetings favourites for leadership positions don't emerge owing to their vocal presence and perceived ability to achieve a consensus behind their proposals. Candidates emerge from the dynamics of the assemblies, and those who prefer not be elected sometimes decide not to attend.[10] However, since MAS has been in power, becoming a leader has become vastly more attractive owing to the possibility of moving up and obtaining a position in government. This has led to a more open electoral competition. From a Western perspective, one instinctively welcomes this as a positive development increasing transparency and account-ability, but it is unclear whether it really helps in bringing the most dedicated and trustworthy people to the top or simply favours those who have oratorical or financial means of convincing others.

Evo Morales and other *sindicato* leaders stress that the movement's leadership differs in another respect from Western representative democracy, as they perceive it: *dirigentes* have no flexibility to make individual decisions, but are supposed 'to be one' with the bases and follow their lead. This principle of *mandar obediciendo* means taking the views of the bases to higher levels of decision-making without adding personal spin to them. Conversely, it entails giving nearly verbatim presentations to the bases regarding discussions at higher levels. Thus a leader is regarded more as an instrument or facilitator for the bases than as an autonomous legislator. A leader needs to ensure that the extensive discussions somehow generate consensus, and must be able to guide the discussion with care and subtlety without pushing his personal opinion. This model of leadership is not very different from that of Rosa Luxemburg (1940), who stressed equality of the proletariat and rejected a hierarchical ordering within an organization (i.e. a communist party). The various demands of the coca growers are made equal in opposition to an external other, namely the repressive state. The absence of a hierarchy of demands convinces all members that their individual demands are important, and helps to stimulate a sense of community within the movement, which is a crucial factor for the effective mobilization of the bases.[11]

Morales has become a successful leader of the movement due to his skill at projecting clear leadership that defines an external other and his ability to take on board diverse viewpoints but nevertheless achieve consensus. Leadership is more complicated than in organizations where conflicts can be resolved by voting, or by top-down imposition. Though Morales may indeed sometimes impose decisions, he has at least to go through the elaborate process of presenting them as taken at the grassroots by consensus. This does not render the decisions better or more democratic, but it has the potential to do so, which is far from the case with Bolivia's other mainstream parties.

Yet Morales's discourse about a 'truly democratic' organization constructs an image of the organization at least as much as it reflects an actually existing practice. One may question how much of the local consensus is retained in decisions made by the Coordination Committee of the Six Federaciónes (CCSF), composed of the six *ejecutivos*. In addition, we have seen that the actual hierarchy of the meetings contradicts the idea of a bottom-up dynamic, since the highest level meets first. This might imply that leaders have to build a consensus in their organizations for decisions that have actually already been made. Grassroots proposals that are communicated a month later might therefore come too late to influence decisions. Be this as it may, it is not the aim of this chapter to produce a final verdict on how democratic the movement is. Instead, I have used the hegemonic discourse of the movement to show how this has influenced Evo Morales as a leader. From such a perspective we can understand that the image of a grassroots, consensual form of decision-making has been central to the creation of a shared community of coca producers in which most of Morales's socialization and political learning took place. The discourse accompanying this idiosyncratic form of leadership convinced the bases to put a great deal of energy into supporting the candidature of Morales. It also proved politically very beneficial for Morales since he could effectively present himself as a very different (i.e. more responsive and accountable) candidate compared to all other candidates in the country's elections.

The discourse regarding the consensual style of the movement does not mean, of course, that no internal conflicts exist or that people do not criticize each other. The most frequent complaints about leaders are that they are not participatory or transparent enough, that they lack personal effort, or even that they are authoritarian or corrupt. Such criticisms arise when leaders fail to meet expectations, which may not surprising given the demanding requirement that a leader must be *mandar obediciendo* and 'at one with the bases'. For this can be difficult to achieve, as leaders need to find a consensus at higher levels of the movement, which may entail altering the standpoint of their own *sindicato*.[12]

As with any other leader, Evo Morales has to face criticism from the bases, and my interview partners from the *sindicatos* and Central Matanzas duly raised issues on which they were unhappy with him. There seemed to be more criticism in late 2007 than during 2005 or, especially, 2002, when enthusiasm following MAS's good electoral performance prevailed over criticism. In subsequent years, expectations increased and therefore so did criticism. A recurrent theme was that Morales was so busy that he did not spend sufficient time with the bases, thereby distancing himself from the grassroots. With the growth and political success of MAS, people started to ask more questions about how its candidates were selected and why it had established alliances with other parties, especially after the opening up of the party in 2004. In general, there seems to be a healthy degree of open debate and internal criticism of leaders, including Evo Morales.

Evo Morales is known for his outspoken criticism directed at other politicians or the authorities in regions or municipalities controlled by parties in opposition to MAS. However, he is no less frank concerning other leaders or ordinary members of the movement. Much of his criticism is directed at what he regards as an insufficient level of mobilization for collective actions. For instance, he pointed out that the electoral campaign in the Tropic was not always well organized.

> How is it possible that our transport workers do not carry their little flags or at least some kind of identification, like a 'sticker', for example. This is important, it is the best form of campaigning, *compañeros*. For this reason the protest against the Federación de Centrales Unidas: I could not see any flag, except in the headquarters in Shinaota. How is this possible, *compañeros*? I said to Compañero Toco, Compañero Tito, that they should follow the example of Compañero Licenciano and Julio [Salazar] and see how it is in Villa Tunari. It is not possible *compañeros* that in Shinaota the population is better at protesting than at showing the flags. This is the fault of the leaders, *compañeros y compañeras*. (Evo Morales)

For Morales, the main culprits for this sub-optimal mobilization are the leaders of the *sindicatos* and *centrales*, who failed to convince their bases to show support for the movement. This is fairly routine criticism; however, taking into account the movement's bottom-up ethos, the idea that leaders have to mobilize the bases might be interpreted as somewhat paradoxical, given that the grassroots ostensibly rule the organization. Such quotations show, furthermore, that mobilizing the coca producers is an ongoing task for the leaders, and that the political success of the movement to date has to be attributed to the efforts of the leadership, particularly that of Evo Morales.

In conclusion, the most manifest element of the movement's internal organization is the emphasis on grassroots participation, including the large number of leadership positions, extensive communication and consultation with the bases, and a decentralized structure. It might be said that a general principle of the movement is 'subsidiarity'.[13]

> The most important principle ... is that the bases rule. This means that the *dirigentes*, the leaders, have to listen and follow what the grassroots decide. The organizations of the coca producers have

a decentralized, non-hierarchic and participative structure. (Evo Morales)

One could argue that leaders obviously will aim to portray their organization as participative and grassroots-driven. Yet ordinary members share this conception, which is based on their experience of fulfilling leadership roles. This model is predicated on free speech during meetings and the constant stressing of the principle *las bases mandan* or *mandar obedeciendo*. We can characterize this as a 'grassroots discourse' (Panizza, 2005a) since it constructs an understanding of democracy that prioritizes horizontal politics and new forms of political participation that give voice to civil society. Morales obviously regards the decentralized and bottom-up participation in decisions in the coca growers' movement as a method applicable to the national level in order to deepen democracy.

Coca discourse: defending the sacred leaf

The root of Morales's political success is defence of the coca leaf. How could such a stigmatized special issue become the motor for one of Latin America's most remarkable careers? Moreover, Morales and other coca-producing peasants initially defended it purely as an economic demand: this was about making a living, not about abstract issues such as democracy or quality of institutions. The fundamental demand of the *sindicatos* is that coca should be legalized in order to create a legal market for coca leaves for traditional consumption and its legal derivatives such as tea, soap and toothpaste.

> With all those arguments – being legal, moral, scientific, and so on
> – we will defend *la hoja de coca*. And with coca we defend our dignity
> and our sovereignty. (Evo Morales)

The arguments for the legalization of coca are: that coca is not cocaine; that it is possible to produce coca in Bolivia while guaranteeing that none will go to the drugs trade; and that coca consumption is good for the economy by giving poor farmers a livelihood.

Over the years coca became linked to much broader issues. It incorporated other unmet demands through the rejection of the narrow definition and the rearticulation of the crop as a symbol of defence of national sovereignty and natural resources. In other words, from the very particularistic demand of coca as an economic issue arose an increasingly broader political demand, which was ambiguous or 'tendentially empty'. In this way it was able to include other demands within the 'chain of equivalence' (Laclau, 2005). Morales's discourse employs the word 'coca' to demonstrate the existence of a large group of people, who hitherto had not been considered legitimate political actors in the existing political system, and then to articulate the idea of a radical inclusion of the previously uncounted. Hence, the process of naming a subject (i.e. the coca producers) that had not been named before is an important feature of MAS's discourse.

My argument is that the cause of the rearticulation of coca was a repressive strategy by the authorities to eradicate coca, which caused a severe crisis for the population of the Tropic. Their livelihood was threatened fundamentally, while they were not offered any viable economic alternative (Blommaert, 2003; Coca Antezana, 1999). The repression and denial of rights in the war on drugs unmasked for the coca growers the real form of domination behind a facade of liberal democracy. This triggered a process within which the *sindicatos* moved from organizing community self-help to being the grassroots cells of a political party they had founded. Hence, the war on drugs marked the start of the political activism of the *sindicatos*, whose collective actions[14] were intended as non-violent enforcement of their demands to bring the authorities to the negotiation table. However, the rejection of negotiations by all governments since 1985, based on a portrayal of the movement as illegitimate and non-political, strengthened their conviction that the type of democracy sold to them by the ruling elites was not what they understood by the term. They grew firmer in their belief that they could obtain their demands only under a more substantial form of democracy. Before this could happen, they had to elaborate this notion and then practise it at the local level. Consequently, but not without initial resistance, they took part in programmes of decentralized democracy and elected candidates to local government following the institutional reforms of the mid-1990s. At the same time, they kept questioning the repressive strategy of coca eradication and criticized the failure of free-market-oriented economic policies, which brought no tangible benefits to the rural population. Despite objective improvements in the structure of political opportunity, the *sindicatos* continued to articulate their collective actions as a struggle against political exclusion and repression by an antagonistic other. This articulation was central to the changes that were introduced to the opportunity structure, but this did not lead to the demobilization of the movement (as the MNR had hoped). Instead, the *sindicatos* became better organized, with clearer objectives and more concrete propositions in order to achieve political change at the national level.

I will discuss in more detail below the process whereby a narrowly defined demand, which was left unmet for some time, developed. That is, we will see how the demand for cultivating coca became a progressively emptied signifier that included other unmet demands.

Uniting people against the establishment

The discourse of the *sindicatos* positioned the coca producers as a united bottom-up force representing the disenfranchised population.

> The *sindicatos*, *centrales* and *federaciónes* are the united grassroots organizations that struggle for all those excluded. (Don Manuel, former *sindicato* leader and member of the staff of the municipal administration of Shinaota)

The coca producers had emerged from beyond the borderlines of official political society; their internal heterogeneity, while united against the authorities, sanctioned the inclusion of other social actors. In this regard, there is a structural element that increased the credibility of the discourse of the *sindicatos*: their grassroots were not a close-knit rural community, but a heterogeneous melange of people from different origins and backgrounds. We always talk about 'the coca producers', or 'the *cocaleros*', but this is really the view from outside. On the ground, there are important differences even between *sindicatos* that belong to the same *central* – for instance, how their leadership functions, how they perceive and support MAS, how they view alternative crops. Even within individual *sindicatos* we find people with different identities; for example, though some would accept being called *cocalero*, others reject this term and see themselves as farmers, ex-miners, indigenous people, or even taxi drivers who need to supplement their income by cultivating coca. The range of their identities is reduced to the fact that they grow coca, which is only one aspect of their livelihood, which may also include subsistence farming involving a number of other crops (Blommaert, 2003). Yet, through the war on drugs which caused a severe dislocation as it threatened their livelihoods,[15] and through discursive concentration on this particular aspect of identity, the peasants from the Tropic of Cochabamba emerged with a common overarching identity as *productores de coca* (coca producers).[16] This identifies an enemy as being responsible for the eradication of coca, against which the *productores* can be united. This 'other' was the authorities, and within them the 'traditional political elites', who were seen as responsible for all the problems associated with the war on drugs. Since repression and political exclusion by the authorities were key elements of this identity, the *sindicatos* could ally themselves with relatively little effort to other groups, who also felt marginalized, excluded or repressed. Thus the *sindicatos* could make the universal claim that the existing system was not fully inclusive, and indeed sidelined particularities of the differing demands of other groups.

This served to unify the grassroots movement as the victim of an exploitative status quo. The coca producers became equal through their defence of an ancient Andean plant – an important 'natural resource' – against the 'traditional' political elite, which exploited Bolivia's riches on the back of the indigenous peoples. Whereas previously, different *sindicatos* attempted to have their particular demands met through individual negotiations with the state and thus accepted it as the legitimate interlocutor, the dislocation caused by the war against drugs changed their perception of the political system. The perception of an antagonistic other occupying positions of power implied a questioning of the democratic status of the existing political system, and led the coca producers to launch themselves into what had hitherto been a restricted arena of official politics. They framed their collective actions as a movement committed to democratizing Bolivia and making it a more just place. The *sindicatos* presented themselves as a bottom-up force representing the disenfranchised population and as defenders of natural resources and national sovereignty, symbolized by the right to produce coca.

> Whenever I visited relatives in other *sindicatos* or when I attended meetings of the *federación*, I talked to the other leaders and told them: 'Look we are not different. We all want the same. We are all excluded by this system. Let's forget about the differences in our demands and unite against those who repress us.' (Don Nestor, leader of a *sindicato*)

From stigmatized plant to symbol of sovereignty

The specific mode of Morales's articulation made coca a political issue of national importance, while helping MAS to become a major national political player. What happened was that the demand for the legalization of coca was framed in a discourse based on coca as the symbol of national sovereignty: 'The defence of coca is the defence of the sovereignty of the *pueblos originarios*' (Evo Morales). This idea was paramount in deconstructing the image of the coca producers as apolitical criminals, and in establishing their identity as unjustifiably excluded from political society (i.e. as victims of an oppressive status quo). With coca as a national Bolivian symbol, its producers became defenders not only of a natural resource but also of national sovereignty. The logic is simple: coca was cultivated by the ancient cultures of the Inca Empire and ever since has been embedded in popular culture in Bolivia. However, for Morales, this 'important' and 'innocent' leaf became threatened with extinction due to the inability or unwillingness of Western societies to solve their domestic problem of drug abuse. Another factor was the existence of a system of international relations which made it convenient for powerful nations to impose unpopular measures on 'peripheral' countries. Thus the eradication campaign was portrayed by Morales as an 'imperialist intervention', especially by the USA. In league with an 'anti-national' political elite, this interventionism 'victimized' a large part of the Bolivian population since their cultural traditions and livelihoods were threatened. The most obvious legacy of this articulation is the name of the MAS predecessor, Asamblea por la Soberanía de los Pueblos (ASP, Assembly for the Sovereignty of the People), which was co-founded by the coca growers as an explicit means of defending the sovereignty of the Bolivian peoples. Similarly, in the official name of MAS (MAS–IPSP, Instrumento Político por la Soberanía de los Pueblos) and in the subtitle of its political programme (MAS, 2004a), we find again the notion of 'sovereignty of the peoples'. This is linked to national sovereignty through the political project of MAS to construct a 'plurinational' nation.

In this rhetoric, 'coca' can stand for a range of other unmet demands, such as the recognition of co-operative modes of production, of indigenous forms of political organization, of the demands of urban dwellers betrayed by the neoliberal promise of jobs, and so on. Since the prohibition on coca was, with justification, put down to foreign dominance over Bolivia, all other unmet demands were articulated likewise as the consequence of the failure of Bolivian governments to determine their policies autonomously. Coca came to be a symbol that represented a series of (ostensible) binary oppositions such as Andean culture/Western capitalism, national sovereignty/ US dominance, local repression/democracy on the national level, and income for the poor/decadence of the rich. On this, it is worth quoting at length from of an interview with Evo Morales:

> I will explain to you why we defend coca: it is not that we, the coca producers, are involved in drug trafficking; on the contrary, we have always said coca must be legalized and industrialized to benefit from its immense economic potential as a natural product. There are scientific studies of people like you, published in Europe, in the United States, which also say that we need to benefit from all the alternative products that can be made from coca. And we have always said, let us legalize coca and we, the *sindicatos, centrales* and *federaciónes,* will guarantee that none of the coca goes to the drug trade. But the traditional, neoliberal politicians are the ones who profit from the drug trafficking, also the banks, because it is never controlled who launders the drug money. It is they who benefit from drug trafficking, not the small producers ... and in this way the United States and the traditional, anti-national politicians oppress us, mistreat us, kill us, aiming to eliminate Andean culture with their 'zero coca' [the coca eradication programme], with the imposition of the capitalist, neoliberal, Western model, and with so-called representative democracy, which is against the poor, in favour of those who have always been rich....
>
> With our defence of coca, we are the first *instrumento político por la soberanía de los pueblos* [political instrument for the sovereignty of the peoples], and for this reason our name, MAS–IPSP, is important; and they do not like it that we say: it will not be that the US embassy rules this country. (Evo Morales)

These binary oppositions each contained a series of unmet demands (e.g. 'Andean culture' encompasses demands as diverse as those of leftist or indigenous intellectuals, or of those disappointed by neoliberalism). They created two antagonistic poles: coca producers and their allies versus the authorities and the elites. To make this simplification of the political space possible, a crop associated with narcotics became a symbol of national self-determination against foreign interference, and stood for the defence of Bolivia's culture and natural resources. This metamorphosis is quite an achievement on the part of the coca producers, and the new symbolic value of coca has achieved official status in the new constitution (2009).

This discourse is characterized by the tension between rupture and order. The latter refers to the *sindicatos*' explicit claim to hegemonically represent – or, better, to constitute – society in the Tropic of Cochabamba by radically including all political differences within the community. The former is related to the establishment of a sharp political frontier between the coca producers, unified around the defence of coca, and the authorities, who became an external other threatening the livelihood strategy of cultivating coca. For Morales, this frontier was between the coca producers, and all explicitly sympathetic to their cause, and the rest of the outside world.

With the growth of MAS and with Morales reaching out to other interests we find a constant tension between trying to redefine and establish this internal unity and the construction of the external boundaries of this group. The result was the appeal of Morales' discourse to 'the people' as a unified community, with sharply defined frontiers separating them from the 'oligarchy' of 'traditional politicians'.[17] Hence, Morales discourse is rooted in the discursive logic of the *sindicatos* with its tension between exclusion and inclusion.

PART II

CHAPTER 4

Morales's political instrument?
The creation of MAS, early 1990s

The success of MAS as a party that presents itself as having been founded in a bottom-up manner to articulate the interests all those disenfranchised by the main parties raises a number of interesting questions concerning political institutions and the way politics is conducted in Bolivia. For instance, why did it take twenty years after the return to democracy for a party of the indigenous majority to challenge effectively the hegemony of upper-class, *mestizo*-dominated parties? What is the relationship between the crisis of Bolivia's political system, especially of the party system, and the rise of MAS? How does the party's trajectory relate to institutional developments in Bolivia? That is, what role did institutional reforms play in facilitating its success? One might summarize these questions under the overarching question of this chapter: how do we explain the existence and success of MAS?

One central argument of this book is that both the party's formation and its electoral success should be credited much more to its leadership, internal characteristics and political strategies than to institutional circumstances. The founding of a party by the coca producers can be explained by the particular characteristics of their social movement (see Chapter 3), which functioned as a quasi-government in the Tropic, and by their political strategy to reach out to other social interests. The success of this 'political instrument' can be explained by its idiosyncratic characteristics, which include the lack (for a long time) of an institutional party structure, close links with social movements, and having one foot inside official institutions and the other outside them. Moreover, its success can be attributed to the political strategy of including a number of unmet demands in its discourse, and presenting a united challenge to the status quo. This was possible due to the existence of a 'crisis of representation' (Mainwaring et al., 2006) in Bolivia. Citizens lost their trust that politicians would represent their interests. They perceived political parties as acting only for the exclusive benefit of a privileged few. Disaffection with the existing political parties grew so deep and widespread that people began to participate in anti-system popular mobilizations, and started voting for political outsiders. In a nutshell, the 'crisis of representation' was a key precondition for the success of MAS with its anti-establishment discourse. It was then the leadership of Evo Morales that enabled MAS to exploit these external circumstances. The most significant achievements of Morales's leadership were to maintain close links with an increasing number of social movements and thereby to steer MAS to become a nexus between official and street politics.

Brief history of the *instrumento político* MAS

MAS is not a political party. It is the political instrument of the social movements. In the beginning when we wanted to organize a political instrument of the *sindicatos*, there was great resistance from the bases. (Evo Morales)

I remember ... when some leaders said that we needed a 'political instrument' to defend our interests. I believe they always used the term 'political instrument' in order not to say political party, because they were very badly regarded. Always in those years, everything that was politics was seen as oppression, exploitation and corruption. For this reason we said, why get involved in this? There is nothing good, nothing for us, is there? ... There were very few comrades who wanted to form a 'political instrument' in those years. (Don Manuel, former leader of a *central*)

Although in retrospect it may not be clearly evident, members of the social movement of the coca producers were extremely sceptical when in 1986 some of their leaders started to discuss the idea of getting directly involved in politics. High politics was not the sphere in which the social movement wanted to stage its activities: maintaining autonomy and avoiding being co-opted were the guiding principles under which demands were put forward. In that respect, the *sindicatos* did fit the conventional picture of a social movement as seeking no place in the existing political system and refusing to participate in the game of conventional politics in order to avoid the risk of being co-opted. From the perspective of ordinary members, each leader who proposed seeking a deal with political parties, or even to set up an independent party, was regarded as ready to sell the movement out. As members of the social movement recalled in my interviews, this suspicion was held especially by former miners who had migrated to the Tropic and who had experienced the co-opting of their union leaders. In other words, the main surprise is not that MAS grew so large, but that it was founded at all, given the suspicion that existed about establishing a party. So, how did the formation of the party come about?

> The seeds of MAS were sown in 1986–87. In these years a number of leaders began to work with the notion of forming an IP [*instrumento político*, political instrument]. There was at that time no reference to the phrase *por la soberanía de pueblos* [for the sovereignty of the peoples]; nothing more than a 'political instrument' was discussed. It was in 1990 that the concept of the sovereignty of the peoples was introduced. In 1995 MAS was launched as a 'political instrument'; 1997 saw the first parliamentarians. But of course there is a history that informs this political moment: that of a country more or less colonial, wherein the structural conditions for the growth of MAS were created. (Ivan Iporre, National Coordinator of MAS and later director of the National Service for the Administration of Public Personnel)

In 1987, the first leaders of the coca producers' social movement suggested becoming involved in party politics, not as the junior partner of an established party but with their own organization. One of the first leaders to propose the establishment of a political branch of the movement to pursue their demands was Evo Morales, in 1989. However, it took the organizations until 1993 to achieve a consensus on the issue, due to the anxiety on the part of some about the loss of the autonomy of their social movement.

Once the coca producers' social movement had agreed on this change of strategy, its strong position within the national peasant union, CSUTCB, gave the latter organization no option but to follow suit. It duly approved at its seventh congress (25–27 March 1995) a motion, the *Tesis del Instrumento Político*, which stipulated the formation of the Asamblea por la Soberanía de los Pueblos (ASP) with the colours green (coca) and brown (*tierra y territorio*). This was confirmed by the new organization's first congress, *Tierra y Territorio*, in which CSUTCB, CIDOB (indigenous people), FNMB (miners) and CSCB (peasants) participated.

However, interference by the dominant political parties (ADN, MNR, MIR) within the politicized National Electoral Court (CNE) led to its rejecting the registration of the ASP citing minor procedural infringements. The coca producers circumvented this hurdle to its participation in the 1995 municipal elections by standing under the banner of the earlier, electorally unsuccessful, Izquierda Unida (IU). (IU had been formed in 1988 as a coalition of MBL, the Partido Comunista Boliviano (PCB) and parts of MIR in order to unite Bolivia's left. The IU had supported the demands of the coca producers and had received a large proportion of the peasant vote in the Tropic of Cochabamba.) The result was a landslide win in the local strongholds of the movement and the election of social movement leaders. In eleven municipalities peasant candidates were elected as mayor, forty-nine became municipal councillors (*consejales*) and six were elected to department-level councils. In addition, ASP won a majority in five other municipalities, but

---

Poisoned relations

In 2005, Véliz stated that MAS was not the 'political instrument' of the social movements but remained closely linked to the ideology of the fascist FSB. In 2009, Véliz said that he would never ally himself with Morales and defended his alliance with the NFR by claiming that Morales had been a candidate for the MNR in 1985.

---

coalitions of other parties prevented it from obtaining the post of mayor.

In the national elections of 1997 the coca producers made gains, and the IU/ASP slate won four seats in Congress. While IU/ASP obtained 3.7 per cent of the vote nationally, in the department of Cochabamba the party achieved an impressive 17.5 per cent of the departmental vote, and became the second largest party.

Prior to the 1999 municipal elections, the ASP split into two following a painful and personal leadership contest when Alejo Véliz – ASP's presidential candidate in 1997 – refused to pass the leadership of the 'political instrument' to Evo Morales, who had been appointed by the social movement's bases. Although retrospectively both argued that the split was due to a difference in strategic thinking, it is clear that at the root of the conflict was a clash of personalities, one that continues to this day. This got to the point where large parts of the coca growers' movement decided not to vote for Véliz in the 1997 elections. Hence many put a *voto cruzado* (crossed vote) for ASP candidates for parliament but not for its presidential candidate, Alejo Véliz. This explains why he failed to be elected as a *plurinominal* MP. In the end, an *Ampliado* of the Six Federaciónes of the Tropic of Cochabamba therefore decided to leave Véliz with the ASP[1] and to contest the 1999 elections as Instrumento Político or la Soberanía de los Pueblos (IPSP). Véliz and the ASP subsequently became allied with the Partido Comunista Boliviano (PCB) and other parties in order to contest the municipal elections. Once the bases decided to support Morales over Véliz, the latter felt that he would not retain his candidacy in the next national elections and moved on to become a candidate for the populist Nueva Fuerza Republicana (NFR), leading Morales to accuse him of being a traitor. The leadership dispute between Morales and Véliz left deep scars and their relationship has never recovered.

Once again, the CNE seemed to be placing obstacles in the way of an independent peasant/indigenous party, for it not only rejected the registration of the IPSP but also annulled IU's electoral licence. As before, the coca producers found a creative solution to the obstruction denying them ballot access by operating under the banner of the Movimiento Al Socialismo.

Ironically, MAS had originally been established in 1985 as a splinter group of one of Bolivia's oldest right-wing parties, the nationalist and at times fascist Falange Socialista Boliviana (FSB). Using Spain's General Franco as model, the FSB had been founded in 1937 and organized several plots after 1952 to overthrow the MNR. The former presidential candidate of the FSB and then founder of MAS, David Añez Pedraza, failed utterly with his 'national socialist' project and MAS became no more than what Gamarra and Malloy (1995) aptly coined a 'taxi-party'. 'Taxi-parties' are so small that they could host their national convention in a cab. In the period 1990–94, MAS counted about twenty permanent members, according to Sabino Aroyo (*sindicato* leader and former mayor of Shinaota), who claims to have been present during the takeover negotiations. Facing serious illness, Añez Pedraza offered to hand over MAS to Evo Morales and the Six Federaciónes. After an extraordinary congress, the members of the Six Federaciónes approved this handover. This time, the CNE permitted the manoeuvre on condition that nothing concerning the party's name, symbols, statutes or programme would be changed. The peasants did stick to this ruling – on paper – as we will see.

MAS's first electoral experiment, in the 1999 municipal elections, was quite successful: it won seventy-nine municipal council seats and ten mayors. The movement received approximately 70 per cent of the votes in its stronghold, the Tropic of Cochabamba, while on a national level MAS won 3.3 per cent. Having gained valuable experience in local government, MAS and its former social movement leaders prepared more thoroughly for the 2002 elections. Social movement networks provided volunteers, who worked hard to compensate for the lack of finance available for such a large-scale campaign. MAS could not afford to give away flags, stickers and T-shirts, like the other parties did. Instead, its militants organized and paid for the production of these items and sold them for the benefit of the party. As a general rule, the candidates contributed two months' salaries to support the party. From their base in Cochabamba, volunteers travelled to all the other departments – except the remote Beni and Pando – to campaign for MAS, and to form alliances with other social movements in order to obtain their support. One such alliance was with the indigenous peoples of the lowlands through the Coordinadora de los Pueblos Étnicos de Santa Cruz (CPESC), which provided organizational resources and popular candidates in Santa Cruz.

Yet, although the MAS leaders knew that the work of volunteers, the clever use of social movement networks and alliances, as well as the mix of indigenous and leftist-intellectual candidates would pay off, 'nobody had dreamt of coming so close to winning the elections in 2002' (personal conversation with Oscar C. Antezana, MAS minister). Garnering 20.94 per cent of the vote (581,884 individual votes), MAS was only 1.5 per cent behind the winning MNR. MAS became the largest party in the departments of La Paz, Cochabamba, Oruro and Potosí, winning eight seats in the Senate in addition to its twenty-seven lower house seats.[2] The elections were somewhat overshadowed by an incident involving foreign interference, which once more aroused fears of rigging or annulment of the elections. The US ambassador, Manuel Rocha, 'reminded' Bolivians that a vote for Evo Morales, 'a person with links to drug traffic', could result in the cessation of all US aid to Bolivia.[3] Ironically, it seems that Rocha's statement may have delivered as much as an additional 2 per cent to MAS, enough to relegate the Nueva Fuerza Republicana (NFR) to third place.

After this, expectations were very high that MAS would perform well in the municipal elections in December 2004, especially considering the crisis of the other major parties. In the event, however, MAS did not win the mayoralty in any big city, not even El Alto. A major reason was that many MAS candidates were excessively ideological and lacked the necessary pragmatism to convince municipal voters concerned with the daily problems of their cities. In this regard, Álvaro García Linera (2004) – before he became a candidate for MAS – pointed out that the 2004 elections made evident the failure of the party to form durable alliances with the urban middle class in the main cities.

The electoral performance of MAS was, however, not so poor in other respects: it achieved a clear increase in its representation compared to the 1999 municipal elections and became Bolivia's largest *national* party with 28.6 per cent of all councillors, which translated into approximately 500 elected MAS candidates. MAS won an absolute majority in 15 per cent of the municipalities and expected to be able to control 36 per cent of them. It had at least one councillor elected in 70 per cent of all municipalities.

The criticism concerning the party's electoral performance in 2004 – whether justified or not – became irrelevant when the results of the 2005 national elections were announced: with 53.7 per cent of the national vote, MAS achieved a result unprecedented since Bolivia's restoration of multiparty elections in 1982. It rendered obsolete the parliamentary bargaining process of exchanging support for the election of the president by Congress in return for public offices. Yet this was a comparatively minor issue compared to the fact that Bolivia now had an indigenous president for the first time in its 180-year history as a republic. A man who used to be a llama herdsman in his youth was elected head of state with his own party and with Álvaro García Linera, one of the country's most capable intellectuals (who was at pains to emphasize his subordinate role) as vice president. Amalia Pando is representative of many political analysts in her view that having 'an indio as head of state has the enormous significance of the marginalized majority coming to power', which she sees as comparable to the story of Nelson Mandela.

MAS: a bottom-up perspective of the party

From the time the coca producers took over MAS in 1995 until 2004 (when party lists were radically opened up), MAS was ruled in the same manner and had incorporated the same organizational culture as the coca producers' movement in the Tropic. When the *federaciónes* took over MAS they were not allowed to substantially alter its organizational structure. Consequently one must not be misled by the clear and elaborate structure outlined in its statutes. In reality, MAS was an empty shell: there was no independent party organization. It was the political branch of the *sindicatos*, which means that it was run through the social movement structures of the coca producers. This was done by simply adding '*instrumento político*' as an item on the agenda of their monthly meetings. The coca producers used the symbols and legal status of MAS in order to obtain the electoral registration that allowed them to present their own candidates.

> MAS is for us our political instrument.... When we could not register a party of our own, we used the legal personality of MAS. Before that, MAS was a party of other people, you see? But it was dead and we could use it. But the electoral court told us that we had to keep the acronym and the colours to be able to participate in the elections. (Don Manuel, *secretario de hacienda* of a *federación*)

> It simply belongs to our movement and it is for us to have our own candidates. And to have our own candidates, some paperwork had to be done, some documentation and all the rest. It is only for these things that we have MAS: to confer the legal status that gives us the right to have our own candidates in the elections. (Don José, coca grower)

Instead of characterizing MAS as a party based on social movements, a more accurate description – at least for the first years of its existence up to 2004 – would have been a social movement participating in elections through the creative avoidance of ballot restrictions under cover of a political party. MAS served to provide the social movement with the legal status to present its own candidates, and the coca growers did not perceive it as an independent organization. Thus MAS was, in the early stages, the political expression of a social movement seeking to present its demands more effectively at the political level.

As a consequence, all issues concerning the 'political instrument' were discussed as an integral part of the meetings of the social movement. From the local-level *sindicatos* upwards to the highest organ, the Comité de Coordinación, all tiers of the coca producers' movement involved themselves in the decision-making process of the party. Tito Rivas, leader of a *central*, informed me that his own *sindicato*, which was fairly small and remote, had conducted detailed discussions about the formulation of demands, about the right strategy to obtain them, and about electoral slogans, as early as the 1990s. The leaders of different *sindicatos* within a *central* would then present their members' point of view at its monthly meeting, where they would decide which issues their leader should raise at the *federación*. For Rivas, the functioning of the 'political instrument' was initially identical to any other mission of the social movement, be it concerning agricultural issues, land rights or internal solidarity.

During my fieldwork in *sindicatos* of Matanzas, the bases would receive information from the top of the organization; for example, that they contemplated some collective action. The members would then discuss the issue at length and a bottom-up dynamic would produce a consensus at each level of the movement compelling the top to follow this 'mandate of the bases' (of course this mandate may not differ from the leadership's initial proposal). Thus, between 1995 and 2004 MAS was not so much an independent party established by a social movement as – and this is what makes it such an interesting case – an integral part of the coca producers' movement. As such, independent party structures were completely irrelevant to the functioning of the party; decisions were taken by consensus in the general assembly of all *federaciónes*. For the coca producers, then, MAS was 'their political instrument', in organizational terms parallel to the *federaciónes* and somewhat subordinate to the Comité de Coordinación de las Seis Federaciónes (CCSF).

Old wine in new bottles, or something genuinely new?

What exactly does the term 'political instrument' mean? The term is peculiar inasmuch as it can be interpreted as an 'instrument' to further Morales's political ambitions. So, to what degree is MAS just an instrument for an ambitious individual, as for instance the ADN was for General Bánzer, or PODEMOS for Jorge Quiroga, or the NFR for Manfred Reyes? I argue that what makes MAS special is the fusion of political party and social movement. This idio-syncrasy entails – as is stressed constantly by Morales – a reliance on volunteerism, which has clear implications for the movement's leadership, as we shall see. Morales manoeuvred the party between social movement radicalism and party-political pragmatism. A key feature was the strategy of having one foot in the official political arena and the other in that of the informal politics of civil society. In short, MAS is a coalition of social interests and not Morales's private tool. The interests of the two are necessarily intertwined: the movement's success is closely linked to Morales's leadership, while this leadership cannot be understood without taking into account the disposition of MAS.

President Morales: a product of his adversaries' reforms?

The argument outlined above implies that the rise of Evo Morales and the MAS was not the passive outcome of favourable institutional changes. Indeed, I think it would be inaccurate to attribute the success of MAS to an effective response to a more permissive insti-tutional context resulting from reforms such as the decentralization and creation of municipalities in 1994. The problem with such an explanation is that there were a number of possible courses of action in response to this political opportunity and not every political formation responded successfully. Indeed, the success of MAS is an exception; many other attempts to set up a party faltered. So it would be going too far to argue that the more favourable political climate determined the success of MAS. Indeed, it was rather the political strategies of the relevant actors allied to MAS at the time that enabled the project to succeed. I would emphasize, therefore, the importance of the political strategy adopted by the coca producers and their political instrument of reaching out to others disaffected with the status quo. The effect of some institutional reforms is rather ambiguous, and they may appear positive only in retrospect. The process of political decentralization set in motion by the Popular Participation Law (Ley de Participación Popular, LPP) was a case in point. For many observers, it was one of the factors that helped MAS, but for its leaders at the time it was a political manoeuvre to fragment the indigenous-popular vote and to shift the attention of anti-establishment actors to the local level. Furthermore, explaining MAS as the outcome of favourable institutional changes fails to take into consideration the internal dynamics of the social movements, and indeed those of the party itself.

The strength of the party should be ascribed primarily to the discourse of the movement and the party. This created a common identity and activated social movement networks for mobilization. The organizational–political resources of the social movement of the coca producers and its allies, once activated for political purposes, were robust enough to engage directly in national elections. Evo Morales had already travelled, during the 1995 municipal elections, through various departments (most notably Cochabamba, La Paz, Oruro and Potosí). His aim was to convince leaders of local social movements to participate in the elections under the banner of the Izquierda Unida (IU, United Left). Morales's travel costs were financed by the (limited) movement resources of the *sindicatos* of the Tropic, while food and accommodation were provided by local organizations. Once those organizations were convinced, they started to organize their own campaign activities, for which they used social movement or indigenous structures to elect candidates and movement members as campaign volunteers. What in the end limited the electoral success (IU received very few votes outside the department of Cochabamba) was that Morales's attempts to 'convince other social movements were too close to the elections' and the organizations had 'insufficient time to agree on candidates and to promote their candidature' (interview with Evo Morales).

Long-term grievances

Another argument against the view that the success of MAS was due to favourable institutional changes, and in favour of an explanation that focuses more on its internal characteristics, is that MAS is part of a long-term political strategy. When looking at institutional reforms it is necessary to analyse them in terms of the relation between short-term dislocations and long-term grievances. In the case of MAS the long-term grievance has been the exclusion of the indigenous people, and the party developed in reaction to this griev-ance. Explanations that stress the positive effect of reforms brush aside the long process of internal discussion and effort involved in setting up a political party. According to Ivan Iporre, it had always been the intention to set up a political party to compete at the national level, for this was seen as the only level at which the movement's demands could be met. Thus, it was not success at the local level that inspired them to compete on the national level, but the long-term grievance of a 'crisis of representation' on the part of the indigenous–rural population which felt it was not represented in national politics.

Whilst it is true that ballot access was far from easy and an independent party for the coca producers had been ruled out four times by the electoral court, changes to the electoral system should not be overemphasized as a determining factor. At the time any measure proposed by the national government was regarded with great suspicion among the social movement in the Tropic. In fact, they saw the municipalization effected by the LPP – not without reason – as an attempt to divert their political energies away from the national level. Sabino Aroyo, former mayor of Shinaota and elected on an IU sheet, remembers that *sindicato* leaders had accommodated themselves to using the IU as an electoral vehicle for their candidates, and so as far as possible took the party over from within. Instead of perceiving municipal elections as an opportunity, they saw them as thwarting their efforts to achieve a national presence by building into the system an intermediate level at which they had to compete first. Consequently the opportunity arising from decentralization only appears as such in retrospect.

It is futile to try to build a counterfactual scenario around what might have happened without reform, but it doesn't seem far-fetched to suggest that the internal dynamics of the *sindicatos* produced a political strategy geared towards involvement on a national political level. I would argue that this strategy was more important than short-term dislocations or opportunities. For every change in the political institutions there were a number of possible courses of action; choices were made according to the political strategy of the movement. This could involve, for instance, engaging in national politics through the vehicle of a defunct but legally registered party or by utilizing the proper organization; these options perceived as merely a difference in form not in content. Moreover, we should not forget that the LPP was designed primarily to shore up MNR's popularity and enhance its chances for electoral success against the backdrop of the unpopular privatizations in the early 1990s. That is to say, the MNR calculated – incorrectly – that its relatively elaborate territorial structure would make it the prime beneficiary of local elections and that the electoral success of the IU/ASP was an unintended consequence, attributable to the political perseverance of the social movements.

Furthermore, it would be incorrect to state that without the reforms Morales and MAS would not have become successful. For that would ignore the existence of a 'crisis of representation' with an underlying long-term grievance on the part of the indigenous population regarding its exclusion. The dominant parties failed in their efforts to link society and the state in an effective manner. The population, especially in rural areas and poorer urban neighbour-hoods, increasingly felt that it was not represented. This manifested itself in a lack of trust in representative institutions and erosion of the once dominant political parties (see, for instance, the data in the Latinobarómetro, 2003). Emphasis on the positive effect of institu-tional reforms risks overlooking the development of the discourse of Morales, who was able to mobilize these disenchanted voters. When frustration with national politics grew due to unpopular policies and unfulfilled promises, Morales promoted awareness of the gap between official politics and the people in order to generate support for MAS (as will be detailed in the next chapter). He united the dif-fering demands of all those disenchanted with the status quo behind a defence of national sovereignty and natural resources. Morales's strategy successfully articulated the unmet demands, which derived from the failure of the state to produce the growth and employment promised by its neoliberal discourse, with the long-term question of the lack of political representation of the indigenous people. With his defence of natural resources in the name of the people as victims of neoliberal politics, his discourse linked from the very beginning the local with the national, and was geared towards turning MAS into a national political force.

In a nutshell, the electoral strength of Morales and MAS is the result of a process of organizational maturation of one social move-ment, involving a far-sighted strategy on the part of its leaders, including Evo Morales. Through a degree of moderation and further strategic thinking, Morales was then able to build alliances with other organizations by highlighting what they had in common. The introduction of municipal elections was not a necessary pre-stage of national political success. Morales's discourse presented it as an attempt to confine activism to a sub-national level and prevent a broad challenge to the dominant political parties. It has always been the express intention of *sindicato* leaders, such as Evo Morales, to engage in national politics in order to fulfil their demands. To that end, they developed a discourse that linked national issues to daily hardship. They then broadened the discourse to appeal to a wider constituency. Yet this is not to say that the reforms had no bearing at all on the success of MAS. Indeed, its experience in local government in particular has helped the party develop proposals that are more realistic. Furthermore, the efficiency of some MAS administrations have given it credibility among wider sectors of the population, who began to perceive MAS as a viable political alternative. Most fundamental in the relationship between political institutions and MAS was, however, the malfunctioning of the former, especially the failure of political parties to persuade citizens that their demands were being taken into account. This motivated the more moderate and far-sighted social leaders such as Morales to form their own party, and enabled Morales to present MAS as a new way of doing politics that spoke for all those who felt that the mainstream politicians did not listen to them. Hence, MAS arose as a protest party. It is important to keep this in mind in order to understand certain aspects of Morales's political strategy and discourse.

With regard to the 'crisis of representation', it is not difficult to discern that there was potential support in society for a party setting itself up against the detested mainstream. Yet, at the same time, there were many voices at the time criticizing this state of affairs, including from within the 'traditional' parties; hence it is was far from self-evident that Morales would succeed with his anti-establishment position. One important reason for his success is that he maintained, even cultivated, the idiosyncratic organizational characteristics of MAS, including the close link with the social movement of the coca producers and the lack of an institutionalized party structure. So, the main reason for the success of MAS can be said to be the party's shrewd political strategy and determination to see it through. The second-generation reforms of the mid-1990s, for their part, were not as important a factor as they might appear in retrospect.

CHAPTER 5

Outside challengers rise amidst waves of protests, 1995–2002

Second-generation reforms

Despite its crisis of representation, Bolivia was seen by some Western analysts in the 1990s as the valedictorian graduating from the Washington Consensus school. Bolivia's 'second-generation reforms' achieved international recognition as an important attempt to 'get the institutions right' with market-enablement measures and equity-oriented programmes. The process began after the 1993 elections in which Sánchez de Lozada (MNR) and his ally, the *Katarista* Víctor Hugo Cárdenas,[1] achieved an impressive victory. Cárdenas's candidature was a symbolic gesture towards the indigenous population, but their actual influence remained small. MNR's presidency depended on the help of the small parties Movimiento Bolivia Libre (MBL) and Unidad Cívica Solidaridad (UCS). The coalition lacked internal coherence, for it consisted of a core of MNR neoliberal technocrats surrounded by leftist allies who demanded that the government should have a 'social face'. This came in the form of the *Plan de Todos*, intended to redesign the state apparatus, making it less top-down and paternalistic, and to open channels for participation.

The Sánchez de Lozada administration revised thirty-five articles of the constitution, established a voting system that resembled that of Germany,[2] and formally acknowledged Bolivia as a multicultural and multilingual country. The best-known reform is probably the Ley de Participación Popular (LPP, Law of Popular Participation), which included decentralization measures such as moving the administration of health, education and infrastructure to 314 newly created municipalities and extending their jurisdiction into rural areas. The LPP included the direct election of mayors and members of the city council, the direct allocation of funds to municipalities according to population size, and increased popular involvement through participatory planning and budgeting at the level of local communities. Although one might see this reform as an essential part of any long-term solution and as changing the structure of political opportunity in favour of formerly excluded social sectors, care must be taken in accounting for the mixed results of the reforms. There are serious 'structural limits to what municipalities can achieve after the decentralization since national policies exclude them from key economic processes' (Kohl, 2002: 465). Local elites may be able to use these reforms to preserve their power, whereas indigenous people have been marginalized after an initial inclusion (Albó, 2002a: 69, in Assies and Salman, 2003: 4). An educational reform introduced in 1994 aimed to recognize build upon Bolivia's cultural diversity, but culture was restricted to its linguistic aspects. The effects of the reform have been disappointing owing to the lack of local participation and the top-down manner in which it was conceived. Mixed results also followed the 1996 land reform, which was intended to give land titles to indigenous peoples but ignored the reality of communal occupation by the indigenous population.

The 1990s brought economic reforms, which included further privatizations (*capitalisación*), whereby state enterprises acquired a mixed identity: 50 per cent of stock was sold off in the markets; the balance was destined for an innovative pension scheme (BONOSOL), which suffered from serious operational and liquidity problems. The Ley 1689 de Hidrocaburos (Law of Hydrocarbons, 1996) and the Decreto 24806[3] dealt with the privatization of Bolivia's natural gas.

This issue became the focus of substantial protests in 2003. While the reforms failed on their own terms to produce sustainable growth in GDP, they benefited above all MNR members and Sánchez de Lozada, who became the country's largest mining entrepreneur. The continuing structural adjustment contributed also to an expanding informal sector and a reduction in the importance of organized labour, a side effect that didn't displease the government since it made effective popular protest more difficult.

After the deeply unpopular economic liberalization programme, a key impetus behind these 'second-generation' reforms was the regaining of popular support whilst preserving the privileges of the political parties. Yet in the end this was futile: the privatizations had made the MNR so unpopular that it lost the 1997 elections, receiving only half the votes (18.2 per cent) it had won in the previous ballot. In contrast with the mood of the electorate at the time, many foreign observers saw in the impressive set of reforms the signs of substantial progress towards modernization in Bolivia. However, while the reforms were certainly important, they were insufficient to bring about the institutionalization of democracy and the opening up of the political culture of the elite. This shows that simply changing the institutional rules does not automatically bring about a more democratic system, since vested interests are able to circumvent such efforts by utilizing informal means of obstruction. Indeed, I would argue that decentralization was intended to engender political stability by shifting the focus of the social movements to the local level. The reforms thus promoted the fragmentation of the opposition while democratic participation became a matter of competition for limited revenues (Kohl, 2002).

For many another hopeful sign of Bolivia's progress towards democratic consolidation was that ex-dictator Hugo Bánzer waited until the electoral victory of his ADN in 1997 to assume the presidency once more. He formed a programmatically incoherent 'megacoalition', which included MIR, UCS, Conciencía de Patria (CONDEPA), and Nueva Fuerza Republicana (NFR). The reward for this support was the new government's increasing the number of ministries from ten to fourteen. Under pressure to comply with the 'certification' process,[4] the Bánzer government put huge efforts into coca eradication (indeed, it might be said that this was the only thing the government did); yet the figures for the eradication achieved are very much contested. In a nutshell, Bánzer's 'institutional reforms added to the confusion, instability and ineffectiveness at all levels of government. It generated the impression that institutional reforms were all about control of political power and not about improving responsiveness' (Oporto, 1998, in Van Cott, 2000: 219). This means that Bánzer will be remembered as Bolivia's only ex-dictator to become a democratically elected president, but who then left no legacy worthy of note besides the notorious corruption and patrimonialism of his administration.

From the 1990s onwards a few new parties came onto the national stage. The most successful were UCS and CONDEPA, both locally based parties under the almost authoritarian leadership of charismatic, wealthy individuals. Both parties relied heavily on these caudillos as leaders, and so, once they were gone, their uncharismatic successors failed to maintain a similar level of support. I would also argue that both parties joined government coalitions too early in exchange for jobs for party members, which discredited them as political alternatives. If anything, the only 'new' elements were party branding and yet more middle-class individuals profiting from the spoils of government. As a result, the uncontrolled growth of the state bureaucracy, which had begun in 1952, continued (Gamarra, 2002).

Party politics: where is the 'silent revolution'?

The idea that political parties are central to the functioning of democracy is hardly new, any more than is the insight that parties frequently suffer teething problems after the transition to democracy. In Bolivia a common problem (and here the MNR is an exception) was that parties had only small memberships, making it difficult for them to win the trust of the electorate and to build networks with grassroots organizations. Historically, parties in Bolivia have functioned primarily to connect clients with political patrons, and are an attractive means to sustain one's livelihood. In the early 1990s, 60 per cent of the population said they wanted to join a party (Gamarra and Malloy, 1995). But engagement entails the risk of being excluded from patronage when the party fails to join a governmental coalition, which is one reason why 85 per cent of the population have never joined a party, according to the same study.

In general, it is important for a party in Bolivia to display a large following in order to attract voters based on the expectation that their engagement with the party will help them financially. A means to get people to show up at campaigns is to hand out small individual gifts or to deliver goods for a community (e.g. raw materials for building a school). Hence performance in office becomes less relevant than the fact that 'politicians have to deliver before they get the vote' (Lazar, 2004: 234). Most parties do not even discuss their programmes at their rallies. Instead of looking at the programme, voters try to establish personal contact with politicians, and judge them according to their capacity to deliver goods. Successful candidates have to combine the instrumental (i.e. patronage payments) and the affective (i.e. having an emotional appeal) dimensions of politics to be successful. Hence it is not surprising to learn that there is a very low level of trust in the political system (as reflected particularly in the pre-2005 Latinobarómetro polls), given that parties serve merely to distribute benefits to a small following and taking into account the exclusionary style of party negotiations.

This means that some analysts (e.g. Mayorga, 1997) have been rather modest about what can be expected from political parties in a country like Bolivia. Governmental coalition-building and the rise of new parties such as UCS or CONDEPA were, in this sense, regarded as progress towards democratic consolidation. Indeed, political parties taking part in elections and agreeing on post-electoral power-sharing represents a great advance when viewed against a history involving 170 *coups d'état* since 1825. Post-transition Bolivia came to be governed by a 'parlamentarised presidentialism' (Mayorga, 1997: 147), a term used to describe the election of the president in Congress by a governmental coalition. This produced a pattern of coalition politics, a moderately fragmented party system,[5] and the expectation that the popular vote was merely a measure of bargaining power in the process of electing the president in Congress. However, whether this is sufficient to justify the description 'silent revolution' (Mayorga, 1997) is debatable. It seems that overly optimistic views have been disproved by the advent of social protests since 2000, and by the success of MAS in the elections between 2002 and 2005. As I argue throughout this book, this success owes much to Evo Morales's discourse of constructing an antagonism between MAS and the 'traditional' parties and the incorporation of diverse demands behind his political project.

Until 2002 political grassroots initiatives found it particularly difficult to gain a foothold in the party system. This relatively closed system did not encourage trust in official political actors, and in turn their efforts to connect with civil society organizations met with scepticism and fear of co-optation. Bolivian parties tried broadening their membership only after the mass protests in 2003, when it was too late. At that point the 'traditional parties' had lost their attractiveness due to their appalling handling of the crisis and as a result of the revised electoral law making it easier for 'citizens' associations' to participate in elections. Another problem was that political life existed only in the major cities, while the rural areas, which were host to various active social movements, were blank spots on the official political landscape. In sum, the absence of bridges between the state and society remained after the transition to democracy. More and more citizens realized that parties and the party system were not more open or accessible than under the previous regime. Whilst at the top executive dominance and technocratic decision-making remained, access to influence shifted from corporatism to party clientelism without making much of a difference to ordinary people. Another problematic aspect of Bolivian party politics was the regularity of 'coalitions of convenience' (Horowitz, 2000), serving just to elect the president, while lacking programmatic coherence and being too unstable for the executive to be effective. They were intended mainly for securing posts and patronage payments and dissolving quickly after the distribution of the spoils. The participation of citizens through elections has been a rather marginal aspect of Bolivian politics. The politically powerful have found ways to disconnect from the electorate, and determine among themselves who will form a government and at what price. Party leaders, for instance, were able to impose the results of top-level coalition negotiations on the rank and file due to the closed party list system (Domingo, 2005: 1731). In other words, what had been conceived of as an advance in the process of democratic consolidation was the result of closed competition between established parties. This situation has been aptly summarized by Gamarra and Maloy:

> Bolivia stands out as a would-be democratic polity suffering the reality that elections serve mainly to circulate personnel and factions, and have little to do with producing governments that can govern.... It is one thing to win an electoral plurality, an entirely different thing to be chosen president and yet another thing to govern.... Political parties in contemporary Bolivia are closed, hierarchical organizations. Power is concentrated in a few individuals; party members have no say in policy-making, and they do not play any part in party decisions.... The MIR, ADN and MNR adopted a modern party structure, but retained key patrimonial dynamics. (Gamarra and Maloy, 1995: 413–19)

As with certain regimes in central and eastern Europe (see Luckham et al., 2003), in Bolivia the major parties were transformed into instruments of control. They failed to produce ideological or programmatic alternatives to the hegemonic neoliberal economic policies, and debates had little substance. Bolivia was dominated for twenty years by three parties (ADN, MNR, MIR). The opportunities offered by this continuity were, however, thwarted by factionalism caused by internal party competition for jobs and offices.

De jure improvements in institutional arrangements and a nominally well functioning party system did not translate into a *de facto* system able to represent more effectively the interests of ordinary citizens or effect a greater degree of responsiveness by the political class to popular demands. This is because 'commitment to a democratic project has been only half-hearted and served the interest of a ruling political class, which ... proved unable to shed illiberal practices' (Domingo, 2005: 1729). Elections did not create parties as mechanisms for representing the interests of the citizens. Instead, weakly institutionalized governments depended for their survival on the patrimonial dynamics of the party system. As an effect, parties were in the late 1990s more disconnected from society than in 1985 and suffered from very low approval rates. The 'spread of democratic institutions [did] not necessarily mean the spread of democratic politics' (Luckham et al., 2003: 14). This gap between legality and legitimacy became a condition of possibility for a populist rupture in a democratic environment.

On the basis of the 'second-generation' reforms, some have argued, there was from the mid-1990s a belief that Bolivia could become a liberal-democratic, capitalist and multicultural nation. Yet such an interpretation fails to probe beneath the surface of these policies and their architects. I would argue, rather, that the twin processes of neoliberal reform and democratization did not hold out the promise of constructing a new nation. In Arze Cuadros's (2002) encyclopaedic analysis of the MNR, no imagining of the nation can be found for the post-1985 period, marking a sharp contrast with what he found for the period 1941–64. Paz Estenssorro's recollection of the period shows that his government was exclusively concerned with the disastrous economic situation and not with constructing a new nation.

Even if the MNR had retained a vision of the nation, the party was sidelined in the process of designing the reform policies of the

1980s and 1990s. Instead policies were devised by small policy units of the executive supported by external advisers, all with practically no connection to the MNR party apparatus. The speed with which the reforms were put together (less than three weeks) and the lack of attention to symbolism[6] indicate that those in power did not care very much about larger political projects such as nation-building.

A closer look at the constitutional reforms reveals that they are not the expression of a liberal democratic and multicultural nation. According to Zambrana (2005), this is true especially for the Reforma Educativa (1994). Despite introducing Quechua and Aymara, the education reform maintained the hegemonic status of Spanish education. Multiculturalism was basically restricted to a linguistic triptych (Spanish, Aymara and Quechua), while ignoring not only other indigenous languages but also, and more importantly, everything else that constitutes a 'culture' (e.g. norms, values, customs, rituals, forms of authority, etc.). The reformed education system did not endeavour to pass on indigenous knowledge or to tell history from the perspective of indigenous peoples. Besides, the symbolic recognition of indigenous languages in the educational system had no egalitarian effect, due to the remaining differences in quality between urban and rural schools.

Formal recognition of Bolivia as a multicultural country did not stem the persistence of negative stereotypes and informal discrimination in the labour market, which forced many indigenous parents to opt against educating their children in their mother tongue. Another example of the lack of a serious effort to construct a multicultural nation is the 1996 land reform, which was intended to give land titles to indigenous peoples, but which ignored the reality of indigenous communal usage.

Similarly, the municipalization effected by the unpopular Law of Popular Participation was supposed primarily to engender political stability in the face of deeply unpopular privatizations of national companies by shifting the focus of social movements to the local level. Another rationale for the LPP was a political power calculation

whereby the MNR expected to benefit electorally from municipalization since it was the party with the most stable (corporatist and
patrimonial) connections to rural voters.

Overall, it appears that there was no explicit notion of nation-
building during the twin process of democratization and neoliberal
reform. Having said that, the reforms implemented between 1985 and
2002 moved capitalism to the centre of the Bolivian state and thus
implicitly of the nation. Yet this is quite distinct from an explicit
nation-building project by the MNR and from the 'plurinational'
project of MAS. The relative emptiness of the imaginary of the
nation during the 1980s and 1990s made the MAS's imagining of
a new nation more appealing. This was even more the case when
several waves of popular protest shook the very foundations on
which post-dictatorship Bolivia was built.

Consideration of the context in which MAS was founded illustrates that we should not be blinded by overly formalistic accounts
of the functioning of political institutions – here political parties
and the party system. In fact, political institutions can tick all the
right boxes and appear perfectly democratic, behind which facade
political elites alter their behaviour so as to fit their personal or
partisan interests. Whereas the stability of a minimal structure of
democracy is an important requirement for subsequent political
and economic development, Bolivia shows that a system of non-
substantive electoral democracy was indeed quite stable whilst at
the same time showing no signs in fifteen years of engaging in
self-motivated moves towards qualitative improvement.

Having said that, I would add a note of caution. How democratic
the performance of institutions is depends on the local context,
especially the power configurations in which they are introduced.
While in some municipalities in eastern Bolivia old elites used the
new structures to maintain their power, in other municipalities
(e.g. in five municipalities of the Tropic of Cochabamba) social
movements showed how effective they can be in improving local
governance and the distribution of resources. Yet the overall picture

shows that, despite encouraging developments, the population grew more distant from the process of national decision-making under the MNR and ADN governments in the 1990s.

Waves of conflict

The lack of bridges between political institutions and civil society, and the gap between legality and legitimacy, have been among the causes of the waves of social protest since 2000. Another underlying factor was dissatisfaction with the results of the economic liberalization and the perception that these policies benefited only a small minority. The five years prior to the first electoral victory of MAS (2005) saw the emergence of a large popular movement on the public stage. This is a movement that with all its heterogeneity has united previously isolated groups in a shared sense of being 'the people' as a collective victim of neoliberal economics and unresponsive institutions. Although the protests were often spontaneous responses to specific policies and not centrally orchestrated, they formed in their heterogeneity a collective body that generated a rare degree of popular power. 'The people' that arose from the protests was not the result of organic growth, but a deliberate achievement of the discursive strategy of Evo Morales and MAS. The principal reason for the success of MAS was not so much its actual role in the social conflict – indeed it would be mistaken to attribute leadership to a single individual such as Morales; rather, it can be explained by the role its *discourse* played in enabling a splintered social movement to congregate behind shared demands, and around the new common identity of 'the people' as victim of the status quo. Hence the significance of the Water War (2000) and the Gas War (2003), the most dramatic incidents in a series of popular protests that included actions in July 2001, February 2002, February 2003 and June 2005, is that they marked the culmination of a discursive struggle through which various local social movements were reconstituted with a renewed capacity to challenge the hegemony of

Las wawas crecen con mucha bronca

The eyes of the children are most telling: full of hatred and fear. I don't think I have ever seen this again, such eyes that seemed to belong to adults and not to 4-year-olds.

It is the daily ritual in Chimoré: at dawn, huge old US army trucks, carrying loads of young Bolivian soldiers, the *leos* of the coca eradication squad, pass along the main Cochabamba–Santa Cruz road that cuts through the Tropic of Cochabamba. The old engines and big tyres make so much noise that you can hear them from afar. You can cut the air with a knife. All life in the village stops for a moment when everybody watches the trucks, hoping that they will enter another village to do their destructive work.

What a strange moment: full of ambiguity between solidarity among all coca growers and the individual hope that their coca would be spared this time. But just a minute later, when the fifteen trucks or so have passed, everything is quiet again and life resumes its usual slow pace. Normality in the war against drugs…

the political elite in the name of the disenfranchised. At the core of this development is the resistance of the organizations of the coca producers (the *sindicatos*) under the leadership of Morales to the eradication of their crops.

War on drugs

Bolivia suffered between 1985 and 2005 from the consequences of the 'war on drugs', usually defined as the repressive counter-narcotics strategy of the United States to eliminate the supply of drugs, which is regarded as a threat to national security. In Bolivia, the war on drugs is based on the Ley del Régimen de la Coca y de las Sustancias Controladas (1988), which converted an ancient activity into a crime and made the coca producers 'societal delinquents' (Healy, 1991: 90). The issue of coca and of the social movements of the coca-growing peasants figured large in the chapter dealing with the life of Morales. The *sindicatos* have a long history of protest against the forceful eradication of coca, which they see as a symbol of national sovereignty. Already between 1984 and 1991 they used collective actions such as symbolic occupations of local government offices, roadblocks (on the vital *Transamericana*), as well as hunger strikes, mass marches (as far as to La Paz) and demonstrations to protest against the eradication of coca. Virtually everybody in the Tropic of Cochabamba has a story to tell about suffering verbal and physical abuse during the eradication of their coca crops or when the military crushed largely peaceful protests.

> I was in my *chaco* harvesting *yuca* when the *leos* entered. They had not been in the area, so nobody suspected that they would come to our *sindicato* for eradication. Also they had come just a year before and we thought they would not come before the end of the second year. They came in swiftly and there were many soldiers, maybe fifty or so. Many were still very young – you know, those doing their military service, just boys of 18. And they were afraid, but the officers shouted at them and made them aggressive. On their way to my coca they passed through the place where I had planted my pineapple. One of them kicked down one plant and when I cried 'No!', they all suddenly turned against my crops and destroyed everything! I tried to protect the crops but then they started kicking and beating me; even when I fell to the ground they continued until I was bleeding. I just lay on the ground without moving and they kicked me! At some point one shouted 'Let's go, take down all the rest!' They then went and quickly destroyed my coca before hurrying away. I remained on the ground for a long time before I was able to sit up, and only much later did I have the strength to return to my house [an hour's walk from the field]. I was just glad that my wife and children had not been with me this time, because these *leos* would have beaten them too.... Imagine how children react when they see their father return home covered in blood and with bruises everywhere... There is nothing you can do; they are growing up with a lot of hatred. (Interview with coca producer Don Augustino)

The resistance of the coca producers to eradication made them the most active part of civil society. Yet, until the early 1990s these direct actions were purely reactive in nature. Only on the issue of proposing alternative legislation for the use of the coca leaf and in advancing its cultural signification were the *sindicatos* more proactive. Yet this did not add up to a coherent political project. The important factor was that collective mobilization and defence of the coca leaf first unified them and then amplified their protests, leading to the incorporation of other demands. By the end of the twentieth century, the *sindicatos* had proved to be the sole social sector able to sustain confrontation with the government over a number of years without being co-opted.

Although Bolivia has become formally democratic, the coca producers' movement articulates a popular discontent with the quality of that democracy. For them, the 'war on drugs' fundamentally represents part of an ethnic hierarchy hidden behind a facade of democratic institutions. This ethnic hierarchy is determined to prevent the indigenous peoples from ascending to national political power. This discourse has stimulated the forging of alliances with other social movements, because the coca producers broadened their appeal and developed their own political project in order to progress 'from protests to proposals'. With a discourse that articulated the defence of coca as a defence of all natural resources and of national sovereignty, the *sindicatos* could achieve cross-class alliances and establish their own 'political instrument', the MAS party, as a voice of all those disenchanted with the status quo. The first successful alliance, which challenged the fragmentation of civil society at least temporarily, was forged during the *Guerra del Agua*.

The year 2000: a turning point?

For some analysts (e.g. Assies and Salman, 2003: 24; Gutiérrez et al., 2002) the year 2000 was the turning point for popular mobilizations, as by then the problems of lack of coordination, competition for state attention and conflicting demands had been overcome. Indeed the events of April 2000, July 2001, February 2002, and February and October 2003 indicate a reconstitution of various regional social

For our water and for our lives

We could not believe what we were seeing: this was no longer our city but resembled Gaza! No traffic, all the roads covered with stones, burning cars and tear gas.

The centre was full of people, of various kinds, protesting: students, peasants, workers and middle-class people. And then you had the heavily armed police and military, with their shields and helmets and rifles. They used them [the guns] to fire tear gas, but there were always rumours that some would shoot real bullets at us, and that in the buildings around the central square there were snipers.

We were all really afraid, but we were also angry. How could they sell our water to a foreign company? Water is life! You should not sell it and even less to a foreign multinational. And what did they do with it? Nothing! They only increased the prices ... more than double ..., so much that even for us [a middle-class family] it became too expensive.

We had accepted so much, so many privatizations, because we believed they would bring jobs. But water, that was too much! What next? Air?

So, many middle-class people joined the protests spontaneously. We could not accept that no politician took our demands serious. There was such a big gap between what they said and how we saw all this. It was almost as if they spoke another language.

And then all this violence! How could they do this? The army is supposed to defend against foreigners, not to kill its own people. I thought we were living in a democracy, but then it felt like war, like Gaza that you see on television. (Nelida Zuares, inhabitant of Cochabamba)

movements with a renewed capacity to challenge the hegemony of the political elite. Yet the notion of a 'turning point' may not be wholly appropriate, as there is a danger of glossing over fifteen years of accumulated grievances, combined with the organizational and discursive development of the *sindicatos*, which enabled them to forge an effective alliance with urban social forces. Central to this alliance were a shared understanding of the symbolism of the conflict and a clash between official and popular discourses regarding the meaning of natural resources.

Guerra del Agua in 2000

Ostensibly, the Water War in Cochabamba was straightforwardly a massive social protest against the huge (over 100 per cent) increase in the price of water from the municipal supply following its privatization, despite the lack of any investment or improvement in service. The licence had been sold to the consortium Aguas del Tunari, behind which stood the multinational company Bechtel. The water supply had been a divisive issue between urban and rural areas in the Cochabamba region since the 1990s, because urban consumption competed with agricultural use for the scarce water resources. This resulted in a vicious cycle and in the 1992 *Guerra de Pozos* in Vinto. There had long been a proposed solution, but only one international consortium could be found that was willing to make the investment required to execute the ambitious plans, and only then after drastically scaling back the project and guaranteeing a return on investment of 16 per cent.

However, behind the immediate conflict lay a clash over the very definition and use of natural resources. For the Bánzer administration water was an 'economic good' that had to be exploited and used to attract foreign capital. By contrast, for the population it was a 'social and ecological good that guarantees the well-being of families and communities' (Omar Fernández, leader of the Coordinadora por el Agua y la Vida). The governmental discourse rejected any questioning of the project, and reduced it to a legal–administrative issue. The symbolism intrinsic to water, as articulated in popular discourse, was beyond the field of representation of the official discourse. In other words, these popular demands were not representable within the discursive logic of the government, because they fundamentally contradicted the neoliberal understanding of natural resources.

TABLE 1 Chronology of the Water War

Date	Social actors	Government	Analysis
1996–97	Citizens are informed post hoc about the decision to seek private investment in Cochabamba's water supply.	Sánchez de Lozada seeks to obtain private investment due to institutional difficulties and lack of economic resources.	Technocratic government does not consult citizens; ignores material and symbolic importance of water.
April 1998	Organizations issue a common declaration demanding inclusion in negotiations and proposing a definition of water as a 'social and ecological good that guarantees the well-being of families and communities'.	Bánzer government inherits privatization plans, defining water as an 'economic good'. Start of negotiations with the only interested consortium, Aguas de Tunari.	Clash of definitions of water apparent, but governmental discourse reduces project to legal norms to avoid meaningful discussion.
19 November 1999	The Coordinadora por el Agua y la Vida is founded, an unprecedented urban–rural alliance against government plans.	As the Coordinadora lacks a 'legal personality', the government determines that it is not a legitimate organization.	Civil society plays no role in the official political culture. Yet it is active politically, leading to a bifurcation of the political realm.
3 January 2000	First protests start in Cochabamba, when water bills are issued and the scale of price increases becomes apparent.	700 police deployed to control the major roads for the 'security of the citizens'.	Protests outside permitted areas are deemed illegitimate; use of legal mandate to discipline the citizens.
4 January	Protests are suppressed; city becomes a battlefield; violent clashes for fourteen hours.	Government appeals for 'law and order'; denies the existence of price increases.	More than a clash of interests: two realities. The dynamic produces non-negotiable demands.
February	Coordinadora organizes a peaceful 'symbolic occupation' of Cochabamba.	Official discourse cites economic damage and loss of international aid.	Novel collective actions clash with traditional neoliberal discourse.
6 February	It seems that the protests are successful when the government signs an agreement with the Coordinadora.	The government, however, signs the agreement merely to stop the protests and does not comply with it.	Old pattern of negotiations to contain mobilization; serious talks only with the Civic Committee.

27 March	Coordinadora organizes a public consultation, which shows that the overwhelming majority are against the privatization.	Government rejects the conclusions of the consultation as illegitimate and misleading.	Church and ombudsman deem consultation fairly representative. With the consultation, social actors do what they expected from the government, i.e. consult and deliberate.
4–10 April	General strike announced. Total blockade of Cochabamba.	Government continues to reject Coordinadora as legitimate and uses repression instead.	Inflexible official position produces an escalation of the conflict.
5 April	Symbolic occupation of Civic Committee and Aguas del Tunari offices.	Government disqualifies social movement as having 'personal' and 'political' interests.	Government depoliticizes the conflict; political interests are deemed inappropriate for social actors outside the official arena.
6 April	Coordinadora agrees to meet for negotiations.	Government arrests leaders that came to negotiate.	Ombudsman and Church protest; government unwilling to negotiate.
7 April	Daily protest marches; central square occupied by youth, who maintain blockades against the military. Too late for negotiations: the government has lost all legitimacy.	Prefect annuls the water contract, but is replaced by the government, which rescues the contract.	Repression fails, party discipline dissolves, but despite all, government continues with top-down imposition of policies.
8 April	Protesters claim that a army sniper in civilian clothes has killed an adolescent.	Government declares state of emergency.	Despite the loss of life, no side is willing to give in.
10 April	Nothing moves in the city, protesters control all strategic points.	Government has lost control over the city; decides to accept all demands and signs agreement with the Coordinadora.	Conflict escalated according to warfare logic of absolute victory; government defeated on all fronts.

In the Water War the Coordinadora por el Agua y la Vida emerged as the key social actor protesting against an unresponsive style of governance that gave priority to party clientelism over the symbolic and material interests of those affected by its decisions. The Coordinadora was a flexible alliance of social movements that existed at the margin of institutional channels of participation. Its greatest achievement was to bridge the old rural–urban faultline, which had long dominated the conflict. The Coordinadora picked up on the discourse and the collective actions of the *sindicatos*, demanding its inclusion in institutional channels of negotiation, and emphasized the importance of political equality and participation in civil society.

> At first the protests were dispersed and unorganized, but then I got together with some other social leaders, some from neighbourhood organizations and others from peasant or indigenous organizations from the countryside. We had heard about their protests, some people in the city have a plot of land and belong to peasant organizations, so they informed us about it. So we invited them and we saw that we all were against the selling out of our water to a transnational company. For sure, there were many differences but we discussed and came to a consensus and united against this theft of our water. There were also former miners amongst us and they said: not again! We cannot let them sell our resources again to foreigners. So, we decided to set up a Committee to coordinate our protests. By working together we learned from each other: you had miners who knew how to organize demonstrations, middle-class people who were good at fundraising, and from the *cocaleros* we learned that the water privatization was the symptom, not the problem. The problem was that politicians did not want to talk to us, they did not even want to hear us. So, the *cocaleros* said, 'there is no democracy if the government ignores so many people. They always ignored us, but now they ignore you too. So where is the democracy?' I think to realize this was very important for us to never give up even when there was so much violence. (Omar Fernández, leader of the Coordinadora por el Agua y la Vida)

El Mallku

Felipe Quispe Huanca, who likes to give himself the title *El Mallku* (prince or leader), is one of Bolivia's most radical and colourful social movement leader-turned-politicians, being the founder of the Movimiento Indigena Pachakuti (MIP). Quispe regards himself as no less than the president of the Republic of Kollasuyo – an Aymara alternative to Bolivia – and has frequently demanded to meet Bolivian presidents 'as equals' with the same level of authority.

Quispe is notorious for his fierce rhetoric, and for the tendency in interviews to use the first question as the trigger for an avalanche of language, burying the questioner under a mountain of accusations and statements, most of which are unrelated to the issue initially raised.

After studying history, he began a long involvement in the *Katarista* movement of Aymara intellectuals. He has been accused of racism and totalitarianism for arguing that all *q'aras* (whites) should be expelled from Bolivia in order to reconstruct an empire of indigenous peoples. He was elected as the secretary general of the national peasant organization, Confederación Sindical Única de Trabajadores Campesinos de Bolivia (CSUTCB), in 1998. Under his leadership the CSUTCB saw both a crisis of internal scission into three factions and renewed protagonism on the part of of his own faction in social protests; the factions led by Alejo Véliz and Humberto Choque, meanwhile, were prone to co-optation by established political parties.

Political parties tactically avoided debate in order not to 'politicize the issue'. Their participation was reduced to general statements, and positions were determined by national leaderships and not by local politicians. Already in the pre-election period of October 1999, parties had avoided the issue and thereby lost an opportunity to channel social demands. It became evident during the conflict that parties in Bolivia no longer fulfilled their function of aggregating and representing the interests of citizens (García Orellana et al., 2003: 85). A notable exception was MAS, which took a position in the conflict owing to the participation of its militants in the

Coordinadora and through the repeated declarations of its city council representatives and members of parliament.

The Water War was the paramount social conflict in 2000, but the year also saw the concurrence of other conflicts, including road-blocks set up by the coca-growing peasants, teacher demonstrations in La Paz, mobilizations of the CSUTCB in Oruro against the land law (INRA), and land occupations by the Movimiento Sin Tierra (MST) in Tarija. In July 2001, road blocks were set up in the de-partment of La Paz by peasants organized in the CSUTCB) faction led by Felipe Quispe Huanca. The next wave of massive protests came when President Quiroga, who had succeeded Hugo Bánzer when the latter was diagnosed with cancer and had to step down in August 2001, issued a decree on 15 January 2002 that prohibited the sale of coca in the market of Sacaba. The conflict ended in bloodshed: three peasants and two soldiers were killed. In the end the government retreated from the introduction of further measures to restrict the commercialization of coca (Romero Bonifaz, 2004: 15), but only after expelling Evo Morales from parliament by means of a somewhat dubious procedure.[7] The expulsion of Morales was experienced by many as a humiliation and as further confirmation of the merely pseudo-democratic character of the political class. Partly in reaction, the fourth indigenous march set out from Santa Cruz in May 2002 demanding once more that an Asamblea Nacional Constituyente (National Constituent Assembly) be established to redraft the constitution. Bolivia underwent another crisis, the so-called *impuestazo*, in January and February 2003, when the new government imposed a 12.5 per cent increase in income tax. The ensuing protests, partly organized by the police, escalated; there were thirty-three deaths, and mobs attacked the offices of the three powers of the state, and of political parties, as well as shopping centres (Romero Bonifaz, 2004: 16; Albó, 2004: 45). In the end, the government had to withdraw the law and the president reshuffled his cabinet. However, this does not mean that the government had become aware of the scale of the popular rejection of its handling

---

MASsive force?

There is no official monument to the deaths of the 2003 Gas War. But just before you descend to La Paz from El Alto a multi-tonne concrete pillar and a huge rail lie oddly beside the road, although the railway line is several hundred metres away. They are silent reminders of the incredible force a multitude of people were able to mobilize in order to utilize these objects, without any heavy equipment, as elements of a roadblock.

---

of the socio-economic crisis, or indeed more responsive to public sensitivities, for it subsequently refused to approve a second term for the *Defensora del Pueblo* (ombudsman), Ana María Romero de Campero, who was widely regarded as extremely competent (Albó, 2004: 46). President Morales's decision to revoke the 2010 *gazolinazo* law (up to 80 per cent increase in gasoline prices) has to be understood in this context too.

In the social conflicts of 2000–2003 we see a pattern of convergence of many local and particularistic mobilizations towards a nationalization of collective actions aimed at a macro-level reform of politics. In order to accommodate local and specific demands, it appeared increasingly necessary to stress their universal or national aspect. The pioneers of this discursive development were the coca producers, who had shown with their 'political instrument' (i.e. MAS) how particularistic demands could be unified to form a common challenge to the status quo. However, it took new waves of conflict for demands to be articulated in a broad enough manner to persuade the middle class to form an alliance in opposition to the status quo.

Guerra del Gas or *Octubre Negro* 2003

222 years after Tupaj Katari besieged La Paz from El Alto, a series of popular protests – later known as the *Guerra del Gas* (Gas War) – immobilized La Paz once again. The city's location in a steep valley

surrounded by high mountains, with only one major road connecting it to the rest of the country, makes it vulnerable to sieges. Anyone who has visited La Paz arriving at the world's highest international airport in El Alto knows the spectacular descent into the city. Yet the route is also a potential bottleneck: a six-lane road with a vertical drop on the city side and steep cliffs on the other, which makes it ideal to block and to defend. For most traffic, in particular trucks, there is only one other road up to El Alto, and hence to the rest of the country via the southern end of the La Paz valley. But this road is even steeper and easier to block from above. To make matters worse for the city's inhabitants, most vital depots, such as gas and fuel, are located in El Alto, and most of the goods consumed in the capital enter via its satellite city. When protesters have been able to mount and maintain an effective siege of the city, the normally congested and noisy north–south axes of Bolivia's capital have quickly become empty and a ghostly silence has fallen over the city, interrupted only by the frightening war-like sound of clashes between protesters and the armed forces.

> In our neighbourhood there was nothing to see of the riots, but you could see the smoke over the centre of the city. At night, the sky was red and the mountains around the centre were illuminated from the fires of burning cars and buildings. The rest we only saw on television, but then the media started to make people afraid that La Paz would be entered and occupied by protesting *campesinos* [peasants]. This was of course ridiculous; the protesters never wanted to occupy private homes and could never have done so. It was a campaign by conservative media to make people afraid, and many people believed it.... When we saw all the violence and suffering on television, the middle class followed people such as Romero de Campero [the former ombudsman] and marched through the south of La Paz. We all painted our hands white and held them up as a sign for the government to stop the violence. (Marcelo Rosales, middle-class resident from the south of La Paz)

The events brought the small Latin American country some unusual attention: suddenly CNN and BBC were reporting live, and all major international newspapers that hitherto had covered the country from regional offices sent a correspondent to La Paz. What puzzled international observers was that the popular protests were shaking the democratic institutions, which were believed to be in the process of consolidation. Some reports even speculated on the possibility that Bolivia would return to military dictatorship.

The protests, which would lead to the resignation of a democratically elected president, were at first directed against President Sánchez de Lozada's revived plan to export natural gas (LNG) to the United States through a Chilean port. The beginning of the *Guerra del Gas* was on 19 September 2003, when various social movements followed Evo Morales's call for demonstrations in all departmental capitals to protest against the terms for the export of gas. Operators would have to pay a *regalia* (fee) of only 18 per cent for newly discovered reserves plus a 12 per cent tax on the value of gas at the *boca del pozo* (when it comes to the surface), based on a price of just $0.70 per 1,000 British thermal units (BTUs). This was well below the market price at the time; furthermore, transportation and distribution costs were deductible from the final sale price.

The conflict had already begun to escalate by 20 September, when the minister of defence, Sánchez Berzain, personally supervised a military operation to 'rescue' some seventy tourists, who had were stranded by roadblocks in the village of Sorata. The transfer of tourists with a military escort provoked heavy clashes with protesters in Warisata, costing the lives of seven peasants (including one 8-year-old girl) and leaving seventeen wounded. Whether the situation of the tourists was really as desperate as the minister claimed is questionable. According to the manager of the hotel where some of the tourists stayed, they were *bien y tranquillo* ('fine and calm'; interview with the author, October 2004) until the actions of the minister exacerbated the issue. Had the government accepted the offer of the Church to mediate, it is not improbable that the violence could have been avoided (Suárez, 2003: 37). Instead, the repression spurred a broad wave of protests and extension of the roadblocks.

From 25 September onwards other marches, demonstrations and roadblocks protesting against the sale of gas began to spread from El Alto to other regions, including a big demonstration organized by the revived Central Obrera Boliviana. At this point more and more voices started to urge the president to stand down. The president in turn presented himself and his administration as the sole safeguard of democracy, denying the use of repressive violence, identifying the protesters as insurgents with links to drug trafficking, and accusing them of planning a *coup d'état*.[8]

On Wednesday 8 October, an 'unlimited strike' was declared in El Alto to protest against the plans to export the gas and against the violence. The government reacted by playing down the mobilizations as the actions of a minority and stated that it would resolve the conflict through negotiation in parliament. On 9 October a clash between miners and police in Huanuni saw three people (including a boy) killed and twenty-one injured, despite the fact that two members of parliament and a priest (who was subsequently injured by a bullet) had tried to convince the police not to use excessive force. On the same day, many spontaneous demonstrations came together in El Alto with the common strategy of gaining control of the gas and gasoline plant at Senkarta,[9] which is vital to La Paz's fuel supply. A day later, the blockade of the fuel depot caused gasoline scarcity in La Paz.

The worst confrontations of the *Guerra del Gas* occurred on the weekend of 11 and 12 October when the government decided to deploy the military in order to supply La Paz with gasoline from Senkarta. The military operation, popularly coined *carvana del muerte* (death convoy), caused dozens of deaths and injured hundreds, all of them civilians and all victims of gunshot.[10] But not all civilian victims had been protesters: as a strategy to spread fear among the population and to stop the trend of ever more people joining the protests, the military began to attack private houses, with the consequence that two children received gunshot wounds inside their homes (Suárez, 2003: 45; Amnesty International 2004). In addition to suppressing and discrediting the opposition, the government confiscated critical newspapers and attacked opposition radio stations.

On Monday, 12 October, while El Alto was under military occupation and on a day when another gasoline transport protest caused twenty-six deaths, massive mobilizations arrived from El Alto, the Yungas, the Altiplano and mining centres in the city of La Paz to demonstrate alongside inhabitants of the city in 'defence' of gas and to demand the resignation of the president. On the following day, Evo Morales rejected the government's offers as too little, too late. His insistence that after such a death toll the only solution could be the resignation of the president achieved general consensus over the next few days. On Wednesday, 15 October, the middle class definitively joined the opposition. A group led by the ex-*Defensora del Pueblo*, Romero de Campero, reaching about 700 participants, including intellectuals, artists, priests and businessmen, began with a hunger strike to demand the constitutional replacement of the president. In distant Buenos Aires, 10,000 Bolivian immigrants demonstrated in a march from the city centre to the Bolivian embassy. The European Parliament passed a resolution on the situation in Bolivia which, among other things, pointed to the exclusion of the indigenous and peasants from political and economic life.[11] This was the first time that a popular protest in Bolivia had seen such a clear repercussion abroad.

The government reacted to the protests in its tried and tested manner of strengthening the security forces, suppressing protests, seeking international support, and establishing pacts between party elites. In the face of the violence used by the government the middle class joined the protesters, and demanded the president be replaced. On 16 October, some 100,000 people (according to conservative estimates) demonstrated in La Paz to demand the resignation of Sánchez de Lozada, while large parts of the country were paralysed by strikes and roadblocks. Yet still the president insisted in interviews that he was a victim of an anti-democratic conspiracy by Evo Morales's *cocaleros*, supported by Columbian and Libyan terrorists (Dangle, 2003; *Miami Herald*, 17 October 2003; *El Mercurio de Chile*, 17 October 2003). Government spokesperson Sánchez Berzain maintained that

> October was the culmination of a long process of sedition, conspiracy and armed uprising against democracy, ... with overseas finance brought by Evo Morales from Venezuela, with international logistical support provided by Cuban advisers, and including people linked to the FARC, they have initiated a process to overthrow President Sánchez de Lozada.
>
> There have been deaths, but I maintain that the deaths have been deliberately sought and caused [*buscado y producido*] by the people who want to overthrow Gonzalo Sánchez de Lozada. (Indymedia Bolivia, 23 September 2007)

Sánchez de Lozada had tried to depict protestors in 2003 as a small group of individuals with links to 'organized crime' and with the intention of 'provoking deaths' to make the government fall (Pérez, 2007).[12] In contrast, the actions of the MNR government were presented as representing the will of 'the people'. For it is only the government, and never popular collective action, that constitutes the political expression of the people as the ultimate source of sovereignty. While it is, of course, correct that democratically elected governments can claim a certain popular legitimacy, when Sánchez de Lozada claimed he was acting on behalf of the people his approval rating was below 10 per cent. Without wishing to argue in favour of politics guided purely by opinion polls, the point is that the government was completely unresponsive to popular sensitivities; furthermore, there were occasions (including the 2000 and 2003 protests) when popular collective actions had the support of the majority of the population (Albó, 2004).

We can interpret the pronouncements of the Sánchez de Lozada administration in defence of discipline (e.g. 'upholding the rule of law', 'defending the constitutional order'; cited in García Orellana et al., 2003) as perceiving the actions of the people as a threat rather than its democratic expression. Luis Tapia (2005: 106–7) concludes, in his analysis of the discourses of President Sánchez de Lozada and Carlos Mesa, that there was a pattern of describing the decisions of the administration as 'rational' and asserting that the construction of 'rationality' was the exclusive right of the political incumbents. This implies, according to Tapia, that 'the people' were viewed by the authorities as lacking the capacity to act rationally, meaning that they were supposed to accept the established order as it is.[13]

As the conflict progressed, initially divisible and negotiable demands became indivisible and non-negotiable as the two sides formed antagonistic poles. The stakes were raised by the violence used by government forces intent on breaking the demonstration: 80 deaths and 411 injured (Albó, 2004: 51). Although political violence has long been a factor in Bolivia, indignation over the highest civilian casualty rate since the return to democracy cut across classes, and rendered the Sánchez de Lozada administration unsustainable. He tendered his resignation and left the country by helicopter and then plane to Miami on 17 October. The resignation was accepted by Congress and democracy survived with the constitutional succession of Carlos Mesa as president.

The conflict possessed an important symbolic dimension of threatened natural resources and lost wars; the bottom line was not to allow the issue with gas to develop as in the cases of silver and tin, which were being exploited for the benefit of foreign actors and a tiny national elite. Gas also stood for petroleum, and thereby echoed the disastrous Chaco War (1932–35). Moreover, the gas pipeline project through Chile evoked the collective memory of the War of the Pacific (1879–83), when Bolivia lost its access to the sea as well as another vital resource (nitrate) to Chile. In the words of Eduardo Galeano, 'the people have risen up because they could not accept that the same would happen with gas as what happened before with silver, saltpetre, tin and all the other raw materials' (2004: 221).

Conclusion

Despite important advances, such as regular elections, an authoritarian legacy and novel forms of exclusion limited the reach of Bolivia's democracy. For the twenty years of formal democracy, the political culture largely remained in the service of the powerful. The absence of a radical break with the past led to a patrimonial state, whereby the political elite treated the state as their private property. The centrality ascribed to official institutions did not allow for the autonomous expression of popular demands. The institutions did not fulfil their functions adequately. The reforms of the 1990s were insufficient in the long run to satisfy the need to institutionalize democracy, because the electorate perceived them as serving merely to distribute patronage among parties more effectively. Democracy in Bolivia failed to equalize access to political power, and one could even argue that it had negative consequences for subordinate groups in so far as they were excluded by coalitions representing only the elites (Mainwaring, 1988).

The most fundamental problem has been the malfunctioning of political parties, but their deficiencies were symptomatic of the state of democracy more generally. Over the years, the failure of parties to represent social interests beyond an intimate club of party affiliates served to make political parties the least trusted of all institutions. The political parties and the public had become divorced. As in many divorces, the outcome was an unhappy one: the two sides spoke the same language but their underlying assumptions and their interpretations of what was being said were fundamentally different, leading inevitably to mutual distrust, accusations and deep-seated disenchantment. As a result of this 'crisis of representation', the people took politics onto the streets. By 2004 Bolivia was the country in Latin America with the highest percentage of people who had participated at least once in a public protest.

The waves of conflict were therefore not a sudden eruption of popular fury, but the result of a long chain of mobilizations against

the way in which politics in Bolivia functioned. While the significance of the *Guerra del Agua* was its novel urban–rural alliance, that
of the *Guerra del Gas* was its large mobilization of the middle class.
The rejection of popular demands during the conflicts constituted
a shared negative dimension though which various social sectors
became united, notwithstanding their continuing differences. A
key factor in this broad alliance was the symbolism inherent in the
conflicts, namely the exploitation of Bolivia's natural resources and
the lost wars – later to be articulated by Morales as the defence of
national sovereignty. MAS, and Morales in particular, presented
coca, water and gas as symbols of the natural resources that the
Bolivian people had 'lost' to foreign interests without benefit to
themselves.

This implies that natural resources and sovereignty had become
the most potent discursive construction since the revolutionary
nationalism of the 1950s (see Chapter 4). Whereas Evo Morales was
not the leader of the protests, he most successfully exploited the
discursive potential of the conflict as part of a process to broaden
the narrow focus of his single-issue party and movement, with a
view to persuading other popular sectors to get behind its demand
for structural change and a redefinition of citizenship.

The most significant achievement of Evo Morales was leading
MAS in such a way that it retained a foothold within official institutions while participating in collective action in extra-institutional
public arenas. Through this strategy, he built a bridge between the
official and extra-institutional spheres. Morales thereby attracted
people who did not want to participate in a (particularistic) social
movement, but who saw the necessity for political change. Hence,
as an elected MP with at times a more moderate way of formulat-
ing demands than the protesters, Morales brought a legitimacy to
popular protest that could never have obtained otherwise.

CHAPTER 6

MAS assumes political dominance, 2002–05

Reaching out to other social movements

Over the years, MAS has grown to become a political organization embedded in social movements and unions. It has formed alliances wherein associates can determine who will be their candidate for MAS and enter into shared programmatic work. Once a grass-roots organization has decided to become involved with MAS, its members have a duty to be available as volunteers if needed. For this reason, MAS presents itself as organizationally rooted in social movements throughout the country. Its discourse lumps together all the organizations that support it under the vague concept of 'the social movements', which also includes unions and traditional indigenous organizations (*ayllus*).

What is MAS? MAS are the social movements. (Evo Morales)

MAS are the social movements, you see? It is impossible to think of MAS without understanding that MAS is by definition, and in practice, the 'political instrument' of the social actors. This means that, although it has its own structure with national and departmental leadership, and so on, the real structure is the social movements. I think you were present at a meeting of the national leadership; but the leadership happens also during the meetings and congresses of the social sector. (Morales Olivera)

The discourse of MAS's leaders present it not as a political party but as the 'political instrument' of *the* social movements. It describes the double organizational structure of MAS: there is a political party structure but this is not always the place where the most important decisions are taken. Instead, decisions are (ostensibly) the outcome of a bottom-up process of decision-making in social movements, which refers to a dynamic of free-floating demands and the absence of a hierarchy between them. The description of decision-making within the party resembles Rosa Luxemburg's (1940) idea of free-floating revolutionary spirit: no organization determines the priorities of demands; rather, the bases 'consensuate' them through extensive discussions.

> For us as the bases, it was always important that the 'political instrument' remained in our hands. This means we did not want something separated from the *sindicatos*, because that would be the same as all the parties that offered everything to get our votes and at the end never fulfilled their promises. For this reason, I believe that it was obvious that MAS should remain under the control of the CCSF, and in this way under the leadership of the bases.... You know that all the candidates of MAS were former leaders, above all of the *federaciónes*, and they were also members of the *sindicatos* where they had to listen and deliberate to reach a consensus... I would like to say that they were the leaders of the 'instrument', but the bases told them how to manage the politics.... In this way, the political instrument was run as we always ran in the *sindicatos*: the leaders have to listen to the bases. (Don Teofílio)

Introducing the so-called 'political instrument' as no more than an item on the agenda of the meetings of allied social movements, and using social movement networks as structures to channel participation, has persuaded a large number of people that they 'own' the party. Hence the lack of independence from the social movements represents both an important aspect of the party's success and a challenge ever present in the background. Only because the party has remained for a significant period indistinguishable from the social movements' structures has it been able to gain and maintain the trust of its core supporters, who are in general keen to keep politicians at arm's length.

An important aspect of this structure is the 'equivalential' articulation of demands (Laclau, 2005), which means that all individual demands have a status equal, and no one is forced to submit to an internal hierarchy of demands. All supporters are interpellated as equal in their opposition to an oppressive status quo and to 'traditional' parties. Avoiding an internal hierarchical order on the model of a 'proletarian vanguard' helps the party to grow through the incorporation of the demands of other social movements. These movements continue to exist relatively autonomous from MAS and maintain much of their bottom-up dynamic, while using MAS as an additional tool to press for their demands.

The process through which this growth occurs is gradual and is effected largely through grassroots contacts. The Tropic of Cochabamba is linked to communities elsewhere, because the majority of its inhabitants migrated from the Altiplano and the Valleys of Cochabamba to the Tropic from the 1970s onwards. In addition, the Andean cultural practice of working on different *pisos ecológicos* (roughly: geographical and climatic levels) is still alive in the Tropic, and part of its population moves between different *pisos* to diversify its livelihood. That is to say, part of the growth of MAS can be related to the particular cultural pattern of mobility of its members. People from the Tropic travel beyond local boundaries and, using links with other communities, they persuade other social movements to support MAS.

We always go to the North Potosí where my family lives – I have a brother who stays there. We take fruit, and there we have potatoes that we can sell in the Tropic, because they don't grow there.[1] When we had achieved our first MPs with the political instrument, the people there asked us: 'Why do you organize yourselves? Why do you block roads and organize demonstrations? What is the political instrument?' And we explain that we have to organize ourselves, because nobody listens to us, and that it is better to have our own instrument than political parties, and that we will not let them cheat us again. (Don Manuel)

It seems that they talked in their organizations, and in time leaders from other places came to our Ampliados to learn how we ran this political instrument. And our leaders said: you have to organize yourselves well and work organically and we will be able to have your candidates in our political instrument. (Doña Bartolina)

Thus, grassroots contacts help to spread information about the 'political instrument' and prepare other organizations to support it. This does not mean, however, that leadership has been unimportant: Evo Morales and, up to 2004, other leaders of the *federaciónes* played a key role. They initially persuaded their bases to use contacts within other communities to defend what their movement was doing.

Furthermore, Morales makes it his personal priority to travel to other communities in order to forge alliances and unite them behind the common political cause. In particular, he has rallied support in the region of Oruro where he was born; but since his election as a MP he has also sought support in other regions. Increasingly leaders accepted his invitation to attend the Ampliados. Cooperation with the *instrumento político* thus proceeds in a decentralized manner. Once local organizations decide they want to take part in MAS, they are allowed to do so on their own terms, the only condition being that they support the organization's general political project of 'transforming Bolivia'. This grants them considerable freedom regarding the election of candidates, campaign organization, and how to integrate discussion about MAS into their organization.

In some communities special committees are formed; others opt to discuss issues relating to MAS as topics during their meetings. We find here an important distinction with other attempts at developing comprehensive territorial party structures. The MNR, for instance, has proceeded in a centralized and homogeneous fashion, trying to operate identical local party outlets across the country, which must follow the instructions of the central party command. The contrasting laissez-faire approach of MAS seeks to benefit from specific local dynamics, as opposed to coercing these organizations into adopting a predetermined organizational style.

As a consequence, large parts of MAS at the local level function according to the rationale of rural communities. Ivan Iporre argues that MAS can only be understood if one looks at the *campesino* logic of structuration, because before 2002 the principal organizational axis has been primarily peasant organizations. The growth of MAS follows a horizontal logic in the sense that all organizations are welcome to join if they subscribe to a common opposition to the status quo, notwithstanding their at times contradictory particular demands. The tabling of positive proposals started only after 2002, and it was not until 2005 that this happened in any structured way within MAS. MAS benefited, above all, from the crises that blew up between 2000 and 2005 and from the unresponsive behaviour of other parties during these events. In order to unite a diversity of interests, MAS had to do no more than present itself credibly as an alternative to the status quo.

Finally, it must be noted that MAS establishes alliances with other social movements in a decentralized manner. Sometimes it instigates these; on other occasions they follow the requests of other organizations. Since 2004, however, there have been more cases of alliances forged between leaders, with the partnership put into effect by top-down organization. MAS has no template for these alliances, which do not necessarily follow a strategic plan put together by top leaders. We might understand the growth of MAS as a mushrooming at the grassroots, with an additional snowball system operating at the leadership level. This most likely delays the growth of MAS and prevents a more coherent alignment of allies. The latter might mean that whilst MAS will find allies in one community, it does not follow that it will do so in a neighbouring one. A broad appeal is necessary for electoral success. However, it is not certain whether a development based exclusively on the cooperation between leaders would have achieved a more coherent distribution of allies. It can be argued, furthermore, that this slow growth is in the end more successful, since it preserves the image of MAS as the political instrument of a diversity of social organizations. This presents an image of MAS as allowing a degree of grassroots participation similar to that practised in the coca producers' movement. Basically, participation in MAS gives citizens the right to attend party rallies and open meetings, and to express their opinions freely and comprehensively. The most important forums for participation are the monthly *Ampliados* of the *sindicatos* in the Tropic, where MAS's leaders deliberate with the bases during for up to three days about decisions concerning the *instrumento político*. Nowadays, these conventions are also fairly open to outsiders, although foreigners in particular still need the permission of an *ejecutivo* of one of the six *federaciónes*.

However, the coca producers' movement is not the only forum for participation. Other social movements and allied organizations (e.g. unions) also provide a platform for expressing ideas and demands concerning the party. Usually the MAS representative who has been elected by the organization in question has to be present during these meetings. In addition, albeit less regularly, Evo Morales still visits these organizations during their conventions, or at least sends a deputy to note the content of the discussions and explain the position of the Morales government. A related point is that the organization of MAS after 2004 can be characterized, by Bolivian standards, as fairly open to the enlisting of new groups and new demands, the forming of political alliances, admitting volunteers, granting journalists access to internal documents and meetings,[2] and the discussion of internal problems. This contrasts with the founding social movement of the coca producers, which had an organizational culture of distrusting outsiders and of emphasizing self-reliance and self-help. Nevertheless, maintaining openness and participation is a difficult task for MAS, because there are increasingly advocates for reducing the degree of participation within the party.

Lack of clear structures: a new way of doing politics?

MAS is an organizational chaos.... The name of a commission or function of an individual can be just as relevant as irrelevant for the matter at stake. (Manuel Morales Olivera, adviser to MAS and president of YPFB, the state oil company)

Sketched above is a picture of the somewhat disorganized pattern of growth of MAS, with its – for a political party, atypical – emphasis on grassroots connections between its different parts. The consequence of this development is that MAS lacks the clear and hierarchical structures that top-down founded parties (e.g. MNR, ADN, PODEMOS, UN) in Bolivia tend to have. However, this is not the result of negligence or organizational incompetence: MAS leaders welcome and sometimes even encourage this state of affairs. The reason for this is that they try to practise in the 'political instrument' a new politics guided by an *originario* (roughly: indigenous) logic of organization. This includes the primacy of the led over leaders and the rotation of offices. It is of less importance who occupies a leadership position, because the leader must follow the consensus of the masses; and rotation prevents the misuse of power, in the sense of manipulating the organization for personal ends.

They attack it a lot for being what it is.... They say: 'But how will MAS govern if it has no clear structure, visible in serenity?' MAS is a chaos of distinct organizations, but it has an organizational logic. It has strength precisely because it is a new conception of politics, intermediate between the political realm, the state and society. The organizational logic is related to an 'originary' logic [*lógica originaria*]. The leadership of the communities is rotational. This is a large part of the concept. And then when it is viewed from the perspective of Western logic, there is great amazement [*maravillaza*]. It might be that a leader is a very good administrator but nevertheless stands down. So, you might ask, 'But, why? If someone is good, why not re-elect him?'

The answer: because somebody else has to stand. Why? Because the issue is not whether you are at the top or below. The one at the top has to obey. If the one at the top is not a clear thinker but those below are, the system will continue to function, because those below will tell those at the top what they have to do. It is a different logic. This logic exists in reality. I talk about the logic of the 'instrument'. The leaders all obey the bases. Whether it the best pickaxe or the oldest pickaxe that is used, it will function in the same way. (Morales Olivera)

MAS is a rather chaotic alliance of distinct organizations; its leaders present this as facilitating grassroots involvement and Andean communal organizational practices. That the lack of clear structures has a number of significant disadvantages, however, is self-evident. Most important here is a 'certain inefficiency caused by the duplication of some tasks' (Héctor Arze, former minister for coordination with civil society), and the neglect of other tasks, such as the failure to set up a professional and sufficiently staffed press office.[3] MAS compensates for this inefficiency by deploying a huge number of people from the social movements as unpaid volunteers for the party. However, now MAS has entered government, reality requires it to raise its level of efficiency. At the same time, though, it becomes more difficult to mobilize volunteers, as they demand compensation for their work owing to MAS's access to state resources. Overall, 'organizational chaos' has helped the growth of MAS and encouraged strong links with the grassroots. Nevertheless, once MAS assumed governmental responsibility the negative effects of a lack of clear structures became more apparent.

Institutionalizing party structures

Since 2004 the party has embarked on a process of institution-alization of its organizational structures. This has progressed but is not yet complete; structures still give the impression of being improvised and provisional. Notwithstanding this continuing state of affairs, MAS boasts a more vibrant and relatively autonomous party structure, characterized by mushrooming commissions, established at national, departmental and local levels to develop programmatic proposals. Its most powerful body is the Directorio Nacional (National Directorate), which has been for most of Morales's first government composed of ten people,[4] including Evo Morales, Álvaro García Linera, F. Santos Ramirez, Ivan Iporre, R. Quintana, M. Morales Olivera and Julio Salazar representing the six *federaciónes* of the Tropic. The Directorio Nacional is the body where most strategic decisions are taken and which coordinates party activities. Another important organ is the Comisión Política Nacional (National Political Commission), which basically coordinates and approves the proposals of other national and sub-national commissions – on education, health, natural resources, rural development and so on. The determination to institutionalize party structures is expressed also in the creation of the Direcciones Departamentales, linked to the Directorio Nacional, which is intended to support the con-solidation of structures such as the Comités Zonales (for different urban 'zones'); these are coordinated first at the urban district level and then through Direcciones Regionales, which are assumed to guarantee a supply of militants in every city.

Opening up the party lists

In 2004 an important decision was taken to open up the party lists and to devolve control to local organizations in order to attract as many supporters as possible in common opposition to the status quo. By opening up its ranks to include urban intellectuals, MAS has become attractive to parts of the middle class who want an alternative to the other major parties, which are either on the right or centre-right. In general, the process has two related aspects. One is to put an increasing variety of demands on its agenda, but to unite them under the common theme of the defence of natural resources and national sovereignty. The second is the principle that where other demands are articulated within MAS, these will be articulated most effectively if their sponsors are part of the actual organization. Hence the decision to open up the party's electoral lists to local organizations, which can autonomously decide whom they select

Alvaro

I keep reflecting that this is probably my most peculiar interview with a MAS leader: we are sitting in a small but comfortable room, furnished with leather sofas and modern paintings, on the third floor of MAS's campaign building in La Paz. And my interviewee is indulging himself by eating Nutella (Germany's most popular chocolate spread, extremely expensive in Bolivia) with a spoon!

Already, after the second question, our discussion has taken the form of an academic discussion where both sides elaborate at length their point of view. At first I tried to stop myself from talking too much, sticking to the role of an interviewer, but he kept asking and probing, challenging the assumptions of my questions.

Alvaro García Linera really seems to be enjoying this exchange; he is not the cold, distant or even arrogant person often characterized in the media. Rather, he creates a warm atmosphere during the conversation and seems genuinely interested in my point of view. By the end, I had stayed not the scheduled fifteen or twenty minutes but an hour and twenty minutes, during which he finished the glass of Nutella...

to articulate their interests within MAS. In practice, this implies that in every electoral district a popular organization can request the departmental party leadership to adopt their representative as a candidate of MAS. In rural areas, where there exists either the MNR-introduced *Sindicato Campesino* structure or a more traditional but revitalized organization in *ayllus*,[5] the issue is clear-cut. The hegemonic territorial organization elects a person; once elected, they will not be challenged.

However, the decision to open up the party lists also applies to the cities, where competing organizations (e.g. *juntas vecinales*, (neighbourhood committees) and professional associations dispute the right to nominate a candidate for MAS. The different social structure in urban areas causes a number of problems with respect to the selection of candidates (see 'Organizational Problems' below).

It is hard to believe that the leadership of MAS did not foresee this; presumably it was thought that the benefits of appealing to the urban middle class by attracting new players would outweigh any problems with proposed candidates.

According to a senior leader, a number of influential people within MAS warned against the dangers of opening up the party without having control mechanisms in place. Their concerns fell on deaf ears among the top leaders, who were convinced that an electoral victory for MAS required attracting the middle class even if that entailed the risk of losing voters from its rural core. Thus the decision to open up the party *radically* was motivated primarily by strategic, electoral considerations: to maximize its chance of winning the 2005 and subsequent elections. Many long-standing militants and some cadres of MAS told me that they disagreed with this strategy, since they feared the party could lose 'face' by attracting too many people not directly interested in the core demands of the organization. For them, the responsibility lay with intellectuals like García Linera, who has not been a member of the social movements in the grassroots of the party.

Born on 19 October 1962 in Cochabamba, García Linera is actually a mathematician with a degree from Mexico's prestigious National Autonomous University. He explains this unlikely profession by reference to his fascination with and talent for maths in high school, adding that this background helps him to approach complex problems in a rigorous and systematic manner. But García Linera was not apolitical during his studies, and recollects reading 'most of the Marxist classics, as well as their adaptation to a Latin American context'. Upon his return to Bolivia, he decided to put into practice some of the Marxist ideas he had read about and joined the *Ponchos Rojos*,[6] which began as an Aymara experiment in communitarian Marxism in Altiplano villages around La Paz. Today a lot of myths surround the *Ponchos Rojos*. They are sometimes referred to as Morales's 'guerrilla army', because they are suspected of being 100,000-men strong and armed with old Czech and German rifles. (Though a significant number of unregistered arms circulate in Bolivia, most of the old Mauser rifles supposedly in the possession of the *Ponchos Rojos* would by now be defunct.) However, whether or not they are really organized and politically motivated to an extent that justifies the label 'guerrilla' is the subject of speculation. In any case, if they are connected to any nationally known politician then it is Felipe Quispe and not Morales. García Linera participated together with Felipe Quispe in setting up an armed branch of the *Ponchos Rojos* in the late 1980s, the insurgent Tupac Katari Guerrilla Army (EGTK), which mounted a few small-scale attacks on infrastructure. During one such act, intending to destroy an electric power pylon in El Alto, the group was captured, and García Linera was sent to jail for five years on charges of terrorism and insurgency. He made good use of his time in prison, studying sociology (including the work of the French sociologist Pierre Bourdieu) and reading very widely. Consequently, discussions with him are an interesting experience.

Despite García Linera's tendency at times to indulge in abstract theoretical disquisition, he is also able to express himself in a manner comprehensible to everyone. Most of his many publications, produced in the 1990s and early 2000s when he was a university professor and columnist, contain illuminating but not always very accessible Marxist-inspired analyses of the social and political situation in Bolivia. To a degree, the rather removed and abstract but highly intellectual work defending the rights of indigenous people resulted from debates in the Comuna group of leftist intellectuals, which García Linera co-founded. 'The Commune' gathered together some of Bolivia's most renowned leftist intellectuals, including Raúl Prada, Luis Tapia and Oscar Vega. The group combined academic work, political commentary and advice to indigenous politicians such as Felipe Quispe and Evo Morales. Raúl Prada, a sociologist (specializing in demography) and professor at the Universidad Mayor San Andrés in La Paz, became later MAS deputy in the Constituent Assembly and vice minister of strategic planning in the Ministry of Economy and Finance in the Morales government. Together with the

MAS, the *Comuna* organized the *Estado Mayor del Pueblo* in January 2003 in which the most important unions and social movements united to press and prepare for a Constituent Assembly.

Although García Linera had advised the MAS on previous occasions, preparing the *Estado Mayor* was probably the beginning of the closer collaboration with Morales that would lead ultimately to his nomination as a vice-presidential candidate in 2005. García Linera devotes much energy to nurturing urban and middle-class voters, and he also regards himself as a bridge between them and the poor, indigenous and rural supporters of MAS. In his pre-MAS publications, he observed that any indigenous party would have to be able to attract urban middle-class voters in order to win general elections. Although rural and indigenous support alone would in theory suffice to win elections in Bolivia, where a majority of the population define themselves as 'indigenous', the value of the symbolism of having García Linera alongside Morales should not be underestimated. It adds an urban, intellectual and middle-class ingredient, which plays well in MAS's appeal to voters from a range of backgrounds. It probably helps to persuade rural indigenous people to vote for MAS, counteracting the tendency among them to be sceptical about the ability of one of their peers to govern the country effectively.

During the 2005 electoral campaign there were many rumours about the team of *Evo y Alvaro*. For example, since both are bachelors, some saw fit to speculate on a homosexual relationship. By contrast, both have a large number of female supporters: García Linera seems to be popular among middle-class women; Morales, for his part, makes the hearts of Aymara and especially Quechua women beat faster. However, neither has been implicated in scandals concerning relationships. Instead they have focused their energy on making the MAS government work, which is an enormous task, not least given the lack of executive experience of most core MAS officials.

The tough reality of governing with an inexperienced cadre has tempered García Linera's initially high expectations of what the

Morales administration could achieve (although he always said that project to change Bolivia would take twenty or more years), and he has become generally much more moderate. Yet, notwithstanding his moderation and his distancing himself from violence since his release from prison, García Linera is still labelled a terrorist by opponents of MAS. On the other hand, his radical past comes in handy when he needs to persuade potential supporters of MAS who are suspicious of a white urban intellectual as vice president of the party. Many observers still suspect that Morales might be simply a puppet, with policy in reality determined by García Linera and other intellectual 'newcomers'. It is a fact that these new cadres influence policy – after all, that is one of the main reasons why Morales chooses them for important positions, acknowledging the limited executive experience of core MAS militants. Yet, none of them would have been elected without the nomination of MAS and the support of Morales, and no one comes near the latter in terms of popularity and legitimacy. Both the 'newcomers' and Morales know this very well, and he uses this to control his ministers. In addition, his presidential power helps him keep a relatively tight rein on the 'newcomers'.

What we can conclude thus far is that the opening up of the party certainly helped it to win the elections by a large margin and to increase MAS's capacity to formulate policy. Intellectuals, who previously were only loosely connected to MAS as advisers, are now at the centre of the party. At the same time, introducing new people and ideas brings frictions and contradictions into the organization. For the social movement of the coca producers, the opening of the party means, above all, a loss of influence over the course of MAS, since they have seen their direct influence turn into representation in the National Political Commission.

Since 2005, more measures have been taken to establish an institutionalized party structure with greater independence from the social movement. This is a necessary move to try to bring some order to the overlapping parts of MAS. The intention is still to uphold a decentralized structure which incorporates the significant influ-

How indigenous is MAS?

How could I be so wrong? Having met a few leaders of MAS, I apparently still had this stereotype in the back of my mind that they would not be dressed in suit and tie. The location should have been an indicator: a café in the upmarket business district of La Paz.

And there I sat with my wife for an hour waiting for Ivan Iporre to show up, only to realize that he was sitting in the corner all the time: well dressed, working on his laptop while constantly talking into one of three mobile phones (one reserved for Morales, one for García Linera and MAS leaders, and one for his wife, as I later learned).

Well, this interview opportunity was lost, but we met him several times afterwards; he always took time to explain in his clear and methodological manner the functioning of MAS. Ivan Iporre is an engineer with a degree from Mexico's Universidad Nacional Autónoma (UNAM); he further specialized in strategic planning and worked in a business consultancy (IBIS). After working closely with Morales for several years, where he managed the ever growing team of people around the leader, it came to many as a surprise that Iporre was not nominated as a minister. However, he always insisted that he was not interested in a political position and that his essential role was to reform the system for training top-level civil servants; for the key to reforming Bolivia is, for Iporre, to bring about a change in their attitude and behaviour. He therefore became the director of the National Service for Personnel Administration and then of the Escuela de Gestión Pública Plurinacional (EGPP, School of Plurinational Public Administration).

ence of grassroots organizations. However, the requirement to work more effectively on policy proposals and to channel the activism of the large body of supporters calls for a stronger centre to keep a tight rein on allied organizations and committees. This gives more power to the La Paz-based bodies such as the National Political Commission and the Central Executive Committee, within which Ivan Iporre Salguero, later the director of the Servicio Nacional de Administración de Personal (SNAP), tried to coordinate the activities of all the different branches and regional committees of MAS. However, the establishment of an independent structure is an ongoing process. Hence my observation that the set-up had a somewhat provisional feel. Informal conversations with MAS leaders after the elections indicated that the process of institutionalizing party structures has not received much attention since Morales became president, and it seems doubtful whether many of the initiatives have had a lasting effect.

All considered, the opening up of the party to people with no direct link to the social movement of the coca producers leaves us with an ambiguous picture. On the one hand, it helps the party to achieve electoral success, and to attract people who do not identify with the demands of the rural and/or indigenous population. On the other hand, the process has been too hasty and uncontrolled, allowing weak or inappropriate people to obtain positions and threatening to undermine the structural protection of the interests of the founding social movement. Nevertheless, if MAS is to survive as political party, it must go further down the road of institutionalizing the participation of other social sectors within an independent party structure.

Leadership

Descriptions of MAS as a populist party where leadership is personalistic and held by a strong, almost authoritarian figure, such as Hugo Chávez, ignore the constraints placed on Evo Morales by a bottom-up grassroots culture that mediates the relation between leader and the people.

The following description by Ivan Iporre illustrates well the model of leadership that MAS seeks to promote:

> the national leadership is composed of representatives of the social movements. Evo never takes decisions alone. He is always with his people. Why? Because this is the form of governing that is practised in the communities. In this community they elect you so that you are

their representative. But what you have to do is to reach a consensus – to take decisions with the people in your community. If you take decisions alone, the first time they will let it pass, but thereafter not: you will be considered as not belonging to the community. The community is a collective unit. This is how it functions in the political leadership of MAS. Decisions ought not to be individual. (Ivan Iporre, adviser to Evo Morales)

The key statement here is that the national party is run collectively, by 'representatives of the social movements', which implies that the MAS leadership resembles the *mandar obediciendo* style of social movements – a Bolivian version of the Zapatistas in Mexico. This means that Evo Morales is to a degree restricted in his ability to impose decisions: he cannot take decisions unilaterally but needs to build a consensus. Thus, even though president, he undertakes regular – sometimes daily – visits to meetings and assemblies of social movements with the aim of strengthening the face-to-face relationship that is such an important element of his leadership style.

Decisions within MAS are officially taken by consensus, representing the interests of all involved – that is, by the leaders of the social movements. In the discourse of MAS, decisions reflect grassroots demands; the nature of these demands, however, is often vague. The detail of a particular demand may not register as such, as, according to the logic of MAS, a number of demands may be amalgamated in the decision-making process in order to reach consensus. Within this logic it is therefore not necessary for all social movements to be represented proportionally through their leaders; it is assumed that all social movements agree on the broad goal of 'changing the politics'. According to MAS, social movements have accepted it as the only viable alternative to the status quo and therefore agree on its role as vehicle for change.

For MAS the social movements are synonymous with 'the people', which stand in opposition to the 'traditional parties'. The argument is that the protests of 2000–2005 represented a general dissatisfaction with the status quo, for which the 'traditional parties' are held responsible. The discontent and the protests were so widespread that, in effect, 'the people' were hailed as having emerged as a single collective actor. Thus, in a simple discursive operation the grassroots of the social movements are equated with 'the people', thereby allowing Evo Morales to speak in the name of 'the people'. In consequence the decisions made by a small group of leaders within MAS can be presented to the public as decisions made by the entire people.

Thus we have the logic of 'hegemonism' (Aboy Carlés, 2005b), which here refers to the aspiration to include all differences within one party. It includes the unrealistic claim that the collective leadership of MAS represents all Bolivians, with the exception of the elites of 'traditional parties'. No doubt Morales sincerely believes that he does represent the interests of all the disenfranchised, or even of the entire indigenous population. However, although MAS can probably count more sympathizers than any other party, it has never had the electoral support of Bolivia's entire indigenous population. Likewise, not all social movements support MAS; indeed, in some cases it is questionable whether MAS is correct in designating certain organizations 'social movements', as opposed to unions, citizens' associations or interest groups.

Characteristics of leaders

Broadly speaking, MAS has two types of leader. The first are those who have a background in the social movements (e.g. coca producers), unions (e.g. miners, transport workers, teachers), neighbourhood organizations (*juntas vecinales* in El Alto), and indigenous organizations. These leaders are by and large rural, indigenous activists who were elected by their local organization to take part in MAS. The second type of leader is the leftist urban intellectual, who joined MAS as an individual for idealistic reasons. For the most part, these individuals do not themselves belong to an indigenous group but support the cause of the indigenous people as part of their ideology. Alvaro García Linera is an example of this relatively new group within MAS, who have helped the party to develop an ideologically more coherent – though still rather eclectic – programme and used their experience with other parties to support MAS's electoral campaign. In general, leaders such as Carlos Villegas[7] favour a more hierarchical party organization than do social movement leaders, and their sometimes more pragmatic approach has been the object of fierce criticism from the grassroots. Although from its very beginning MAS could count on a number of sympathetic intellectuals, they have functioned primarily as advisers; only after 2004 did they become active leaders in the party. As will become apparent later in the chapter, the existence of this type of leader within MAS has given rise to significant benefits and problems for the party.

Evo Morales in fact unites both leadership currents within MAS, owing to his background as a social movement leader and his defence of the more moderate positions held by some social movements. As MAS's top leader, he not only serves as a role model or ideal type of leader for many others;[8] his trajectory, culminating in his arrival at the top of the organization, is also telling, for it indicates which characteristics contribute to the success of a leader within MAS. For many people outside the party, Morales's identity is determined by his indigenous and rural background and his activism around the defence of coca. It seems that this background is also important within MAS, but here it is framed by the idea of Morales as an autodidact who has been able to direct the organization's remarkable development from social movement to political party. That is, activists identify with Morales by virtue of a shared background (rural/ethnic), but more importantly because he stands as an example of a successful leader without much formal education or economic resources. As such, both MAS militants and the man himself present Morales as exemplary of the dedication and conviction of the best social movement leaders, who undergo considerable personal sacrifice to serve their organizations.

What is interesting about this articulation is that MAS does not depict Morales as an 'ordinary man' or as a 'man of the people'.

It is obvious to all Bolivians that Morales does not come from the elite. To highlight this fact would therefore not create additional followers. The emphasis instead is on stressing how much Morales has learnt despite adverse circumstances, often resulting in more moderate positions than may be assumed, and how he manages the difficult task of leading the social movement of the coca producers. This serves to refute claims that Morales is incapable of governing, instead arguing that he has proven leadership qualities and that all else can be learnt. Prior to MAS's assumption of governmental responsibility, the key learning opportunities for Morales and his fellow leaders were the World Social Forums in Latin America. These events provided a platform for the exchange of experiences and helped to broaden the horizon of early MAS leaders beyond the boundaries of individual social movements. In recent years, Morales has learnt much from dialogue with the broad range of people he meets as president: whether by way of exchanges with sympathetic journalists (he is, it should be noted, notorious for ending interviews where overcritical questions are posed in the absence of an appropriate understanding of Bolivian realities) or in discussion with other leaders, Morales seems quick to learn and develop.

However, this stress on Morales's personal qualities is complemented by the determination to show – or at least give the impression to outsiders – that decisions are not taken alone but, rather, based on consultation, deliberation, teamwork and consensus at the grassroots.

> The leaders had to have credentials as good leaders: listen to the bases, inform them well, be able to negotiate, talk well, and so on. With twenty-seven MAS MPs, we all knew each other; and to a great extent we could ensure that no abuses of power occurred, that the bases were kept informed, and that we were always able to present a common position in Congress and defend it coherently. (D. Nuñez, former MAS member of parliament)

In other words, decisions are the outcome of a social process. They take some time to mature, and the social control exercised by the bases over leaders, as well as the consensus among them, secures compliance. Implicit in this is an aversion to the kind of erratic decision-making associated with a personalist form of leadership. This is portrayed as alien to the Andean communal tradition. Whether MAS can entirely avoid such personalist leadership remains to be seen, not least because historically the presidential system has tended to favour a 'cult of the leader' in Bolivia. Nevertheless, one should be wary of attributing all decisions personally to Evo Morales (or, indeed, of assuming he is unduly influenced by advisers). Morales can be a forceful leader, one who instils great respect and, sometimes, a reluctance in others to contradict him, but he has also learnt to listen and learn from other people. At present he is surrounded by people who are prepared to put forward alternative positions. This is to argue, then, that Morales does not fit the conventional description of a populist leader whose political movement is built exclusively around his personality. Morales is a product of the social movement of the coca growers, which will continue as a political actor even without him. Similarly, MAS is a political party that has benefited greatly from Morales's leadership, but the structural integration of social movements and the ongoing process of consolidating party structures mean that it is unlikely that the party will fall apart with the end of Morales's political career.

Election of candidates

> The leader of the social movement, who is at that moment the candidate, is the candidate of the people. As our candidate, [he is] the result of the social struggle, the struggle that we had as the Six Federaciónes of the Tropic of Cochabamba. (Evo Morales)

The way a person can become a candidate is central to the analysis of political parties, because it is probably the clearest indicator of how the organization functions internally. To begin with, the selection of leaders within MAS is similar to that of the *sindicatos* and should be understood, according to Morales Olivera, as following a *lógica originaria* (or indigenous logic). The principle of rotation stands above that of merit, and another person has to take office for the next term. This principle has to some extent also been applied by the Morales administration, which shuffled ministers and political appointees more frequently even than was the case in previous administrations. Although officially this is for the purposes of increasing accountability and improving institutional governance, some European donors have privately expressed frustration with the frequent changes of interlocutor and the negative consequence for the institutional capacity to implement policies.

Thus, a leader is considered to be an instrument for the expression of the will of the bases and has to obey their decisions. It is doubtful that all social movements or unions that participate in MAS are able to live up to this standard. Yet when the coca producers started a political party this was not an issue, and the means of selecting candidates was obvious: they had to be leaders of the social movement of the coca producers and they had to be nominated unanimously by the bases. Before the 2002 elections, it was the *sindicatos* in the Tropic that had the last word in special congresses in selecting the candidates of MAS (or its predecessor, ASP), although during that time the 'political instrument' was not yet a national party.

When the MAS leadership decided to open up the party, the lack of an institutionalized, independent party structure made the conventional mode of candidate selection an unlikely option if the bases were to retain their democratic influence. As a solution, the responsibility for and control over the selection of candidates has been mostly 'outsourced' to local organizations.

> In the campaign of 2002 and the ones thereafter, Evo said that every organization, in every electoral district, should elect its best candidate. No matter if they were from MAS or not, the best man or women, recognized as such by the community or group, should be chosen.... Now, in 2005, it is again the same logic. With the difference that we have the problem that previously these circuits were smaller. Thus they were more communitarian; in the rural areas this selection method was better known. (Ivan Iporre)

This reflects a very idealistic discourse about the selection of leaders, according to which all are social activists who have been elected by grassroots organizations. The following statement is a little more cautious:

> With the uninominal candidacies there was a tendency towards elections similar to those in the *Asambleas* [of social movements]. So far as I am aware, the correct description is 'there was a tendency towards election by the grassroots'.... But let us say the intention was to let the Assemblies organize the election. In the end I know there were problems; they attempted to solve these problems, but I cannot say whether or not this happened. Basically the issue is this: the plurinominal candidates have been elected through agreements with social sectors; the odd one will have been through a political party, but the majority would be based on social sectors. This is to say, there was an agreement with the Movimiento Sin Miedo (MSM) here in La Paz. The logic is this: the uninominal candidates were elected by the Assemblies; the plurinominal ones through agreements. (Morales Olivera)

This means that the influence of the bases is considerably greater in the case of uninominal candidates than in that of the plurinominals, where the leadership of MAS has more control over who will be nominated. The selection of candidates can only be described as a general tendency, to which exceptions exist. In some instances MAS does not have the time to let grassroots organizations decide. What takes place is a mixture of top-down nomination with some form of consultation and consensus, which in fact might have happened in more instances than MAS leaders care to admit. Evo Morales told me in an interview about a case where the departmental political commission of MAS came together and decided in a small circle of leaders who would be the preferred candidate. This person was subsequently presented in meetings with local grassroots organizations, which had to decide either to accept the candidate without reservation or to reject him, with the possible consequence that MAS would fail to present a candidate before the deadline.

So, in this case we can best speak of a process of ratification by the grassroots, with the real decision-making power resting with the small group of top leaders. It is impossible to verify in all cases how the selection of candidates is carried out. My interviews and participant observation inside MAS yielded the impression that the selection of candidates ranges from direct imposition by Evo Morales to completely autonomous decisions by grassroots organizations. In general this paints a rather chaotic picture, and the failure to implement consistently the guiding principles of selection implies a reduction in transparency. Hence the professed 'primacy of grass-roots decision-making' possibly covers up what can be in reality some rather autocratic decisions.

Organizational problems

A common criticism of MAS is related to its internal organization: a lack of clear structures and hierarchies. This is valid: MAS lacks efficiency and consistency in all the traditional party tasks such as recruiting new political leaders, developing policy proposals, structuring electoral choices, and organizing the government. Arguably the only aspect in which the structure of MAS yields positive results is the democratic education of Bolivia's citizens. This, however, might not be deemed a key function of political parties, but rather something that can equally be done by other kinds of organizations, such as the Church or NGOs. Considering the electoral success of MAS and the importance it has for many people, it is probably going too far to argue that its internal problems limit its functioning to such a degree that it could be replaced by another organization. Nevertheless, it remains true to say that there remain severe problems within the organization of MAS. Equally, though, these are the flip side of an organizational structure that has been instrumental in the party's success.

We can divide MAS's internal problems into two categories. The first relates to its roots in social movements and the continuing emphasis on a shared organizational culture, which includes the manifest importance of mechanisms enabling extended grassroots participation. The problem emerges when there are no well-organized grassroots organizations able to guarantee that the participative process of selecting candidates is truly democratic. Meaningful consultation with the bases is a lengthy process, limiting the party's ability to react swiftly and decisively in response to political developments. In addition, the bases sometimes have contradictory demands and, furthermore, can exhibit a considerable degree of radicalism and lack of realism regarding what can be achieved though institutional politics within a limited time frame. Hence their participation may push the party into positions which its leaders know are untenable. Ultimately this means that very little will be achieved, whereas a degree of compromise might have yielded better results.

On the whole, however, it is the great virtue of the leadership to obtain some moderation from its bases on key political questions. An example would be the apparently successful self-limitation of one *cato* (0.4 hectare) of coca growing per family in the Tropic. Nevertheless, the guiding principle that leaders obey the bases involves the risk that one day grassroots radicalism could overrule all moderation. There is no structural guarantee that future leaders will be able to maintain the degree of moderation from the grassroots as Morales. The organizational culture, which combines a 'movement-cum-party' structure and the portrayal of a common antagonist of 'traditional' politicians, is both the foremost reason for MAS's success and its biggest potential stumbling block.

The second category of problems relates to the growth of MAS. When new people joined the growing party, with its social movement structures, the possibility grew that both levels of organization would suffer from the intrusion of outsiders with their own opportunistic agendas. In addition, the opening up of MAS's electoral lists reduces the importance of social movements because many who entered prefer a tighter, more centralized and hierarchical organization that entails clearer leadership over its members. Frequently, new members, many of them urban professionals and intellectuals, bring with them experience of other left-wing parties or managerial skills, which are needed by MAS. This gives them a head start over rural leaders and catapults them after a short time into influential positions, where they advocate a more top-down prioritization of demands. This is at odds with the priorities of the social movements, which privilege an organizational approach without a centralized leadership.

Hence, within MAS two philosophies regarding how to achieve political change come into conflict. Elements of the social movement fraction within MAS perceive the new approach as that of opportunists threatening their political project and not as a different path towards a common goal.

To conclude, MAS is much more than merely a political instrument for Morales's political ambitions. MAS is a coalition of social interests and not Morales's private tool. The two are intertwined: the party's success is closely linked to Morales's leadership, while his leadership cannot be understood without taking into account the idiosyncrasies of MAS. A key aspect of the success of MAS is its fusion of political party and social movement. This entails – as Morales constantly stresses – a reliance on volunteerism, which makes efficient leadership difficult.

Anyone who agrees with MAS's political project of challenging the hegemony of neoliberalism in Bolivia can approach the party and participate in one of its many meetings and commissions. The party offers citizens such a range of possibilities for participation because it retains a social movement ethos. Notwithstanding all the changes it has undergone, MAS still stresses this open and participatory ethos, and by doing so it bridges the gap between official and extra-institutional politics.

The success of MAS in winning the 2005 and 2009 elections can, therefore, be explained to a large extent by this bridging function. For traditional politicians and bureaucrats such an identity is disturbing since it questions the legitimacy of institutions from within. Only because MAS's project is to redesign Bolivia's political institutions (including through a Constituent Assembly) is it possible to maintain this paradox of parallel logics of institutional and extra-institutional political activity without producing a negative spiral of de-institutionalization and democratic de-consolidation. Although MAS's strategy of continuing to engage in street politics has weakened existing institutions, its project of institutionalizing 'two platforms of governance' implies initiating a process of re-institutionalization to prevent the breakdown of democracy.

CHAPTER 7

Compañero Evo,
symbol of the pluricultural people

Politics is the science of serving the people, not living off the
people. I want to ask of you personally, in the name of the
people: zero corruption, zero bureaucracy. We have the task of
dignifying politics. (Evo Morales, speech during his presidential
inauguration)[1]

This chapter outlines the process by which 'Evo' became the
symbol of 'the people', and how this helped him to win the 2005
elections. According to Morales, 'the people' means the oppressed,
marginalized majority – embodied by himself. 'The people' is a
new political identity established by constructing a distinction
between the people and its oppressors. Evo Morales presents 'the
people' as the sovereign owner of Bolivia's natural resources, and as
deprived of rightful control over these resources by a self-interested
political elite. This idea of 'the people' blurs the differences within
the popular sector, because it shifts the focus to what distinguishes
them from the elite. Thus, this chapter will show how Morales
became for the people the symbol of the 'underdog', behind which
he has been able to unify a diversity of interests in common opposition to the status quo. That is, we will see how Morales has
been able to consolidate and advance the cause of the majority
population.

The people

Although 'the people' is one of the most common concepts in politics, it is also one of the least precise. It cannot be defined with essential characteristics such as boundaries; nor is there always continuity. An additional complication is that we cannot determine 'the people' empirically in cases of contested boundaries, since that presupposes knowing the answer *a priori*. A good example is former Yugoslavia. Under Tito all the different groups made up 'the people' of Yugoslavia. In the 1990s we witnessed the tragic process whereby the definition and boundary of 'the people' was changed. Suddenly you had to be a Bosnian to belong to 'the people', while Serbs were excluded, and vice versa. Similarly, who are 'the people' in Kosovo? Or is the population of Kosovo just part of 'the people' in Serbia? Or does 'the people' comprise the population in Kosovo and Albania? These ambiguities make the concept interesting to study: 'the people' is readily available for contesting interpretations, and it can easily become the centre of political competition. Sometimes, such as in periods when the United States becomes electorally supercharged, 'the people' has so many meanings that it becomes meaningless.

As we shall see, Morales used 'the people' as a signifier to challenge the political status quo. If we accept that populism is a 'process of naming that retroactively determines what is the name of the people' (Panizza, 2005: 19), then the discourse of MAS is populist to the extent that 'the people' (*el pueblo*) refers basically to all those 'who consider themselves as disenfranchised and excluded from public life' (Panizza, 2005: 16). However, there is much more to the concept of 'the people', and focusing on it will help to understand the role of MAS in aspects of politics that are difficult to analyse: the dynamics of the mobilization of dispersed groups into a political body which generates power where there was none before.

It could be argued that with the waves of protest in Bolivia after 2000, a new 'people' arose in the sense of an imagined political community, which merged a multitude of interests and origins. What started as isolated protests grew into an organic sum of collective actions as the expression of the sovereignty of 'the people', who took power from a – in its perception – delegitimized government. This meant there was a notion of 'the people' as a political community with a sense of historicity as 'first peoples' (*pueblos originarios*), but without the idea of a shared nationhood. This is to argue that 'the people' as a political community might be conceptualized as a deliberate achievement rather than the result of organic growth.

Who are the people?

In Bolivia, as elsewhere, the question 'who constitutes the people?' has received different answers over time. For example, in the discourse of the MNR in 1952, and for the leftist military governments in the 1970s, it was the new working class. In his quasi-encyclopaedic work about the MNR, Arze Cuadros (2002) shows how the party tried under a bourgeois leadership to organize the new working class of mining workers as a nucleus of 'the people'. After the introduction of neoliberal economics in the mid-1980s, 'the people' became the urban self-employed of the informal sector, for instance in the discourse of Unidad Cívica Solidaria (UCS). Despite changing notions of the people, one legacy of the MNR remained: the people had to be 'moulded' into a unitary system that centrally defined legitimate forms of political organization. As we shall see below, Morales rejected this assimilationist construction of the people, and moved towards a more decentralized notion. The main characteristics of the people became defined according to the diversity of indigenous and rural identities. Morales thus redefined the meaning of 'the people' as well as that of its 'oppressor', which gave him the opportunity to charge the government with not representing the people. This was a powerful accusation, since it was generally accepted that sovereignty rests ultimately with the people. Morales claimed to speak with the voice of the people through his continuing participation in popular mobilizations.

Mobilizing people to become 'the people'

Canovan (2005) has written a very interesting study on 'the people', which is very relevant to an understanding of Evo Morales's claim to represent the voice of the people. In her work, mobilization is central to bringing a people into existence, which implies an understanding of the people as an ongoing process, continuously constructing, deconstructing and reconstructing the meaning of the concept. In moments of large-scale mobilization, the people can enter the public stage as a collective actor, as a body to generate power and exercise sovereignty. This manifestation of the people is likely to be a brief episode, after which the people return to being an 'abstract authority in reserve' (Canovan, 2005: 91). We might say that the waves of protests and the 2005 elections marked a period where 'the people' arose as a powerful political body. Canovan's emphasis on mobilization implies that neither direct nor deliberative forms of democracy can guarantee that 'the people' will assume the form of a political actor. MAS has introduced forms of direct democracy, but these institutional reforms alone cannot bring into being 'the people' as a collective actor. So, how does MAS aim to mobilize the people as a whole?

The people and the exercise of power

> The sovereign people is the protagonist of its own existence and projects its destiny. (MAS, Comisión IV: Soberanía e identidad nacional, 4 July 2005)

Morales and MAS ascribe political power to 'the sovereign people', but how exactly can 'the people' exercise this sovereignty? There has existed a consensus among the elite that the exercise of popular sovereignty should be limited to a liberal, procedural notion of democracy: participation in free and fair elections. This represents the claim 'that the continuing, collective and usually absent people has made its presence felt in the votes of the concrete individual people' (Canovan, 2005: 110), which means that the people surrendered power some time in the past and would use it only in rare emergencies.

What constitutes such an emergency is obviously the central point of the discussion. The MNR and ADN governments rejected the idea of the people acting as the sovereign power outside elections. Morales, by contrast, refers to the protests since 2000 as instances in which the people manifested concrete power through their collective actions. This implied, furthermore, that for Morales elections did not play a crucial role. 'The people' were assumed to exercise their power in a more continuous manner, and should not be limited to isolated acts of participation such as elections. 'The people' manifested themselves in mobilizations and collective actions, which meant the more they could be mobilized for policy initiatives, the more 'the people' would be a continuous political actor exercising its power.

In practice, however, many possible factors cast doubt on the assertion that the people have acted, both in the conventional view and that of Morales. 'The people' as a united actor is a problematic notion in the light of disputes about the internal and external boundaries of a people (e.g. the 'Two Bolivias' discourse and the autonomist movement in Santa Cruz and Tarija), forms of manipulation or corruption of the electoral process, or ambiguous results such as marginal victories or uncertain outcomes in referendums. One example is the referendum on gas exports held on 18 July 2004, which asked voters whether the state should assume greater control over its gas reserves, charge taxes and royalties of at least 50 per cent of the value of the gas, and use gas as a strategic resource to obtain access to the Pacific. However, the convoluted wording of the questions made it difficult for many to understand the meaning. The referendum was phrased in a way that allowed many interpretations and also avoided explicitly use of the word 'nationalization', although then president Mesa portrayed it as precisely proposing such as measure. As a result, two of the five questions received a much lower approval rating than the other questions, leaving somewhat open the question as to which policy the government should pursue.

Similarly, the idea of mobilization and popular initiatives is not without problems: who mobilizes whom and on behalf of which interests? Do those being mobilized know and understand what they are being mobilized for? What size does a mobilization have to be in order to count as 'the people'? Evidence from Bolivia supports the claim that giving politics back to 'the people' through mechanisms of direct democracy is not straightforward.

For Canovan (2005: 113), the claim to hear 'the people' is plausible by virtue of the fact that there will have been widespread public discussion and political mobilization prior to, for instance, a referendum. There has to be a strong sense of common political community, free and fair voting, clear wording, a salient topic, large turnout and an overwhelming majority in the outcome. Obviously these conditions are seldom met in reality. For instance, the above-mentioned referendum on the export of gas does not satisfy all criteria, since the wording was ambiguous and there was no overwhelming majority (taking into account the geographical bias of the results).

The issue of how people are able to exercise their sovereignty remains contentious and cannot be resolved here. Also we cannot assume that elections or even a more direct form of democracy (referendum) by definition captures the voice of a people and can therefore be understood as 'the people' exercising their power.

Construction of identity

As discussed in Chapter 3, the coca producers emerged as political actors in the 1990s through the dislocation of the 'war against drugs', articulating 'coca' as the symbol for the defence of Bolivian national sovereignty. This implied the necessity of defining on whose behalf national sovereignty had to be defended – that is, who the 'us'/'the people' are. The coca producers became politically successful under Evo Morales's leadership when he presented himself and the other coca producers as 'the people'. This served a triple purpose. One, it allowed escape from the stigmatizing discourse of the political elite that depicted them as 'narco-traffickers' (e.g. PODEMOS leader Quiroga, in *La Voz*, 12 November 2005). Two, it helped the formation of alliances with other social movements, which felt equally stigmatized by the elites. Three, it prepared the ground for Morales to campaign for president as the embodiment of the people as the victim of the dominant political class. All this was possible owing to the conceptual characteristics of 'the people', which enabled Morales to challenge the existing meaning of the term and attempt to hegemonize a new understanding of it.

In fact, Morales built upon a long discursive tradition in MAS of constructing the people as 'plurinational' on account of their roots in peasant organizations. This notion has its origins in the political strategy of the national peasant organization CSUTCB, which used the term 'plurinational' for the first time during its second congress in 1983, in which the organizations of the coca producers participated. Since Morales and the other founders of MAS played an increasingly important role in the CSUTCB, the proposal by MAS to create a 'plurinational' nation can be seen as a product of the work of its grassroots organizations. This popular identity was therefore not invented by MAS or Evo Morales. Rather, it was constructed from the bottom up, thereby highlighting the diversity of the inhabitants of rural areas with their different identities as *pueblos originarios* (First Peoples).

To put it simply, there has been a struggle between the reform-orientated project of MAS, with its logic of uniting different demands against the status quo, and the project of the political elite to maintain the status quo, with its belief that all demands could be satisfied without profound institutional change. Whereas for Morales and MAS, 'the people' are all those disenfranchised and excluded from public life by the 'traditional politicians' or the 'oligarchy', in the discourse of PODEMOS, Unidad Nacional (UN) or MNR there is no such social division between 'us' the people and an antagonist, nor can there be.[2] That is to say, these parties do not construct the people in opposition to something, but rather try to emphasize the tolerance of diversity, granting each sub-identity its well-defined place.

The electoral programme of PODEMOS, for instance, spoke of the need for unity, tolerance and equal opportunities for all Bolivians. It constructed 'the people' as the sum of individuals, all of whom have their individual rights and duties, defined by their belonging to a determinate category. As a legacy of ADN's slogan *Orden, Paz y Trabajo* (Order, Peace and Work), PODEMOS deployed *Orden y Progreso* (Order and Progress), which linked the improvement of the economic situation to a well-ordered society (PODEMOS, 2005: 2–3, 62). For Unidad Nacional, the unity of the Bolivian people exists even in its name. Its programme contained several proposals for improving the situation of the poor without fundamentally altering the composition and structure of the people as a whole (UN, 2005).

The meaning of 'the people' remained contested. Although one could argue that Morales was able to strengthen the dominance of his version of 'the people', it did not become hegemonic since it did not constitute the entire space of political solidarities related to the notion of 'the people'. This generalization was contested, for instance, by the civic committees of Santa Cruz and Tarija.

In a situation where the meaning of 'the people' was contested and different interpretations coexisted, it was possible both to appeal to the idea that the people were oppressed by the government, and to legitimize government actions in the name of 'the people'. That is to say, there is nothing inherent in 'the people' that attaches it to any socio-political order or to a particular class. As a result of its being a 'floating signifier' (Laclau, 2005), elections bring the people into government, but simultaneously keep them at a distance.

To give an example, Morales criticized other political parties for using elections as the outlet for the popular desire to participate, and for failing to allow the whole of the community to exercise political power beyond these well-defined instances. In other words, for Morales politics represents the collective action of the whole community. He criticized the existing system for conducting politics to the exclusion of part of the population. That articulation equated Morales and 'the people', while constructing an internal frontier separating 'the people' from 'the oligarchy' as an external enemy.

However, after victory in the 2005 elections, Morales began facing the same problem of a gap developing between the people itself and the people's government. Some grassroots organizations criticize Morales for failing to establish a government for the entire people. As a sign of spreading frustration that Morales cannot meet high expectations and at time contradictory demands, the COB organized a large protest against the government in early 2011. In response, he has attempted to find other channels to through which to connect the people with government, such as the establishment of a *Coordinadora* with social movements.[3] Every such institutional measure remains open to challenge, since there is of course no way to prove whether or not Morales really expresses the voice of the people and represents them. In fact, this ambiguity is one of the most controversial aspects of his presidency, because he presents everything his government does as a decision of the people, whilst this is clearly not the case in all instances. Opponents of his decisions find themselves frequently confronted with accusations that they are defending the interests of 'the oligarchy' and hence are an enemy of 'the people'.

Thus the ambiguity of the concept of 'the people' keeps politics open-ended: even Morales, who is portrayed as the embodiment of 'the people', can be challenged 'in the name of the people'. Morales uses a discourse of 'the people' to oppose the status quo, and yet faces a challenge from Santa Cruz and Tarija, which accuse him of not acting on behalf of the entire community. Hence the struggle over the ability to define the meaning of 'the people' is related to one of the most notorious issues of democracy: namely, disillusionment with a government that is disconnected from the people.

'The people' in Morales's discourse

What makes them afraid is that we now represent the voice of
millions; we are the voice of the people. In rural North Potosí, in the
mines, in the mountains and in all other parts of Bolivia, bit by bit
the always marginalized unite, they decide to remove the neoliberals
and the corrupt from power, supporting their political instrument,
MAS. (Evo Morales, in *Soberanía*, 2002a, author's translation[4])

'The people', for Evo Morales, are the outcome of political mobilization. Over the five years prior to the election of MAS we have seen
the emergence of a large popular movement on the public stage,
a movement that with all its heterogeneity has united previously
isolated groups in their shared sense of being 'the people'. 'The
people' that arose from and with the protests were not the result
of organic growth, but a deliberate product of Morales's discourse.
A very particular identity – Morales the coca producer – gradually
became broader and more flexible by the increasing reference to the
more common aspects contained within this identity (defender of
natural resources and of national sovereignty). Through this partial
'emptying' (Laclau, 2005), the identity of 'the people' represented
by Morales was turned into a single common identity for all those
disadvantaged by the status quo. The antagonism between Morales
and politicians of mainstream political parties was generalized into
an antagonism between 'the people' and 'the oligarchy'. Fundamental
to the emergence of this new identity, where '*Nuestro hermano* Evo'
was the brother of all 'the people', was the discourse of the coca
growers and their MAS party. Morales, together with the other
movement militants, articulated 'coca' as a symbol for the denial
of economic demands and political exclusion. This resulted in a
questioning of the political system. Morales's alternative political
imaginary accumulated force over approximately ten years, during
which time it was completely outside mainstream politics. None of
the main political figures proposed anything close to the ideas of
Morales and his political movement. But in order to become a major
political force, they needed to include other demands. The central

symbols – defence of 'natural resources' and 'national sovereignty' – made this possible. A broad alliance of previously isolated social movements and middle-class actors emerged as a result of political decisions insensitive to popular sentiments, which in turn gave rise to waves of social conflict after the year 2000.[5]

The effect of this was to divide society into two camps: the *pueblos originarios* as exploited, hereditary protectors of natural resources, and political elites seen as *vendepatrias* (traitors). This was frequently reduced to a personal clash between *Nuestro Compañero* Evo as embodiment of the suppressed and the politicians of the mainstream ('traditional') parties, such as Jorge 'Tuto' Quiroga (PODEMOS) and Rubén Costas (governor of Santa Cruz). The creation of these two poles entailed a shift away from the positing of many particular internal frontiers within the people (workers versus employers, peasants versus landowners, etc.) to the creation of a single polarized conflict. This reduction questioned the existing institutional arrangements on the ground that they excluded the population from political and economic power. For instance, the expulsion of Morales from parliament (22 January 2002), for rather spurious reasons, has been used repeatedly by Morales to invoke the impression that the entire people were no longer welcome within official institutions. It was this casting of doubt on Bolivia's institutions that made the drafting of a new constitution such an important item in the programme of MAS.

The principal reason for the ascent of Morales to the head of all those dissatisfied with the status quo was not so much his actual role in the social conflicts; indeed it would be incorrect to attribute such leadership to Morales. Rather, it was the role his *discourse* played in enabling splintered social movements to converge behind a common demand. This facilitated the emergence of a new popular identity as exploited *pueblos originarios*,[6] embodied by '*Nuestro Compañero* Evo'. Through Morales's continuous reference to himself as 'victim', the core of this popular identity is the notion of Bolivia as victimized nation that lost its rightful control over natural resources. In consequence, Western countries have been able to benefit from the exploitation of these resources on the back of 'the people' (MAS, 2004a). This spirit explains to a great extent the decisions of the Morales administration, such as the apparent annual tradition of selecting an industry to be nationalized, preferably by using the army to occupy the premises of foreign companies as a display that Bolivia is no longer a victim but a sovereign actor.

Somos MAS, Somos el Pueblo!

> MAS is not only a movement of the *cocaleros*. It is for all Bolivians. We will fight for the cities, notwithstanding the 150 million bolivianos that Carlos Sánchez de Berzaín has put up in order to stop us in Cochabamba. (Evo Morales, *Soberanía*, 8 June 2002)

> The traditional governments ... have tried to divide us, but now it is clear that they could not mislead us: we are more united than ever and we will fight for our rights, to recover our natural resources. (Evo Morales, *Soberanía*, 8 June 2002)

Between 2002 and 2005, a key electoral slogan of MAS was *Somos MAS, Somos el Pueblo!*[7] Its origins lay in the social movement that founded MAS, and that retains a strong identification with its 'political instrument', as expressed by the statement 'We are MAS'. The slogan *Somos MAS* also means 'be more' – that is, constitute the majority. This is an allusion to the indigenous majority in Bolivia that (ostensibly) supports MAS. It indicates the confidence in having more supporters than other political parties, which is a common campaign tool to convince people to vote for it. The central message is 'We are the People', which aims at erasing the connotation of political party from MAS and at constructing it as 'instrument' or direct expression of 'the people'.

> You know the problem that we have with our sister, the Republic of Chile: it is the issue of the sea. I want to say to you all, until now we have established a certain trust, trust from the people to the people, trust from government to government, from president to president,

under the diplomacy of the people. (Evo Morales, speech at the UN, quoted in *La Prensa* 27 September 2007)

Morales presents himself as the embodiment of 'the people'. It follows that discussions between President Morales and other presidents, such as Chile's Michelle Bachelet, are articulated as discussions between the two peoples. This implicitly denies other parties the status of representing fractions of 'the people', since this has found its political expression already in MAS and its leader. We find also the construction of an antagonism in this slogan, because if MAS equates to 'the people', what can be said about the status of other parties? They have to represent the interests of some 'external other'. A similar antagonism is present in the following statement by Evo Morales:

> Don't let yourself be misled by these traitor [*vende patria*] parties, which only seek to continue enriching themselves. Vote for the candidates of the people! ... Let us vote for ourselves. (*Soberanía*, 2002: 6)

Here, to vote for Morales means to vote for 'yourself', which is an explicit form of equating Morales with 'the people'. To claim that Morales is the voice of 'the people' implies his being more responsive and more democratic than the leaders of other parties. Thus Morales set up a polarization between 'the people' and 'the elites'. This is symbolized by his presenting himself as a political outsider who plays the electoral game under a new set of rules, combining institutional politics with street politics. MAS's equation of Morales with 'the people' has been constructed carefully. An example would be the opening of Morales's electoral campaigns in El Alto, the definitive city of the popular classes.

Who are 'the people' in Bolivia?

The basic premiss of MAS is that 'the people' are inherently a carrier of positive qualities, such as honesty, being democratic, and able to sacrifice personal needs for higher goals, all of which are symbolized by Evo Morales. Being democratic means, according to Morales, that 'the people' have a great appetite for participation in politics through elections, but also through more direct forms such as referendums and citizens' assemblies. García Linera uses the metaphor of water to describe the 'participative energy' of the people.

> What the state does is to construct dams to contain the water. But there were moments when there was so much water that it overflowed. If that is the case, what has to be done is to construct rivers... channel the water so that it can be converted into electricity, so that it generates electricity. Here what has been done is to contain the water, isn't it? What we want to do is produce energy with this water. (García Linera)

'The people' are thus a vast source of energy that the state can use productively. Given the tradition of social protest in Bolivia, it is evident that the main issue is how to contain and direct this energy. Another quality frequently attributed to 'the people' is *humilde*, humility, which carries a positive connotation, in the sense that humble origins such as those of Morales himself are presented as a source of strength, in contrast to the corruption of the elites. What had previously been a stigma is thus turned around to become a source of pride and identification.

> I only believe in the people, who are honest, with a healthy common sense, and will never be confused by this kind of propaganda. (Evo Morales)[8]

'The people' thus possess a healthy common sense (Morales often trusts his own common sense/intuition more than the elaborate analysis of experts). This enables 'the people' to identify what is in their own interest, assuming that there is such a thing as a common interest of 'the people'. These core characteristics – honesty, common sense and shared interest – serve to underline Morales's claim that 'the people' are the basis of sovereignty and the source of all political power. Just political power can, according to the discourse of Morales, only be generated by collective action by 'the people'. He brushes aside any questioning of the belief that the collective action of the poor and disenfranchised constitutes an expression of the voice of 'the people'. Whilst rejecting the notion that his own followers could have been instrumentalized, Morales nevertheless accepts that 'the people' of Santa Cruz have been misled by the political elite in their bid for departmental autonomy. According to García Linera, 'the exclusion of the indigenous peoples has been structurally included in the Bolivian state'. We observe here the Marxist idea that the state as a relation of power reflects the interests of the incumbents. This underlines the construction of an antagonistic relation between the ruling elite and the 'victims' as represented by MAS.

Evo Morales is synonymous in the discourse of MAS with 'the people'; according to this logic, the *guerra sucia* (dirty war) against him and MAS by other parties is an assault on 'the people'. He draws here a comparison with Argentina's *guerra sucia* during the military dictatorship, when people suspected of belonging to the opposition were imprisoned or 'disappeared'. Morales stated in an interview that PODEMOS leader Quiroga 'has taken on the task of systematically satanizing' the MAS party, and by extension the entire people (*La Voz*, 12 November 2005). We also find instances where MAS speaks as if it has been directly affected by the suppression and exploitation of the indigenous population. On the first page of its 'Principios Ideológicos y Políticos', MAS makes clear that

> we have been dominated by the cosmology of Western culture....
> We have strengthened the economies of Europe and the USA ..., but
> have not industrialized ourselves. (MAS, 2004: 1)

Thus we find there is another way of expressing the idea of the people as victim, with the implicit message that only a government of MAS will bring an 'end to the discrimination of the people and make Bolivia a country of dignity ..., because 500 years of oppression are over' (MAS, 2005a: 2). In the words of Morales, 'as the people, we are the victim of this neoliberal class that not only is corrupt, but also has discriminated and excluded the people for 500 years.'

Whereas Morales observes that these negative campaigns are intended to reduce the vote for him and for MAS, it is obvious that the latter's positioning of itself as a victim is an effective method of attracting and maintaining supporters. This is because it invokes sympathy from a majority of Bolivians, who feel they are the victims of the negative consequences of policies pursued by previous governments. Morales extends the idea of being a victim from the personal realm to MAS, and then to the social movements and the entire people. In this way, he links his personal experience to the notion that the majority of the population are the victims of an 'anti-national elite' and of 'internal colonialism'.[9] This latter idea harks back to the Spanish conquest of Latin America and invokes the history of the exploitation of natural resources (notably silver and tin).

Given the painful collective memory in Bolivia, the symbolism of an indigenous presidential candidate challenging the *mestizo* elite on behalf of the 'impoverished people' is indeed very powerful. Evo Morales symbolizes 'the people' as 'underdog' when he appears among black-suited politicians as a disadvantaged outsider, clearly underdressed in his (in)famous red pullover. (Recently, he has started wearing custom-made suits, but no tie, with traditional Andean fabrics.) Indeed, he has turned the stigma of his casual dress into a positive trademark; in consequence, the pullover has become a best-seller, popular on eBay among Bolivians in the USA and Europe. Similarly, the lack of formal education and personal fortune is transformed into a marker of industriousness and honesty. A good example is the biography of Morales, *Evo: A Story of Dignity*, which celebrates his upbringing in poverty. The biography concludes:

> He who was a humble boy, a llama-herdsman, has become a nightmare for the empire, neoliberalism and the transnational companies, but also the source of hope for the people, for the national majorities. (Contreras Baspineiro, 2005: 61)

Morales uses his personal history to portray himself as both victim and symbol of hope, and to generate sympathy for the disadvantaged and those who have lost out to privatization. This serves to construct a new notion of 'the people' from the bottom of the socio-economic order, in contrast with those who stood in the sunlight of economic reform in the 1990s.

Implications of the new articulation of 'the people'

What does it matter that Morales constructs 'the people' differently from other political parties? Have we not observed simply one group replacing another in power, each with a different articulation of who 'the people' is, without any tangible outcomes? The answer to the first question can be found in the idiosyncratic relationship between MAS and a number of influential social movements. Morales and other leaders present MAS as the voice of 'the people' by means of

> a direct relationship with the social movements. It has to be direct even if executing a public office. Through this there will be a greater guarantee that issues will be linked to the entire population and not only to the privileged in a party. (Omar Fernández, MAS senator)

MAS leaders act as a bridge between the party and social movements, thereby also creating a close and direct relationship to 'the people'. This is supported by combining institutional (party) and extra-institutional (social movement) politics. As leader of a political party and subsequently as president, Morales engages in parliamentary debates, proposes or rejects legislation and fights political campaigns to position himself well for upcoming elections. All these activities are stressed in order to create an image of MAS – especially targeting the centre-left of the electorate – as a relatively moderate, reliable and credible political alternative.

Simultaneously, however, Morales challenges the dominant political culture by asserting that a large part of the population have never been citizens in the full sense of the word. Hence he is anti-institutional, in that he questions the assumptions upon which Bolivia's institutions are built. In its 'Principios Ideológicos y Políticos' (MAS, 2004: 1–24), MAS rejects the modern conception of state institutions as neutral arbiters between a plurality of societal interests. For the party perceives institutional 'neutrality' as a particularly modern, and 'occidental', means of concealing the fact that since the time of the Spanish conquest the same minority had ruled the country.

Neutrality in an environment of distinctly unequal power relations plainly works in favour of those with the social and economic capacity to approach power-holders on an equal footing. It is important to point out here that Morales, notwithstanding the actions pursued through MAS as political party, does not completely subscribe to the logic of party politics. He remains highly critical of official institutions and emphasizes the unity of social demands opposed to the status quo. This contrasts with other political projects that discursively and organizationally privilege the logic of difference, and cannot therefore articulate a common signifier that is able to represent a wide range of differing demands.[10]

Conclusion

The emphasis on unity in diversity against a common enemy enables Morales to articulate a new social imaginary that entails the redefinition of what 'the people' means in Bolivia. This implies a redefinition of the notion of citizenship and a reconceptualization of what kind of state would be required to accommodate these new citizens. Challenging the previous political logic of attending to demands meant discrediting the associated institutional mechanisms and the actors using them. However, the central 'empty' signifiers of the discourse of Morales have already shown some flexibility in including other demands. It might indeed be possible that at some point in the future Morales's discourse includes the demands of his contemporary antagonists whilst creating a new frontier. In his 2009 election campaign, there were already some indications that Morales was attempting to include demands from the *media luna* departments (Santa Cruz, Tarija, Beni and Pando). This implies the possibility of articulating a new sense of 'the people' as a shared community among all Bolivians, equal in their diversity and as citizens. The political identity of 'the people' remains in continuous construction through the struggle for hegemony. This involves an understanding of 'the people' as an ongoing process of large-scale mobilization – the key element in Morales's project to bring 'the people' into existence. We can understand this mobilization as a key democratic task for the leader of a political party committed to involving individuals in politics and to connecting civil society to the state.

At the same time, 'the people' as united actor is a problematic notion, because it ignores existing disputes about the internal and external boundaries of a people. As we will see in the next chapter, Morales has attempted to resolve these boundary problems by constructing a common 'plurinational' political community intended to preserve the diversity of the indigenous peoples. However, attempting to form a united bloc opposed to the status quo whilst maintaining internal diversity seriously stretches the limits of a coherent construction of popular identity. Similarly, the idea that 'the people' came into existence through mobilization is not without problems, because of the difficulty of defining whether or not a mobilization counts as an expression of the people. Morales ignores these problems by designating the mobilizations in support of MAS expressions of the people, whilst delegitimizing mass mobilizations in Santa Cruz.

In a nutshell, a central element in the rise of Evo Morales and the MAS is that he has been able to present himself as the embodiment of 'the people' as the victim of the status quo. 'The people' is a new political identity established through the construction of a difference between the people and their oppressors. Evo Morales has presented 'the people' as the sovereign owner of Bolivia's natural resources, and as having been deprived of rightful control over these resources by a self-interested political elite. This idea of 'the people' blurred the differences within the popular sector, because it shifted the focus onto what distinguished them from the elite. Morales became the symbol for the people as 'underdog', through which he was able to unify a diversity of interests in common opposition to the status quo.

The idea of an individual embodying an entire people is, of course, deeply problematic for democracy, because it may signify that only the presidency of Evo Morales can ensure that the people are able to exercise their sovereignty. However, we should note that Morales as symbol of the people works only through MAS. That is to say, MAS as a broad alliance of social movements is indispensable to Morales: only through his position as leader of MAS can he claim to represent the people.

From a more pragmatic point of view, having Morales as a symbol of the people has resulted in some important positive side effects, giving people hope and encouraging them to aspire to the highest offices in the country. An example is the response of a young boy, who, when asked by Morales what he would do with the $25 *Juancito Pinto* family grant introduced by the MAS, replied: 'I will prepare myself to become like you.'

PART III

CHAPTER 8

Bolivia's first indigenous president,
2005–10

Just a few moments after the first exit polls were announced on ATB, one of Bolivia's main television channels, celebrations erupted in El Alto that could be heard deep down in Calacoto, a rich neighbourhood in southern La Paz. Here the news made some anxious; others only said 'Let us pray that Morales does not disappoint them, because if that happens we really will have a civil war'; still others expressed the hope that the election of Evo Morales would end the paralysis of the country.

In a time where the shelf life of news becomes ever shorter, only a few images that make world news remain in the memory of many people. For people interested in Latin America, the night of the elections in 2005 provided scenes that will not be soon forgotten: thousands of people, of all backgrounds, celebrating on the streets of La Paz, hundreds of indigenous Whipala flags and Bolivian tricolours flying in front of the Palacio Quemado. Television pictures around the world would later show Morales surrounded by the masses, embracing indigenous women wearing the traditional bowler hat and multilayered skirt. But Morales's first public appearance was not in La Paz or in El Alto, but on the small square outside the dilapidated building of the Seis Federaciónes del Tropico de Cochabamba (the union of the coca producers). Here, so close to his political roots, the taste of victory was sweetest, while the familiarity of the location seemed to offer him strength and security for the challenges ahead.

Bolivia under President Morales

When Evo Morales was running for president in 2005, great hopes were attached to his election: a MAS government was seen by some as the last chance to include large, marginalized sectors of society while at the same time avoiding the spread and deepening of social conflict. In short, the expectation of President Morales was no less than to break the vicious cycle of conflict that was leading Bolivia to the brink of secession of the *media luna* departments, especially resource-rich Santa Cruz and Tarija.

Morales's campaign picked up on the disenchantment with the status quo among many Bolivians and promised a transformation of the country. His pet project in this regard was to oversee a new constitution drawn up in a participatory manner by an elected Constituent Assembly. The image of a political outsider (although Morales had been in politics for almost ten years) heavily criticizing the political establishment while promising to refound the country was a powerful political strategy. To this we can add the clever use of decentralized support for his campaign, which might have served as a model for Barack Obama's campaign, but without the modern networking and communication techniques. The last ingredient was the discrediting of other major parties and their inability to propose convincing alternatives in terms of candidates and programmes. These three elements are usually cited as the key factors in the election of Morales as Bolivia's president, and for good reason. However, such thinking does not help us to understand why it was Morales and not, for instance, Felipe Quispe, Alejo Véliz or Victor Hugo Cárdenas who achieved political success. My answer to this is that it was Morales's discourse that made all the difference: despite the apparent imprecisions, incoherencies, alternation between radicalism and moderation, there is a very effective logic informing the way Morales presents the world around him. It was the uniting of a wide variety of groups-as-victims in opposition to the status quo that brought Morales his victory in the 2005 elections.

The election of Morales with such a clear mandate from the electorate raised enormous expectations that he would do no less than embark right away on a course to 'refound' the country and that this would yield immediate results. In order to signal right at the start that he was intending to instigate radical change, President Morales reduced his salary and that of all ministers. Of course this was a populist move with no consequence for the economy. However, it was an expression of Morales's deeply rooted belief in the virtues of a relatively modest lifestyle and, most importantly, that those in high office should be guided by a sense of duty and not personal enrichment.

The first cabinet of the Morales government was not so much one of indigenous people but of left-wing intellectuals and activists with a record of defending the interests of the indigenous, workers and the poor. Among them was Andrés Soliz Rada, the *viejo combatiente nacionalista* (old nationalist combatant) and outspoken critic of foreign oil companies, who became the first MAS minister for hydrocarbons. David Choquehuanca was appointed minister for foreign affairs, and would be one of the few who did not move to other positions. He is an experienced adviser to and organizer of indigenous and rural social movements. The key position of the minister of the presidency went to Juán Ramón Quintana, an ex-army officer (influenced by the short-lived leftist military regimes in the 1970s) and sociologist with his own left-leaning think-tank in an upper-class neighbourhood of La Paz. A former Trotskyite militant and intellectual, Hugo Salvatierra, was named as minister for rural development. Salvador Ric Riera, popularly dubbed the 'leftist millionaire', who had been working with MAS for some years, took the ministry for public works and services. Both personalities were also know for their roles in opposition in the Civic Committee of Santa Cruz. Another intellectual and one of the few Aymara in the government, was sociologist Félix Patzi, who had been forced by poverty to migrate to La Paz in his youth. He nevertheless obtained a Master's degree in sustainable development from the University San Andrés and later became the director of the Institute for Sociological Research there. Patzi received the education portfolio even though he had been somewhat critical of MAS before the elections. Other ministries were distributed according to what can be called corporatist criteria. Abel Mamani, leader of the neighbourhood organizations of El Alto and protagonist in the Water War, was named head of the new Ministry of Water. The minister for work was Álex Gálvez Mamani, a factory worker and union leader. The coca producer and mayor of Villa Tunari in the Tropic of Cochabamba, Felipe Cáceres, became vice-minister for social defence, in charge of anti-drug policy. Cáceres was to be another constant in the cabinet; doubtless owing in part to his background, he has been relatively successful as a minister. However, arguably one of the biggest surprises was the nomination of Casimira Rodríguez as minister for justice; a former domestic worker and autodidact, she headed – not without success – the government's legal team during the first wave of nationalizations.

The first landmark policy of this first cabinet came on 1 May 2006, three months after Morales's inauguration, when he announced the nationalization of the country's oil and gas industry (Supreme Decree 28701 – named 'Heroes of the Chaco', recalling the war against Paraguay of 1932–35, which was linked to control over oil reserves). Radical language and the dramatically staged use of the army to surround the Pedrobras–San Alberto site had the desired effect of rallying supporters behind the government (whilst alarming international observers). The measure itself consisted of significantly raising taxes, renegotiating contracts and reviving the state oil company. The Bolivian government negotiated forty-four contracts with twelve different companies, which were reviewed by the Bolivian Congress and approved in April 2007 (a process not undergone in the case of all previous contracts). Yet the measure did not involve the expropriation of assets and was not therefore a nationalization as such. Furthermore, the most important measures concerned only the companies that produced in excess of 100 million cubic feet of gas per day in 2005: namely Petrobrás, Repsol and Total–Fina. Under the new contracts, the overall government share of gas and oil income is about 54 per cent. Another aspect of the measure that has been frequently overstated or misunderstood is that it calls for the state oil company, YPFB, to acquire majority control of the privatized petroleum company operations. Again, this is more significant as a signal than as a change in real terms, because the Bolivian government already owned a 48 per cent share of operations as part of a fund for retired Bolivians (BONOSOL). Hence, instead of a drastic purchasing of shares, YPFB had to buy no more than 3 per cent of the shares of each company. What is beyond doubt is that the measures flooded the Treasury with money: gas revenues increased from US$173 million in 2002 to an estimated US$1.57 billion in 2007.

This has – to some degree understandably – laid bare the worrying inability of the government at all levels to invest the money responsibly and sustainably. In addition, the Morales government still needs to act to increase investment in production and exploration so that production remains able to meet both internal and external demand from signed contracts. Financed by the gas revenues, Morales introduced the *Renta Dignidad* pension scheme for Bolivians over 60, utilizing a maximum of 30 per cent of the gas tax. Another measure was the *Juancito Pinto* stipend, which pays families about US$25 a year for each child in primary school.

Soon after his inauguration in January 2006, Morales began preparations to fulfil his central campaign promise: the refounding of Bolivia through the drafting of a new constitution. To this end a Constituent Assembly was elected on 2 July 2006. The process of defining how the Assembly would be elected proved difficult, and Morales realized that he had to compromise with the major opposition parties – PODEMOS and Unidad Nacional – which resulted in an electoral regulation that privileged political parties and drastically reduced the number of directly elected indigenous representatives. The first eight months of the Assembly were marked by a near total absence of any discussions about the content of the new constitution; instaed all eyes were on the internal regulation of the Assembly, especially the voting system for approving the draft constitution. The ensuing legalistic debate led to widespread public apathy concerning the actual work of the Assembly. This was an opportunity wasted, considering the high hopes initially held by the general public and the Morales administration's claim that the Assembly would be the stage for a 'new social pact', in the words of Vice President García Linera.

On the contrary, the process of drafting the new charter and preparing for its subsequent approval by referendum faltered due to lack of agreement on central political issues. Instead, it heightened the polarization between the Morales government and the opposition. According to the foundation UNIR–Bolivia, there were 156 social conflicts in the first half of 2007, or around 26 per month, 16 per cent of which lasted for more than four days and showed 'marked signs of violence'. In total, three people were killed and more than 250 injured during this period. While these figures aggregate a large variety of different conflicts and underlying demands, most of them were at least indirectly linked to the polarization and stalemate between the government and the opposition. The existing rift became deeper through the highly controversial process of drafting and adopting the new constitution. The initial draft constitution was formally approved by the Constituent Assembly in September 2007, but the vote was boycotted by the opposition. Angry and at times violent demonstrations followed, and four regions declared autonomy in protest. A recall referendum was held in August 2008, which returned high scores for both the president and main opposition leaders. Tensions heightened at the end of 2008 and violent protest erupted in the eastern departments of *media luna* (mainly in Santa Cruz), with general strikes, blockades and the violent takeover of public institutions. In the general turmoil, human rights NGOs were attacked. These tensions threatened to turn into a bloodbath with the massacre of peasants in Pando on 11 September 2008 in which at least 11 people were killed, 50 wounded and 600 fled to neighbouring Brazil. After the government's first attempt to convene the constitutional referendum by decree, the national electoral court (CNE) declared that it needed a congressional law to be able to organize the referendum. Since MAS lacks a majority in the Senate, making it likely that the law would not be passed, social movements close to the Morales government encircled Congress in La Paz to push for the adoption of the law.

The political deadlock over constitutional reform ended in October 2008 when Morales accommodated the opposition by agreeing to some 140 amendments to the draft constitution. Congress approved the revised constitution and decided to hold a constitutional referendum on 25 January 2009. The agreement had been made possible to a considerable extent owing to Morales's acceptance of dialogue with the opposition and his willingness to compromise by accepting some of their key demands. The new constitution was approved by national referendum with 61.4 per cent in favour (90.2 per cent turnout), although majorities in four out of nine departments voted against it. International observers considered that the referendum had been conducted according to democratic standards.

The new constitution (CPE) is a very ambitious, complex and at times vague document that includes the recognition of thirty-six indigenous 'nations'; a wide range of social, economic and political rights; state intervention in the economy (including control over natural resources); and reform of the judiciary (with the direct election of Supreme Court judges and a parallel system for indigenous peoples). Particularly contentious is the creation of nine institutional-territorial entities[1] and four levels of autonomy without a clear definition of the distribution of competences and resources. The most important and controversial aspects of the constitution – concerning autonomy, decentralization, the electoral system and judicial reform – have yet to be clarified and implemented through secondary legislation, which according to former president Mesa will lead to continuance of the polarized political climate and possibly once again the eruption of violence. The Constitutional Court remains inquorate at the time of writing, putting in doubt legislation implementing the new CPE, which requires 'constitutional control'. Recent tendencies in interpreting the CPE have favoured participatory democracy, both through the ballot box and via the direct involvement of social movements in the decisions and machinery of the state. Institutionality and the rule of law are going through a period of uncertainty. One issue of concern in this respect is the lack of a precise definition of treason in the CPE, which makes it rather easy to charge somebody.[2] Another aspect of the uncertainty is that prefects and civic committees of the eastern regions remain opposed to the new CPE, and no advance has been made in dialogue to implement there its provisions for autonomy.

According to the new constitution, general elections were due to be scheduled, but the timing proved particularly contentious. In the run-up to the elections, finally set for December 2009, tensions between Morales and the opposition again developed, to the extent that the European Commission decided to fund a €4 million intervention to promote dialogue and mediation. Particularly contentious was organizing the elections using the existing voter registry. With a strategy to win time to forge a united front against Morales, the opposition demanded a new voter registry before any election could be held. It did so by twisting the recommendations of an earlier EU Electoral Observation Mission, which had indeed proposed a new, biometric voter registry, but as a long-term strategy and while acknowledging the continuing validity of the existing system. In reaction to the opposition's refusal to agree to the organization of elections, the CSUTCB, a key *campesino* organization, announced it was going to surround the parliament in order to force the adoption of the transitional electoral law. Morales then did something that seemed to outsiders an extreme populist and almost anti-democratic gesture: he went on hunger strike for five days in early April 2009 in order to push for the approval of the convocation of elections for December 2009. However, this was a very clever though un-conventional strategy for avoiding a potentially violent blockade of the Congress. Morales invited social movement leaders to join him in the hunger strike, thereby steering clear of the danger of having to use force against some of his allied social movements. He also accepted the demands of the opposition for a new voter registry and to reduce the number of indigenous voting districts to seven from fourteen. After these concessions, Congress approved on 14 April a new (transitional) electoral law convoking the elections for 6 December 2009.

Morales then faced a problem: he had personally committed to the new biometric registry, but there was little more than seven months to the election – by international standards an utterly unrealistic time frame for setting up a new registry. In the end, a small Bolivian miracle happened: although the most distinguished international companies in the field of biometric voter systems were unable to fulfil the contract, and faced with the withdrawal of international funding and support, the government nevertheless managed to sign up a company willing to take on the challenge. The Morales government financed this approximately €20 million exercise by postponing the replacement of the thirty-year-old presidential airplane. To everyone's surprise the company succeeded in registering 5 million people, thereby exceeding expectations by 1.4 million, whilst no major quality concerns were raised by international observers.

The election of 6 December 2009 ended with a clear victory for Morales, who obtained 64.22 per cent of the national vote, even winning a majority in the former opposition bastion of Tarija. Morales also won 75 per cent of the votes from Bolivians living abroad, who could vote for the first time, albeit only in a limited number of countries. The sole exception to majority wins in these expatriate communities was the vote in the USA, where Morales obtained a minority 31 per cent. The impressive show of support for Morales should not blind us to the fact that the country remains deeply divided between his supporters and opponents.

Morales: nationalist and populist?

Evo Morales is frequently named as one of Latin America's new left-wing nationalist and populist leaders. Central to this description are, one, the notion that Morales's government is ideologically incoherent and, two, the common denominators of nationalist intervention in the economy and direct populist appeal to the common people. There are clearly nationalist and populist aspects in MAS's politics, but they differ considerably from those that define the stereotypical populist Latin American leader. The idea of a 'plurinational' nation is in fact an intriguing way of thinking about Bolivia's future. What is more, while there are clearly inconsistencies in MAS's ideology – or, rather, while there is no clear universal ideology at work – the more interesting question is how MAS has nevertheless managed to hegemonize the struggles of many different social interests.

In spite of shortcomings in the imaginary of the new 'plurinational' nation, it seems that MAS's electoral slogan *Ahora es Cuando!/Jichapi jichhaja!*(Aymara)/*Kunanma kunank'a!* (Quechua), which translates as 'Now is the Time' (literally: 'Now is When'), has struck a chord with most Bolivians. The 'plurinational' nation serves as 'social imaginary signification' (Castoriadis, 1987: 135–56) that provides meaning and orientation to a large sector of society, and answers essential questions about the historicity of the community by linking death to the unborn.

Imagining the 'plurinational nation'

How has the Morales government achieved fundamental change without losing popularity, triggering a serious bid for secesion, or provoking an attempted overthrow? One obvious explanation is the flow of national income following the 'nationalization' of gas, from which both government and opposition as well as many of Bolivia's poor benefited. Secessions and military coups are out of fashion in Latin America; many who might have played with the idea thirty years ago would calculate that their chances are presently quite low – at least so long as Morales plays by the rules, as the example of Zelaya, the ousted former president of Honduras, tells us. Also, it is of course the case that many reforms are straightforwardly popular with a majority of Bolivians, who have kept voting for Morales.

However, there is another element to the answer that is often overlooked. Proposing fundamental political change within the frame of imagining a new nation has the effect of reducing the uncertainty that those changes bring with them. This is because it constructs a shared (imagined) community that gives people something to hold on to, and represents a connection to eternal values at a time of change (Anderson, 1983). To articulate this community as 'nation' enables it to seem natural and given, which has made MAS's arguments more persuasive. This is because it articulated somewhat abstract political issues (e.g. changing the electoral system) in more emotional terms (using shared memories and myths) as part of a common identity. MAS's leaders argued that Bolivia lacked an imagined community and that its construction would yield national unity:

> We conduct politics in the field of the construction of national unity, of what Anderson calls an 'imagined community'. This is what we need. We can say that the imagined community in Bolivia has been dismantled. For the gains made by the national revolution [1952], the aim was to construct a *mestizo* society. But this project failed ultimately due to neoliberalism, a very tough concept. (Ramon Quintana, former minister of the presidency)

This statement is interesting in that it shows the reflexivity of the social sciences: the actual 'imagining of the nation' by MAS leaders was influenced by Anderson's theory of the 'imagining of the nation'. It shows that leaders of MAS were conscious of the possibility of creating a politically powerful new sense of national community. This imagining reflected MAS's criticism of the model of the nation that was constructed in Bolivia after the 1952 revolution. For MAS, the concept of the nation was fundamentally flawed due to its being imagined along *mestizo* lines. This led to its collapse following the introduction of neoliberalism as the dominant ideology in the 1980s. In the absence of a widely accepted conception of the nation, MAS presented itself as the vehicle for a new nationhood based on the *naciones originarias* (First Nations), which were suppressed by the revolutionary nationalism of the MNR.

The 'plurinational' nation

> We want to be the instrument and facilitator of a process of reconstructing these nations. (Morales Olivera)

There are three central themes in the imagining of the nation of MAS: one is that of diversity or 'plurinationality' of the various indigenous peoples or indigenous nations; another is 'dignity' as a principle of cohabitation; and the third is 'sovereignty':

> The Bolivian nation has dignity, is sovereign and plurinational with its *pueblos originarias*. (Evo Morales)

MAS seems to be trying to bring together elements that appear at first sight to be mutually exclusive: various (indigenous) nations as constituting one (Bolivian) nation. This means that the national identity is composed of a variety of other identities:

> The common national identity includes and integrates the multi-ethnic pluriculturality of the diverse communities with their own cultures and identities, which is the means of achieving well-being and sovereignty within the overarching group of members. (MAS, 2005a: 33)

MAS defines the nation as a community that integrates 'pluricultural' and 'multiethnic' communities. This means that the nation hosts the great diversity of the *naciones originarias*. The diversity of historical subjects constitutes the nation.

Filling the 'plurinational' nation with meaning

According to MAS, the failure of earlier nationalist projects resulted in a diversity of historical subjects without clearly delineated identities. This makes it necessary to facilitate a process – through a Constituent Assembly – to allow the various identities to define themselves, and then come to realize a common vision for the nation.

> This is the kind of question we ask ourselves continually: who are we? Once an identity is affirmed, we project a vision of the country.... And we are now in this process ... of simply being Bolivians. Those who have a well defined identity, or who exercise and articulate their identity very forcefully, with much initiative, are the indigenous peoples from the Amazon. (Ivan Iporre)

> Now also the professional who is not Aymara, who is not Quechua, who is a *mestizo* but confused, can also have a *mestizo* identity, and generate his own identity. We will start generating an identity based on principles as simple as the love of life, respect for the people, respect for the community, and so on. This will give a new conception and new vision of the nation and the country. (García Linera)

Within a Bolivian identity it is possible for MAS to have co-existing identities. Yet only the indigenous people of the Amazon have already defined their identity clearly, while Quechuas and Aymaras, and even more so the *mestizos*, need to define theirs more precisely. Defining these particular identities is the prerequisite for a subsequent emergence of a common Bolivian identity, and indeed of a Bolivian nation. MAS's approach of a bottom-up process of defining individual identities and then redefining the nation as 'plurinational' stands in contrast to the previous, homogenizing ideology of revolutionary nationalism. MAS stresses the importance of allowing ample room for local peculiarities:

> If we achieve a consensus on two issues in a debate about five issues, this does not constitute a problem for us. Because this is not about a homogenizing model. It is the concept of diversity. You cannot say that the economy has to function through communitarian models,

because if you were to try this in Santa Cruz, you would fail. Or, should we implement an intermediate communitarian model? No, it should be us, here, according to our way, and them, there, according to their way. What this is about is a common historic cause. Then diversity will not make us scared. It does not worry us if there are no large consensuses or if everything doesn't find its consensus. (Morales Olivera)

The prime example is respect for 'cultural diversity', 'different ways of organizing daily life', and different 'forms of political organization' (MAS, 2004b: 20). MAS leaders emphasize that respect for diversity explicitly includes different forms of economic activity. As a concrete example, this means not altering the large-scale, export-oriented economy in Santa Cruz or Tarija. Such statements are of course part of a strategy to win votes in those departments and from the business sector in general; nevertheless, considering the internal diversity within MAS, we should take them as a serious commitment to finding an alternative way of doing politics.

To the MAS this 'plurinational' nation is based on the principle of *intra-culturalidad*, which means recognizing and appreciating the various cultures within the nation.

Regarding intra-culturality, we believe that much has to be done to recognize, value, appreciate what our cultures are. Give them more credit and strengthen them. We need to see them from within. This is the idea. But this is not enough unless there is a certain type of relationship between the cultures. Not only between the national ones; we need to think of the rest as well. Therefore we emphasize the cultural sphere, and don't restrict ourselves to the issue of languages, because this caused the previous government severe problems.... Aymara was considered only as a language in the educational reform; there is this linguistic aspect, but no cultural-educational focus.... We have to have a much broader perspective to appreciate what it is that constitutes our identity. (Noël Aguirre, head of MAS Social Commission)

Constructing the 'pluricultural' nation thus proceeds from the bottom up by having the various cultures define themselves and allowing them to choose their own place in the nation. 'Pluricultural' aims to value existing cultures in their entirety; that is, to add to the linguistic aspect also *cosmovision* (world-view), forms of political organization, legal systems, and so on. Such a nation will prevent the disintegration of Bolivia since 'pluri-nation' does not mean *pluri-estatal* ('pluri-state'), argues Quispe (2007).[3] The reason is that MAS seeks to replace what it regards as the Western model of the nation-state, where each nation pursues the goal of having its own state, with the new notion of a plurinational state in which different nations will coexist as equals but each with a degree of territorial and institutional autonomy:

> What to do? Disintegrate so that every nation can found its own nation-state? No. The solution is to found a plurinational state. This means that all the nations that cohabit in Bolivia recognize each other as equals. And, under equal conditions, agree to create one pluri-national state that represents and expresses the different identities in all its institutions and public policies. Only in this way will it be possible to construct a nation of nations, but with only one state and with territorial autonomy on different levels. Plurinational does not mean pluri-state. Now we have a historic opportunity for the peoples in Bolivia to construct their future, and without depending on the Eurocentric political theories that made the First Nations subaltern to the nation-state. (Quispe, 2007)

'Nation of nations' is a key element in MAS's political project, as can be seen from the renaming of the state and its institutions, where usually the term *plurinacional* is added, such as in *Asamblea Legislativa Plurinacional* (parliament) or the *Organo Electoral Pluri-nacional* (electoral court). A nation of nations would maintain the constituent and autonomous identities of the various communities while providing them with a common roof.

However, the model is also different from the American idea of a 'civic' nation, which is defined by common rules, citizenship rights, political values and a common territory. MAS's 'nation of nations' is an interesting and, thus far, idiosyncratic hybrid model, somewhere between civic and ethnic conceptions of the nation. From the civic nation it takes the emphasis on a common legal framework (constitution, liberal values and citizenship rights) and adds an ethnic element with shared ancient values (complementarity, reciprocity and solidarity). It is an attempt to reach out to both the party's own indigenous constituency, which views the Bolivian nation in the ethnic terms of *pueblos originarios*, and to those sectors that understand the nation in civic terms. For MAS, a common Bolivian nation can only be imagined if it is constructed as an ethnic and civic mosaic.[4]

What holds the diversity together?

As the unifying element for this diversity, MAS constructs an antagonistic relation between its 'national pluricultural identity' and 'the globalized identity of neoliberalism' (MAS, 2005a: 33–5). Hence it imagines the nation as distinct from Western multicultural models. The following statement summarizes how MAS proposes to build a unified nation from the existing diversity.

> It must be recognized that this country belongs to the *naciones originarias*; we also have a lot in common. From colonial times until now we have had a common constitution, and we form together a common social subject. This means that the Bolivian Quechua is not the same as the Peruvian Quechua. This expresses itself in different flags: for Bolivia it is the Wiphala Quechua.
>
> We are not only Aymaras, Quechuas, Guaranís and other smaller peoples; we also form historically a national unity. For this reason the campaign of MAS shows the Wiphala and the Bolivian flag together. And this is the concept: it is not about ending Bolivia, because we exist together as Bolivians historically. We constitute a historical social subject as Bolivians. It is not about including the Aymara, the First Peoples, and so on. It is about all historical subjects together being the foundation of the new nation....
>
> Clearly this is our reality: some are more Bolivian than Aymara, other are more Aymara than Bolivian. The corollary is to begin with an *Asamblea Constituyente*, which would have the capacity to recognize the distinction – that we are Bolivian Aymaras, Bolivian

mestizos, and so on. This is because as *mestizos* we are different from
the *mestizos* of Argentina, Chile, and so on. (Morales Olivera)

Although in Bolivia there exist *naciones originarias*, they still
have aspects in common that make them 'Bolivian'. Again, one of
the unifying elements is the relation to a common external 'other':
Bolivian Quechuas are different from Peruvian Quechuas, as are
Bolivian *mestizos* from those of Chile (who 'stole' Bolivia's access
to the Pacific). In addition, the difference is based on a common
history (of lost wars and lost natural resources) within the same
(diminished) territory, with shared symbols such as the Bolivian
flag as well as the 'Bolivian' Wiphala of the *Qullan Suyu*, and with
shared 'ancestral norms' such as reciprocity, solidarity and respect
for nature:

> The national identity maintains the ancestral values of comple-
> mentarity, reciprocity, service and solidarity, as well as a respectful
> relationship with nature. These values are shared by the thirty-five or
> more cultures of the highlands and lowlands of Bolivia; the national
> identity recovers the norms of *ama sua, ama llulla, ama qella*. Boliv-
> ian women and men have in common an identification with these
> norms and values as well as the citizens' rights of liberty, equality
> and justice that oriented our judicial code and our form of governing
> democratically and in a participatory manner. (MAS, 2005a: 35)

Shared norms such as the *ama sua, ama llulla, ama qella* (don't
steal, don't lie, don't be lazy) are, according to MAS, what binds
this diversity together. In addition to ancient indigenous norms,
a common element of Bolivian national identity is the belief in
universal liberal values such as liberty, equality and justice, which
would govern the 'refounded state' imagined by MAS. From a neoliberal point of view, however, there seems to be an inconsistency
in MAS's aforementioned construction of the antagonism, since
liberty is one of neoliberalism's core elements, and equality and
justice are also important values. The reason why the construction
of the antagonism works despite this inconsistency is that blaming

neoliberalism for all the ills in Bolivia has become hegemonic in political discourses. This means it does not matter what a party proposes, it can always construct its proposal as a positive alternative to *el modelo* (the neoliberal model).

Furthermore, for Manuel Morales Olivera (the son of the lawyer Morales Dávila, who bravely challenged the military dictatorship of García Meza), Bolivian national identity is also based upon a common institutional superstructure, symbolized by the constitution. However, it seems unlikely that many ordinary Bolivians would share his idea that the various constitutions bind them together as Bolivians. Yet Bolivian constitutions could have a role to play in defining the nation, at least in the sense that they are different to those of the country's neighbours. In addition, when social movement leaders argue that the constitutions suppress the diversity of indigenous nations, they function as an antagonist through which the Bolivian nation can define itself.

Thus, a uniform, mono-ethnic constitution is an 'external other' in contrast to which the diverse, plurinational nation is defined. Even if the idea that the existing constitution functions as a common element for the national community is contested, it remained for MAS an important symbol in unifying the country. Consequently, it proposed creating a Constituent Assembly in order to draft a new constitution.

However, the difficulty in constructing a common nation in Bolivia has been highlighted by the regional conflicts (2006–07) between the eastern departments of the *media luna* (half-moon[5]) and the central government, which indicates that MAS's imagined community of the nation has not been accepted in the regions demanding more autonomy. It is difficult credibly to combine indigenous values (presented as anti-neoliberal) and liberal values to which proponents of neoliberalism would refer. The difficulty in squaring this diversity with a common national community points to the tension between the 'foundationalism' and 'hegemonism' (Aboy Carlés, 2005) that render MAS's discourse populist.[6] Foundationalism refers to the fact that MAS radically breaks with the past of a united national community, placing a frontier at the heart of the political community between the people and the elite as oppressor. Yet it also attempts hegemonically to include everyone within its conception of the nation. The presence of both logics lays this conception open to challenge. It should also be noted, however, that it would be difficult at this time for any concept of the nation to gain acceptance in the eastern departments. For these regional demands are not necessarily a consequence of the failure to construct a Bolivian nation. Rather, they are motivated by the financial and political considerations of a regional elite that has lost much of its influence in central government, and that seeks to consolidate its power at the sub-national level.

Imagining the nation: recovering its sovereignty

The other characteristics of MAS's imagined nation are 'sovereignty' and 'dignity', as displayed in the electoral slogan *Por una Bolivia Digna, Soberana y Productiva!* In order for Bolivia to recover its productivity and dignity, it must first become a sovereign nation. MAS defines sovereignty as follows:

> It is the supreme authority or the power to make our own decisions and to carry out actions to reach our own goals and objectives; with independence from external influences. The republic of the criollos practised sovereignty of class and of race. For neoliberalism sovereignty belongs to the capital of finance companies and to the transnational companies.
> MAS will restore the sovereignty of the people and will delegate its exercise to the three powers of the state, as Article 2 of the Constitutions sets out: sovereignty resides in the people; it is inalienable and imprescriptible; its exercise is delegated to the legislative, executive and judicial powers. (MAS, 2005a: 33)

This takes the definition of sovereignty from Bolivia's (former) constitution and uses it against the 'neoliberal' governments that originally drafted it. By claiming that sovereignty in Bolivia used to be exercised by class and race, and by capital and transnational companies, MAS implies that the indigenous population as well as the working class were not sovereign in taking decisions without being subjected to external influences. Yet there is an inconsistency in that MAS does not propose an alternative way of exercising sovereignty. Instead, it refers to the liberal notion of constitutional government, where the people delegate their sovereignty to the three powers of the state. Through the course of the first Morales government, this inconsistency was at least partly removed by proposing mechanisms of direct democracy.

The most important point, however, is that MAS portrays a nation that had lost its sovereignty through the war on drugs. Another aspect of losing sovereignty is dependence on US aid and the conditionality ('certification') of successful coca eradication efforts. According to MAS, the result has been restrictions on the choice of policies. In a logical step for MAS, USAID was told in 2008 that it could close its offices in the Tropic of Cochbamba if it did not subscribe to the new cooperative approach to controlling coca production. In addition, MAS criticized Bolivia's adherence to the rules and policy recommendations of the International Monetary Fund (IMF), which (ostensibly) meant losing control over economic policy in favour of the poor.

According to MAS minister Ramon Quintana, developing the 'capacity of self-determination' would not only help to overcome the 'poverty trap', but would fundamentally empower the nation to become sovereign. As such it would be possible to reconstruct the public sphere in order to develop its political-democratic potential. According to Quintana, achieving 'sovereignty will help Bolivia to find what Anderson calls an imagined community'.

Imagining a 'productive' nation: rethinking development

Through copying and imitating the foundations of Western culture, the state has always been dominated and controlled by the elites of internal colonialism, already during military dictatorships but also under the so-called representative democracy installed by the neoliberal political parties. (MAS, 2004a: 5)

Imagining the nation as sovereign implies the ability to choose economic and developmental policies. MAS proposes more state intervention, but this does not imply a socialist economic policy. There is a degree of economic nationalism in MAS's insistence that Bolivia's resources must first and foremost benefit the Bolivian nation. Yet the 'nationalization' of private companies was initially understood by MAS leaders as simply a significant increase in taxation and government regulations. And, in this regard, we should not overlook the fact that, although the government chose symbolic dates (especially Labour Day) for its nationalizations, most international companies continued their operations in Bolivia. Evo Morales has repeatedly stressed that 'nationalization does not mean expropriation'. MAS envisages a more active state that works in partnership with private companies on the exploitation of 'strategic natural resources' (e.g. natural liquid gas).

The imaginary of the nation entails a vision of an alternative form of development, which can be interpreted as a rejection of the underlying narrative of capitalist modernity. It is assumed that this alternative economic model will make Bolivia 'productive' as a prerequisite to the recovery of its 'dignity', since it would change economic policy to the benefit of the indigenous peoples. MAS's talk of defending coca and later 'natural resources' implies more than calling for the protection of a cultural heritage. We find also a criticism of Western notions of 'development' and its attempt to build a social narrative able to provide qualitative answers to the essential questions of life. This criticism is directed at the work of Western development agencies (especially USAID) and the failure of their 'alternative development' projects to provide viable economic solutions for peasants dependent on coca (see Chapter 3). Their neoliberal notion of development implies for MAS a violation of *Pachamama,* Mother Earth, due to the unsustainable exploitation of non-renewable natural resources, while the paradigm of 'development' does not allow a country such as Bolivia to look for alternative ways to organize its economy, since these would not 'develop' the country.

The existing 'development' paradigm would never enable Bolivia to become economically independent from advanced countries, because, according to the *dependista* analysis of MAS, the international economy is built around a capitalist system where advanced nations at the centre exploit the resources of peripheral nations, which are made and kept dependent on this system. The *dependista* perspective traces the origins of Bolivia's problems back to colonization by the Spanish and sees a problematic colonial legacy in Bolivia's status as provider of cheap (i.e. unfairly priced) raw materials. While the 'North' or the 'Centre' benefits from its precious resources, Bolivia is left with pollution and low life expectancy among its miners. In more traditional Marxist terms, MAS argues that developed countries have an interest in keeping Bolivia at the economic periphery so that they can exploit its resources. The means for this are policy recommendations, conditional credit and development projects. In a word, 'development' is a tool of political and economic domination.

Imagining the nation as 'productive' refers to an alternative model of development, influenced by the Latin American *dependista* branch of Marxism. Yet there seems to be an inconsistency when MAS first defines sovereignty in liberal terms, then puts forward an alternative development project based on a *dependista* analysis highly critical of the same liberal definition of sovereignty.

Dignity

The MAS government decided in 2008 that all 'alternative development' projects in the Tropic should no longer be run by foreign development agencies, and their management should instead be transferred to the Mancomunidad de Municipios (Association of

Municipalities). This was regarded as the first step in implementing another economic policy, required to free Bolivia from its dependence on advanced countries and to fascilitate the recovery of Bolivia's 'dignity', as it would allow for culturally and environmentally sustainable forms of production. However, 'dignity' is not a pure form of indigenous revivalism in the sense of a full-scale return to ancient forms of economic organization. MAS has learnt from the failure of socialist experiments that a state-run economy would not be the most productive and that communism would not guarantee a dignified nation. It therefore emphasizes that a sovereign and productive nation needs to allow diversity among its modes of production.

Yet for large parts of Bolivia, especially those where 'alternative development' projects operate, the most appropriate form of production needs to be more imaginative than what has been designed by 'Western bureaucrats'. MAS's plans combine small-scale production, a recovery of traditional forms of communal land use and mutual assistance (*ayni* or *mink'a*), and modern forms of agricultural cooperative, as well as rediscovery of the productive opportunities of ancient plants (e.g. the coca leaf).

Vowing to recover Bolivia's dignity, the political programme of MAS stresses improvement in the quality of life (*vivir bien*), achieved in harmony with 'Andean cosmology' and 'nature'. Development with 'dignity' has clear limits: it should not be based on the unsustainable exploitation of natural resources. Moreover, MAS argues – inspired by the *Kataristas* – that 'developing' aspects of nature ought not be a social end in itself; rather, it should maintain an 'equilibrium of forces'.[7] Economic policies need to make sense to the population and must provide tangible material benefits to all social layers. But they also have to be part of a larger project that aims to give new meaning to the political community – that is, recovering the 'dignity' of the nation. A key aspect of the imagining of the nation is therefore installing an economic 'model' that will function as a 'real sign' that the nation is emerging as a productive, sovereign and dignified political community.

A new imaginary of the nation:
challenging existing power relations

MAS's imagining of the nation is intended to install new relations of power in order to 'hegemonize the political project behind MAS, not necessarily the party itself'. For MAS state and nation are interlinked, which means that the definition of the nation is not a philosophical problem, but has very tangible political consequences. Redefinition of the nation is for MAS a necessary element in supporting the reform of institutions and making the changes sustainable. Whether or not the proposals are realistic or coherent is another issue, but they certainly have produced alternative structures of thought that challenge the status quo.

According to MAS, the waves of protests after the year 2000 show that the transfer of knowledge and technology from the West has led to a sense of cultural loss. Not all problems in life can be solved by growth and technology or put to rights with the knowledge of Western society. At the same time, some new practices are in direct conflict with the traditional social imaginary of the belief in *Pachamama*. MAS criticizes the copying of capitalism as following a foreign narrative, because it has destroyed the idyll in which the indigenous peoples lived, and failed to provide a social imaginary capable of guiding the people. Indigenous practices have not been eliminated, since they possess more depth than capitalism or neo-liberalism, but they are under threat from the 'globalized identity of neoliberalism' and its 'anti-values'.

> Against the national and pluricultural identity rises the globalized identity of neoliberalism, with its anti-values of competitiveness, corruption, unscrupulous greed, eagerness for immediate profits and the ruthless exploitation of nature and human beings. Separation from our identity and our values produces alienation in the youth, who feel ashamed of their origins and their culture, and imitate and adopt a consumerist, predatory and egoistic identity, which the trans-national corporations try to impose through globalized free trade and unnecessary consumerism. Alienation from our identity produces

in the population inequity, discrimination and exclusion that make
sustainability impossible. (MAS, 2005a: 34–5)

This statement shows how MAS constructs an antagonism between
its model of 'pluricultural' national identity and that of Western,
globalized and neoliberal identity, which introduces a series of 'anti'-
values, destroying the harmony of the indigenous social fabric. With
its stress on a single neoliberal identity, MAS constructs a common
enemy that incorporates a simplified version of all ostensibly negative
foreign influences – inequity, discrimination and exclusion. Against
this, MAS presents the construction of a Bolivian nation as entail-
ing the presence of appropriate institutions, which would indulge
the commodities of modernity without accepting uncritically the
Western model of life.

'Plurinational', 'sovereignty' and 'dignity' produce an alternative
'social imaginary' that seems to provide orientation for the population. As an empty signifier, 'natural resources' links the past (silver,
tin) to the future (lithium[8]), referring to the high culture of Andean
civilization that has become the victim of exploitation of natural
resources. 'Coca' is intended to help regenerate the contemporary
community spiritually and economically,[9] and symbolize a different
form of modernity, one which accepts the benefits of a Western way
of life but simultaneously attempts to fill the 'hole at the centre of
culture' (Castoriadis, 1987: 159).

Such an interpretation helps us understand how MAS appeals to
large sectors of the population disappointed by the failure of neoliberal economic policies to improve their standard of living. Prior
to MAS, there had been no hegemonic ideology giving orientation
to the people within their specific cultural context. The promise
of a 'spiritual regeneration', where both traditional and modern
spiritualities seek an alternative modernity, has been the foundation
of the rejection of the political system and of the appeal for change
articulated by MAS.

CHAPTER 9

Refounding the state: the foundational promise of populism

> MAS–IPSP has the conviction to seek change in Bolivian society, because neoliberalism has come full cycle; in its place we need to construct an economically, socially, politically more just society, within the frame of democracy and national unity. What we are confronted with in the elections is this challenge, allowing all Bolivians to transform Bolivia through their vote....
>
> I call upon all *compañeros* and *compañeras* to unite with us more than ever in the struggle for the construction of our country. With renewed spirit we will work together, in order to eradicate injustice and inequality of opportunity; we will demonstrate that the people know how to work, and we will construct the just Bolivia that we all want, with dignity, solidarity and sovereignty. (MAS, 2005b: 3)

Until now, I have discussed Evo Morales and the MAS with a view to explaining how he rose to become the president of Bolivia, as well as sketching the fundamentals of his first five years in office. This chapter goes a step further and analyses the long-term political project of MAS of 'refounding' the state. President Morales's basic promise is that he will oversee the redesigning of Bolivia's political institutions. His 'refounding' of Bolivia is intended to make the entire political and economic system more just, inclusive, participatory and aligned with the indigenous cultures. The chapter will analyse the process of socio-economic and political change initiated by the government, including the drafting of the new constitution and its most interesting elements. This project is driven by Morales's experience of exclusion and marginalization as an indigenous coca grower, and entails a politically powerful – populist – promise of renewal and the redemption of politics. In addition to seeking to understand the policies of President Morales, I will show in what way he can be characterized as 'populist'. Such a tag does not make him a danger to democracy. On the contrary, populism is best understood as the 'mirror of democracy', which shows us what it is about and what it is lacking.

In short, the defining element of Morales's presidency has been the promise of a new order to reconstitute the social as more inclusive. This has involved establishing a sharp political frontier between a near past considered 'as not representing the people', and as 'anti-national', and a propitious future marking a contrast with the past left behind. Again, I would stress that it is not Morales's style of leadership or policies that make him a populist. Rather, it is the logic underlying his rhetoric that establishes a common antagonist while promising a radical inclusion of all those disenfranchised in the past. 'Refounding the state' is therefore about creating a political structure able to accommodate 'the people' and 'the nation'.

A central element of the Morales administration has been the creation of a 'plurinational' state through a mixture of top-down, behind closed doors decisions and more participatory elements of direct democracy. Of course, officially it is neither the party nor its leaders that change the current system; rather is 'the people' who do so. Indeed, Morales claims that under his government 'the people' have assumed power which had been 'taken away' from them.

Building a new state: what had to change?

Change is an important signifier in the discourse of MAS, and Evo Morales calls his cabinet 'the cabinet of change'. When he assumed the presidency, he pointed out that he had received the 'mandate of the people for change'. (*Informa-tico*, 23 January 2006)

> A way of understanding political change is to associate it with a new
> beginning, with an event that represents a complete rupture with
> the existing order.... In the discourse of populism change as a new
> beginning can be imagined to signify a break with a present condition
> associated with governments that are deeply unpopular or have lost
> their legitimacy. In other words, for populism 'change as rupture' is
> the promise ... of a radical new order... (Panizza, 2007: 7).

Morales proposes to break with the existing order of a state
governed by 'anti-national' elites, and to start afresh by radically
redesigning its political institutions by means of a new constitution.
This follows the populist logic of 'change as rupture' (Panizza,
2007). The rupture is symbolized by the call *Ahora es Cuando*
('Now is the Time'), which was the principal electoral slogan of
MAS in 2005.

On the one hand, *Ahora es Cuando* was directed at those who protested on innumerable occasions against the political establishment
and its unresponsiveness to the demands of the popular sector. On
the other hand, however, the choice of this slogan was a conscious
attempt to win support from the middle class, which also had shown
its discontent with the political establishment, but which could be
expected to reject radical change. Hence, the avoidance of negative
slogans such as 'Enough is enough', 'We can't take it any more' or
'They all have to go' was an important strategic choice. The deliberate vagueness of *Ahora es Cuando* allowed different social sectors to
supply the meaning: for radical workers' unions it meant the time for
revolution has come, while for the middle class it meant it is time to
improve the current situation. Morales avoided stating what change
meant under cover of the argument that a MAS government would
lead the way to a Constituent Assembly in which the people could
define for themselves what they wanted to change.

> Now it is clear: this country will change. And the man who will
> change it will be Evo. And the people will be the government. And
> who is not yet believing it will believe it when we have achieved
> important things. For example, invest in education, in the health

system, right? I think that, yes, it is within reach; one can feel it.
(Ivan Iporre)

The signifier of change is Evo Morales, who serves as a symbol
that a MAS government is different from the previous ones, owing
to his background as an indigenous social movement leader. This
implies that Morales would establish a social movement model of
governing, which would bring about a government by the people.
The reader might argue now that the statement above, with its
mention of more investment in health care and education, contradicts
the argument that 'change' was emptied discursively. The point is,
however, that the signifier 'change' has become broad and mostly
vague, so that a particular audience can fill it with concrete meaning
without it contradicting other statements. Hence, we find instances
of precise propositions regarding what needs to change, but they
still fit the frame established by the empty signifier.

Recover and refound the state

So, the struggle of the Quechuas and Aymaras, of all the poor in
Bolivia, will be to refound the country. (Evo Morales)

Evo Morales and the other MAS leaders use rather bold (and at
times utopian) concepts to describe the kinds of transformation
they imagine accomplishing. This has not changed since 2005 in
spite of several setbacks and the realization that changes require
time even under a president who is popular and who has a solid
majority in parliament (after the 2009 elections, in both houses). A
core element is the commitment to *recuperar* (recuperate/recover)
the state, which has its roots in the discourse of the MNR. This
includes the idea that for 500 years the state had been colonized by
anti-national and anti-indigenous interests, and that it requires a
major institutional reform to 'decolonize' it. Recovering the state is
central for indigenous peoples, who had never been part of the ruling
class. They felt that Evo Morales, as the first indigenous president,
could give them the state back for the first time since the Spanish

conquest. In this sense, Morales has attracted disenchanted former MNR supporters and the left, especially workers' organizations, because he tempted them regularly with interventionist policies, first and foremost the nationalization of gas.

Recuperating the state also has a moral dimension in defence of a victim: it signals the idea that the state has been taken away from its rightful owners, the indigenous peoples. Morales claims that those occupying positions of power failed to act as they were supposed to, treating the state as private property, and causing harm to the entire Bolivian society. Claiming the state in the name of indigenous peoples therefore carries a 'promise of plenitude' (Howarth et al., 2000) or of 'unconditional justice' (Groppo, 2003) from which the entire community would benefit.

The target of change: defining the state

> We understand the state as a community of men, with its own territory and in possession of an organization from which results a superior legal authority of action, command and coercion over the group considered as its members.... It is divided into three powers. (MAS, 2005b: 7)

As I have argued concerning other aspects of Morales's discourse, through his description of the state before he came to power (or more recently his depiction of the departments) as the personalized expression of those wielding power, he constructs an antagonistic relation between the elite and the indigenous 'victims' represented by MAS. Furthermore, he commonly expresses the idea that the changes pursued by his government will largely be facilitated after MAS has succeeded in establishing completely new relations of power, with indigenous peoples in decisive public positions. It is in this light that the establishment of a university in the Tropic of Cochabamba and of the 'Plurinational' Institute for Public Administration (headed by Ivan Iporre, a key figure in MAS) has to be seen. These initiatives are intended to answer the criticism that MAS has no competent people to run the country. Although Morales acknowledges that it has been difficult to find enough qualified people for his government, his general way of getting around this criticism is that in a country like Bolivia it is not a matter of knowledge, but of honesty and willingness to serve. Thus, for Morales, bringing indigenous people and their allies into positions of state power has been an important first step in constructing a new Bolivia.

Morales often contrasts the state that he inherited with the positive imaginary of a new 'plurinational' state that is intended to come into existence under the new constitution. By contrast, the old state was presented as 'anti-*campesino*', as 'anti-national' and as insensible to the poverty in which the majority of the population lives:

So, when we entered into government, we found not only an anti-national, anti-*campesino* state, and a state that ignores the poverty in which the majority of the people lives, but also a state that was destroyed and de-structured. And, on top of this, with norms, bodies of law, supreme decrees, and so on, that are unconstitutional. (Ivan Iporre)

Morales and other MAS leaders are always careful not to be interpreted as anti-democratic or attempting to destroy the last remnants of stability, and therefore present the state as already destroyed and operating with unconstitutional laws.

A small percentage of the Bolivian population imagined and constructed the country according to the image that they wanted and needed it to be. The rest of us suffered from what those people imagined. (Ivan Iporre)

The two statements quoted above show again the existence in MAS's discourse of the notion of the people being 'oppressed'. The alleged failure of the existing state becomes even more significant when we consider the important role played by the state in MAS's programme. If there is anything that resembles socialism in MAS, then it is the state interventionism that places the bulk of the responsibility for the well-being of citizens on the state. In line with the programme of MAS, Morales presents a vision in which the state assumes an active, interventionist role in the economy, as well as actively promoting ethnic equality. In this he has been influenced not only by Vice President García Linera but also by other leftist intellectuals in his circle of influence. Inspired by *dependentismo* (dependency theory), they have formulated an 'endogenous vision of development' entering a 'post-neoliberal' era of economic policy, which focuses primarily on industrializing Bolivia's natural resources (MAS, 2005a).

Compared to the interventionist model of MAS, the state that existed when Morales came to power was just a shadow of its former self: its core functions had been destroyed and key structures removed by a series of allegedly unconstitutional laws and presidential decrees. To argue that some reforms were unconstitutional is an attempt by Morales to gain the moral and legal right to repeal the reforms. In Morales's logic it is not sufficient to implement institutional reforms, because when the same people remain in power all reforms tend to serve the interests of the powerful. Therefore the only alternative is to achieve a new balance of power in favour of the marginalized by constructing a new political community, redesigning institutions accordingly, and staffing the state with new personnel.

High-minded as this may sound, it boils down to reproducing the same dynamic of filling public offices with those politically loyal and personally trustworthy – for which Morales's government has frequently been criticized. However, the limited number of highly competent people in organizations allied to MAS result in the best officials being moved from one institution to another, often replacing others who have proven unlucky or incompetent. In a similar fashion, MAS leaders like García Linera have talked much about a necessary 'decolonization of the state through a new power correlation'. Yet, considering the above, one may wonder whether it is not just a different group of people attempting to colonize the state. One recalls reports of opportunists seeking state employment who approached the party shortly before and after the 2005 elections, and the story of customs offices at the border with Peru occupied in 2006 by so-called *MASistas*. Indeed, many people in the lower leadership echelons of MAS I met over the years told me that they had joined around 2005. It goes without saying that MAS leaders would strongly reject this charge with the argument that they aim to represent the entire Bolivian people, and their party includes a much broader group of supporters, so they will not allow the state to be used in the interests of a privileged few. However, the politicized bureaucracy gave Morales no other realistic choice than to embark on a strategy of placing people sympathetic to its ideas within the state apparatus. As a leader with a long anti-establishment record, he has not been able to count on the loyal and impartial support of civil servants, especially in the current polarized political climate. Morales's crude calculus of 'if he is not with us, he is probably against us' has therefore been a not unrealistic assessment of the possibilities he has for governing the state effectively.

To sum up, Morales was very critical of the state prior to adoption of the new constitution (2009). At the same time, he reduces a large range of unmet demands to the category of 'victims of the status quo'. However, Morales has never envisaged an end to Bolivia as a political entity, and in fact proposes rebuilding the state in order to preserve the unity of the nation. This is to be achieved by refashioning its institutions in order to make them serve all Bolivians and to ensure a more equal distribution of resources. This can only be achieved, according to Morales, if the changes are so thoroughgoing that they amount to the construction of an entirely new state.

Refounding the new state: an alternative form of modernity

In its programme, MAS emphasizes that the new state needs to be based on 'Andean principles' of equality, solidarity, consensus and equilibrium. This includes economic policies that aim to 'preserve nature and to produce for the common good of all living beings' (MAS, 2004a: 15–17). The most elaborate account of what a new state means for MAS comes from García Linera, who draws on his writings as one of Bolivia's most influential leftist intellectuals. The choice of

García Linera as vice president has given MAS greater ideological coherence and a clearer picture of their aims as a government. The fundamental idea is that MAS seeks an 'alternative form of modernity' (García Linera) for the Bolivian state, one that would be more rooted in the cultural practices of its population; that is, a modern state that can give direction to its citizens by combining traditional aspects with the requirements of life in a globalized world.

> The state this time will be, in a sense, modern – inasmuch as it has the capacity to articulate, sidestep and direct the logics of participation as well as the indigenous, communitarian organizational logics of rotational leadership, accountability, deliberation and near consensus. These have to enter into the system of public decision-making.... A modern state in Bolivia is not so much based on the individual ... An exclusively Bolivian modernity has to come into being ... [combining] realism with communitarianism; articulating the individual logic of political action together with communitarian logics. This is the great challenge of our own modernity for our state. (García Linera)

A modern state has to combine indigenous political logics (e.g. consensus instead of voting) and forms of organization (e.g. rotation of offices) with representative democracy. Related to the idea of 'two spheres of governance' (see below), a new institutional blueprint for the Bolivian state needs to take into account two logics of political action: an individual logic, using voting and representation, and a 'communitarian' logic (practised in *sindicatos* and indigenous organizations), emphasizing deliberation and consensus. Part of the 'communitarian' character of the new state is for Morales the idea of making it less centred on the individual (as in the Western liberal model) and more on the community. This means making the new state more open to different logics of organization and forms of political action. One proposal that became encoded in the new constitution was using rural/indigenous communities as an additional political and administrative unit. Although the description of two modes of political action is probably somewhat idealized and sees communitarian practices in an overly positive light, in essence

it is correct to argue that alternative forms of politics exist, and that
the failure to incorporate them into the official political system has
contributed to the disenfranchisement and disillusionment of large
sectors of the population.

Principles of a new state

For MAS imagining a new state is a form of hegemonic struggle
concerning not merely the rules of cohabitation for society but the
very definition of Bolivianness, including to whom the state belongs
and whose interests it is supposed to serve.

Relationship between culture and the state

A state that is perceived as reflecting the common identity of all
Bolivians cannot be culturally neutral, and until recently it has been,
according to the reading of MAS leaders, the vehicle for *mestizo* cultural dominance. They propose a new relationship between culture
and the state: one based not on the inclusion of the Quechua and
Aymara into an ostensibly mainstream *mestizo* society, as proposed
by reforms in the 1990s, but on the founding of a new state:

> It is about funding a new Quechua, Aymara, *mestizo* state.... You
> cannot include the majority. The majority has to construct its state.
> And the minorities are the ones that have to be included in the state.
> It means that the traditional political vision of the Bolivian state was
> about making the state exclusive. No señor, the state has to be given
> back to the Quechuas, Aymaras and Guaraní. When the *mestizos* and
> the whites are included thanks to the Aymaras and Quechuas, then
> we will have our place in the state. (Morales Olivera)

Interestingly, the view that the state has to be given back to the
indigenous peoples is voiced most firmly within MAS by its non-
indigenous leaders such as Morales Olivera, Ramon Quintana and
Ivan Iporre. This may be partially to bolster their own position in
what is after all a predominantly indigenous party, at least in terms
of their core electorate. But it also represents a shift in parts of the

leftist Bolivian elite to give priority to the indigenous majority, and to abandon their pretension to lead the indigenous population. It seems that leftist intellectuals within MAS have stepped back to allow indigenous leaders, primarily through the new constitution, to define how to include the *mestizos* in their state. In this way, MAS envisages that a new Bolivian state would be favourable to the *recuperación de culturas indígenas* ('the recovering of indigenous cultures'; Noel Aguirre).

This 'recovering' is a very common element in the discourse of MAS and has been adopted in various places in the new constitution. Recovering 'natural resources', 'sovereignty', 'dignity' and 'indigenous cultures' means unifying the diversity underlying these signifiers by concentrating on what they have in common, which is their shared exclusion from the status quo. Such recovering can be understood as a process of radical inclusion in a new state of affairs that has not been – at least in the sense articulated by Morales – part of the previously dominant neoliberal ideology. Recovering indigenous cultures means, therefore, constructing a new state that incorporates the indigenous *cosmovision* (or *Weltanschauung*).

Beyond achieving official recognition, it is thought the amalgamation of modern institutions and ancestral elements – for instance combining a modern judiciary with community justice in the new constitution – will infuse both state and indigenous cultural practices with new life. The state is intended to become more relevant to the daily practices of the indigenous population, while indigenous customs will be institutionally anchored, thus halting their decline. A telling example is the refusal to open the constitution with a statement affirming the equality of all mankind, because this is believed to be an anthropocentric conception of life and alien to the indigenous *cosmovision*. Instead the preamble stresses the roots of the plurality of the Bolivian peoples in *Patchamama*, Mother Earth.

Since the new constitution functions as a broad and vague symbol to unite and mobilize supporters, Morales pointed out that MAS should begin by defining what unites the Bolivian people, which had to be determined beforehand by a bottom-up process. However, in this context he stresses the idea to change the cultural content of the way the state is defined. This entails, as part of the Andean indigenous world-view, a different kind of ethics, accentuating reciprocity as a fundamental value. Hence the construction of a new state is associated discursively with a new ethic of 'how to arrange our individual and collective liberty under a number of common criteria' (De la Arcón[1]). That is, ethics is considered to signpost the way towards a new state, where individual liberty is respected in conjunction with the respect for the liberty of communities. The core principals of this ethic are those of *ama sua, ama llulla, ama qella*.

Alternative logics of political action

Evo Morales presents MAS as an organizational experiment to find new forms of political action through which the gap between official and extra-institutional spheres can be bridged. The central idea is that governance within official formal institutions is not sufficient for guiding Bolivia through institutional change towards a more democratic and stable system.

A strategically important aspect of MAS's discourse on the political system is the notion that in Bolivia there exist two 'platforms of governance', and that the failure to take both of them into consideration led to the downfall of previous governments.

> In Bolivia governance has two platforms, and this neither Sánchez de Lozada nor the Liberals understood. In Bolivia politics is carried out in the political-institutional, parliamentary sphere. But politics is also carried out in the *sindicatos*, unions, associations and companies. These are two platforms. Governance is guaranteed if one forms parliamentary majorities and coalitions and social majorities and coalitions. The one who does not work on both platforms is lost. (García Linera).

Civil society organizations engage in political action rather than trying to obtain influence through their representatives in the official institutions. In practice, this means that these organizations develop

political visions and proposals, which they try to implement within
their limited sphere of influence. They do so because they have
learned to expect nothing from the institutions, and believe that
self-organization is the only way to achieve their demands. Hence
some of the organizations – for example, the *sindicatos* in the Tropic,
the FEJUVE of El Alto and the Comité Cívico in Santa Cruz – have
come to function as, in effect, micro-governments with considerable
influence over the local populations.

Armed with this analysis, it is easier to understand why President
Morales appeals to the social movements to continue pressing for
the ratification of laws – as he did, for instance, when convoking
the Constituent Assembly. For the same reason, he has on several
occasions threatened to join social movements in their protests on
the streets, an unprecedented move for an elected president. But the
boldest example is certainly the five-day hunger strike he embarked
on, together with movement leaders, in the Palacio Quemado in
April 2009. To call upon extra-institutional political actors and to
revert to social movement tactics in order to overcome paralysis in
the official political institutions is certainly one way of countering
opposition and of increasing executive effectiveness. In addition, it
has helped to contain more radical social movement forces and avoid
a number of violent confrontations.

Another important aspect of the equation is that Morales, by
keeping one foot outside the official institutions, can enhance his
presidential powers by uniting various protest movements in support
of his government and against an opposition seen as reactionary.
When García Linera talks about '*una institucionalidad dual de
acción política*' (double institutionality of political action) and the
necessity for the Bolivian state to be capable of articulating this
double institutionality, this implies that President Morales and
his government set themselves the challenge of finding ways to
institutionalize both forms of political action. For this reason, the
new constitution includes mechanisms for direct democracy, such
as the right of citizens to propose laws or to remove politicians by

referendum (*referendum revocatorio*). Yet it goes even further and includes such controversial measures as 'social control' over the state – or over state-funded enterprises, which implies the election of citizens onto the boards of companies. And, indeed, the process of shaping the new constitution has, according to MAS, incorporated the two forms of political action.

The path to change: *Asamblea Constituyente*

The demand for a Constituent Assembly was first voiced by the indigenous peoples from the lowlands and came to national prominence during the 1993 March to La Paz. Bolivia's indigenous minorities, such as the Guaraní and the Chiquitanos, were inspired in their demand by the experience of indigenous peoples in Constituent Assemblies in other countries, especially Ecuador, where indigenous peoples have obtained new rights and the legal recognition of their customs (Van Cott, 2005). In Bolivia, the demand for a Constituent Assembly was gradually adopted by other popular organizations, including the national peasant association CSUTCB. Nevertheless, it took the *Guerra del Agua* and the *Octubre Negro* for the demand to become the signifier for a fundamental reform as articulated by MAS. It was probably one of Morales's most important accomplishments to link the nationalization of gas with the Constituent Assembly, an act that became hegemonic in the sense that even candidates of the opposition parties PODEMOS and UN presented proposals on the issue. Irrespective of the fact that in reality a Constituent Assembly is just about drafting a new constitution, which may or may not produce new institutions, by 2005 it was widely regarded as a process that would fundamentally change the country, although the meaning of change was left vague.

Great expectations: the Assembly as collective ritual

According to MAS leaders, the Constituent Assembly was supposed to be first and foremost a 'collective ritual to form a political community, to nationalize the state and its institutions' (García Linera). The Assembly was envisaged as a process through which citizens would again start to feel part of a larger entity, which would recognize them as the members of a sovereign people. The idea was that they would take ownership of the state and its institutions, because they would feel that they had participated in drawing up its fundamental rules. The collective ritual of drafting a new constitution would therefore be the founding moment for a new political community and a rupture with the old order. It would be different to the only other founding moment in the country's history, the Chaco War, a traumatic event that infused society with a defeatist spirit. After the Chaco War, the only signifier common to the Bolivian people was defeat, translating into a pessimistic outlook of the country. For García Linera, the assembly presented the historic opportunity that Bolivians would be bonded by a sense of success in overcoming particularistic challenges. What García Linera suggested was that the Assembly should help to strengthen political institutions not simply by redesigning them, but by breaking with the existing system in order to bring about a sense of ownership and a more positive attitude towards them.

However, we know now that the Assembly fell far short of this ideal scenario. Contrary to what Morales and García Linera hoped for, the Assembly soon reflected the deep divisions within the country, failed to heal them and even at times exacerbated the polarization. People became rapidly disillusioned and lost interest as the Assembly spent an age debating procedures. To its credit it ultimately produced a draft constitution, which, though not a very coherent and consistent document, nevertheless represents a big step in the direction of transforming Bolivia. In this regard, Bolivia stands out from other countries in Latin America, where similar assemblies have been less successful, with the notable exception of Ecuador.

Bolivia's new constitution

Although issues around the new constitution were discussed previously, the detail has not been considered. The small print is important because, notwithstanding the compromises reached, the constitution carries the signature of MAS. As we have seen, Morales's early career was heavily influenced by the social movement of the coca growers and their critique of the idea of representative democracy. Morales's understanding of democracy has been shaped by the ideal of communication, participation and deliberation as fundamental principles of democracy. It is therefore not surprising that a long-standing demand of Morales is to effect fundamental changes in the system of representative democracy to make it more 'direct' and 'communitarian', adding mechanisms of popular decision-making such as the referendum and the citizen-led legislative initiative:

> See, only in 1952 did we achieve the universal vote with our blood, our lives. And later, with our blood, in 2003, we obtained the referendum. Therefore we will deepen democracy, not only as participative but also as direct and deliberative. So that every Bolivian will not only have the right to elect every five years the president, vice president, MPs, mayors, and so on, with his vote, but can at once shape his destiny, his future. (Evo Morales)

> On the other hand, the participative democracy that was brought about through the mobilizations and implemented by the reforms of 2004 needs to be broadened, not simply remaining 'participative' but carrying forward this process of communitarian or direct democracy. And if this is to be the case, intrinsic to democracy must be the full capacity to make decisions, and through this to guarantee the holistic, comprehensive development of people and their community in harmony. (MAS, 2005b: 7)

For Morales, democracy is more than the election every few years of representatives who remain largely unresponsive during their incumbency. Genuine democracy goes beyond the recently installed, improved form of 'participative' democracy. 'Consensus,

along with respect for and acknowledgement of diverse social organizations, where communities and individuals find their liberation
from poverty and discrimination, need to be added' (MAS, 2004a:
20). Hence democracy is more than a political system, since it
includes socio-economic equality as the fundamental prerequisite for
people to become true citizens and develop themselves in a 'holistic,
comprehensive' manner.

Fundamentally, the new constitution is intended to increase the
capacity of the people to influence politics, facilitate more direct
representation, and enhance accountability. The new constitution
contains 411 articles drafted by the Constituent Assembly over a
period of thirty months. The constitution is ambitious and complex,
with some provisions being detailed whereas others are left very
vague. Interpretation and implementation of the text, as well as
future accompanying legislation (especially the Law of Autonomy and
Decentralization) will be the subject of intense political debate.

Given that it is a large and abstract political document, did the
constitution actually enact any important changes? The answer is
quite clearly yes. To begin with, it details a number of important
new rights, mainly but not exclusively concerned with indigenous
rights. It stresses the importance of ethnicity in Bolivia's 'plurinational' make-up, including official recognition of thirty-six languages (Articles 1–5). Democracy is defined as direct, participatory,
representative and communitarian (Article 11). A whole chapter is
devoted to indigenous rights, including the possibility of indigenous peoples having their own political, economic and judicial
system (Article 30 §14). The constitution also introduces a series of
indigenous principles (Article 8): 'Don't be lazy, don't steal, don't
lie', or 'vivir bien', as general guidelines for all subjects within
the constitution. Furthermore, existing social rights are elevated
to constitutional status, including the right to water, food, (free)
health care, education and housing. There is an obligation on the
state to guarantee food security and provide basic services. And,
last but certainly not least, natural resources are defined as the

exclusive dominion of the Bolivian people, administered by the state (Articles 16-20).

The constitution includes a battery of important institutional changes (Articles 277-296), starting with a very complex decentralized institutional structure. There are four levels of autonomy: departmental, regional, municipal and indigenous. The constitution then defines no less than nine different types of territorial entities, as well as providing for additional local variations. To make matters even more confusing, the units of indigenous autonomy – territory, municipality, region – can be created and delimited by inhabitants, although it is left vague how this is supposed to happen and what the mechanisms for resolution of disputes are. Given that some indigenous communities inhabit areas where natural gas or other resources are thought to be located, the possibility that their territory could become autonomous from the department to which they currently belong has already created conflicts concerning the control of these resources. The implementation of these institutional changes is intended to conform to a long list of sometimes conflicting principles (Article 270) informing state structures. However, what principles such as unity, self-government, solidarity, equality, equity, complementarity, reciprocity and subsidiarity mean in practice and how they are to be operationalized let alone enforced remain to be determined.

An issue that has already caused some controversy has been the provision for two consecutive terms (Article 168) for the president, since Morales has signalled that he might run again in 2014, which is technically possible since his first term was under a different constitution. However, to run again would mean violating a central promise he gave in the process of convincing the opposition to approve the constitution. Another key change introduced by the constitution is abolition of the much criticized election of the president by the National Congress should a candidate fail to win a simple majority. Under the new system, there will be a second round if no candidate wins more than 50 per cent of the vote (or at least 40 per cent with a 10 per cent margin over the next candidate; Article 166).

Concerning the legislature, which is now called the Asamblea Legislativa Plurinacional (ALP), a key compromise with the opposition, which is regionally concentrated and thus benefits from the representation of the regions in the Senate, is the bicameral structure remaining in place whilst the number of senators increases from twenty-seven to thirty-six (Article 148). Strikingly in line with measures Morales demanded during his election campaigns, the constitution changed a number of the rules concerning members of Congress: they no longer have immunity from prosecution in criminal cases; there are no salaried substitutes; and all elected officials are subject to the possibility of recall elections and thus ending their term prematurely. In terms of the electoral system, the constitution foresees proportional seats reserved for indigenous candidates and special *indigenous–originario–campesino* electoral districts. Both the distribution of seats and the delineation of electoral districts are still to be determined, since the law regulating the 2009 elections was only provisional. Political representation can function through parties, *agrupaciones ciudadanas* (citizens' associations – a fashionable disguise for discredited former mainstream parties) and organizations of indigenous peoples, which can select their candidates according to their own (non-electoral) norms.

Particularly controversial were the changes concerning the judiciary, because they established a parallel indigenous judicial system (Article 179), intended to function according to the norms and values of indigenous peoples and with jurisdiction over members of indigenous communities and matters within indigenous territories. The sensitive question of how to guarantee a minimum rule of law and level of human rights, as well as how the parallel system relates to the mainstream judicial system, is still to be detailed in secondary legislation, which was still being drafted in early 2011. One point in defence of such a system must be, however, that many members of small indigenous communities do not make use of the official judicial system, preferring to solve matters within their community. Hence the constitution only regulates what already exists, and one could argue that this is more effective in ensuring minimum standards than ignoring or outlawing indigenous community justice. Another controversial aspect is that authorities in the judicial system, including the Supreme Court and the Constitutional Tribunal, will be elected by popular vote after pre-selection by the ALP (Article 182). Although judges cannot belong to a political party and are not allowed to campaign for themselves, this does represent a politicization of the judiciary. It also seems highly doubtful that an alienated judiciary will improve corruption, accountability and inefficiency.

Following up on Morales's idea of institutionalizing alternative forms of political action, the constitution provides a social control mechanism. This allows 'popular action' (bypassing judicial and administrative remedies) against actions or omissions that violate collective rights or interests related to patrimony, public security and health, and the environment (Articles 135, 136). Formulated in extremely vague terms, this popular action seems to apply to all aspects of life; it threatens to bypass and therefore weaken the rule of law, since there is no requirement to use existing institutions. Similarly problematic is that there are no minimum standards to which these popular actions must adhere. Moreover, the social control mechanism provides for civil society organizations to participate in the design of and control of public policies. In order to improve transparency in the way taxes are spent, they can exercise control over all companies and institutions that use taxpayers' money (Article 241). Once again, this measure has to be set out more clearly in secondary legislation. It is unclear whether or not, or to what extent, social control will be applied in practice.

The economic policies of President Morales are probably one of the most misunderstood aspects of his administration. This is partly a consequence of the misleading name of MAS, which is not a socialist party. There is no doubt that Morales would have chosen a different name were this an option at the time he and the other leaders of the *sindicatos* took over the party. The constitution does not set out to establish a twenty-first-century socialism, as in Venezuela or Ecuador. It does, however, state that a mixed economy will be established that is oriented at improving quality of life. It stresses the important role of the state in general planning and regulation, strategic control over production chains and processes of industrialization of natural resources.

The state can intervene directly in the production chain of strategic sectors, but must respect the law and entrepreneurial initiative. Bolivian investment is prioritized over foreign investment, and foreign companies cannot obtain conditions more favourable than domestic companies. Individual and collective property rights are guaranteed, but property must fulfil a social function and not be detrimental to the collective interest. Expropriation is possible, but only with prior compensation. Similarly, private business is respected and protected, but the emphasis is clearly on the promotion of co-operatives and the 'communitarian' economy (Articles 306–309). There are also loopholes in the protection of private business, because economic activities must not endanger Bolivia's sovereignty; this is linked to Morales's frequent criticism of privatization and the activities of multinational companies in Bolivia. Furthermore, though the standards still have to be defined, all forms of economic activity are obliged to generate decent working conditions and protect the environment. One area where these provisions have already been tested is the *latifundio* or large landholdings. Under the land tenure reform, landholdings became limited by referendum to 5,000 hectares. In general this cannot be applied retroactively, except if the land does not fulfil any socio-economic function or if the proprietor is found guilty of forced or child labour. On 14 March 2009, the Morales government issued for the first time the expropriation of properties of large landowners where indigenous (mostly Guaraní) people live in forced labour. Given the government's weakness in the area and the well-organized (political, legal and potentially violent) resistance of the landowners, the expropriations have not yet been carried out. The most notable case is that of the holdings of Ronald Larsen, a

US citizen who with his family owns some 57,145 hectares of land in Santa Cruz and who has been accused of keeping indigenous people in conditions of semi-slavery. Rumours about the Larson case abound, and the entire issue has become another element in the clash between Morales and the *media luna* governors, given Larson's good political connections with Rubén Costas and the political elite of Santa Cruz. This makes it impossible to come to a final judgement on the merits of the case. Nevertheless, it is arguably the case that expropriations of parts of such enormous territories may make sense, at least theoretically, if evidence of forced labour can be found. This is because forced labour has been one of Bolivia's most serious human rights problems, occurring especially on large landholdings in, for instance, Santa Cruz and Chuquisaca. Previous governments were criticized by the international community for not intervening decisively, and now the authorities have the necessary legal means available. On the other hand, the constitutional provisions (especially with respect to the 'socio-economic function') are still too vague and allow for arbitrary intervention.

To sum up, this extremely ambitious new constitution has the potential to change fundamentally many parameters of Bolivia's political and economic system in favour of the previously marginalized sectors of the population. Yet in Bolivia, as in many other developing countries, legislation and in particular broad constitutional dispositions do not in practice have the desired effect as many laws are simply ignored or not enforced. Hence, the first question is to what extent the many principles of the constitution will be implemented in practice. These caveats notwithstanding, the constitution is symbolically very important and codifies important elements of MAS's programme. It is extremely ambitious and has the potential to realize some important positive changes. However, most of it will have to be operationalized in secondary legislation, which will be a complicated and sensitive undertaking. In addition to the already identified problems, a number of issues stand out. For example, there is no hierarchy between the different autonomous entities; they relate directly only to the central state and not to each other. Mechanisms for cooperation, distribution of competences and resources between different forms of autonomy have yet to be defined in a Law of Autonomy and Decentralization. This will involve extensive discussion and potentially vertical as well as horizontal conflicts. No objective criteria for an act of treason have yet been defined and there are no clear time limits in place for a state of emergency, making both provisions vulnerable to abuse.

Analysing the role of the state

Looking back at Morales's first four years as president, there is an incoherency in his vision of the new state: his discursive logic of unifying a broad range of demands, or what Laclau (2005) calls the 'logic of equivalence', does not fit well with his policies of state interventionism. On the one hand, there is an 'equivalential logic' of unifying a variety of political and economic practices behind the vague concept of a 'new state', which is seen as opposed to and breaking with the pre-2005 status quo. On the other hand, Morales pursues the idea of a strong, interventionist state. Yet a strong state acts, according to Laclau's (2005) 'logic of difference', by defining a hierarchy of demands and by assigning social categories. In Morales's discourse it remains undefined how this 'diversity' will be handled equivalentially within the context of a strong state. This problem of including heterogeneity within a new nation and state points to the tensions between the logic of 'equivalence' and 'difference' that typify populism (Panizza, 2007; Aboy Carlés, 2005b).

Another issue has been how to relate an interventionist government to the idiosyncratic structure of MAS, which remains at a distance from official institutions in order to use social movement dynamics to generate support for its government. Morales argues that he can resolve this problem through MAS's social governance strategy (*gobernabilidad social*), which refers to the capacity of mobilizing civil society organizations in support of certain policies. However, the early years in office have shown that a president who proposes interventionism while using an equivalential discourse appealing to grassroots movements as pillars of support faces a serious balancing act between bottom-up mobilization and top-down implementation. The need to make policy choices in the face of limited resources threatens the equivalential relations of demands. The underlying problem is the tension between MAS's social movement dynamics and the influence of urban intellectuals who are members of Morales's cabinet but who only recently joined the party. These 'newcomers', who have a leftist background favouring state intervention, have brought a degree of valuable experience to public administration. Yet they have entered an organization with a social movement culture which gets its energy from informality and spontaneity.

Conclusion

Evo Morales articulates a strong belief in democracy as an ideal political system that gives citizens a chance to influence decisions that affect their lives. His representation of democracy is a mixture of the utopian ideal of direct, 'communitarian' democracy and concrete proposals to make the political system more representative and responsive. Morales's project of a new state is a way of imagining an 'alternative form of modernity' that ties together respect for economic and political diversity and the 'recovering' of indigenous cultures by changing the guiding principles of the state. Part of the imagining of a new state is the understanding that in Bolivia there exist two spheres of governance: official political-institutional and extra-institutional. Morales argues that any government has to ensure governability in both realms, and that it is necessary for the Bolivian state to be capable of incorporating both forms of political action. This implies that President Morales set himself the challenge of institutionalizing social movement tactics and traditional indigenous forms of decision-making.

More accurately, refounding the state means for Morales and the MAS reforming the institutional identity of the first and official sphere of governance and institutionalizing the second sphere by means of a new constitution. Following Morales's political logic, any reform of political institutions is futile unless accompanied by measures that give civil society organizations regular structural access to national decision-making. In the end the attempt to create better links between society and the state mean for Morales establishing more levels of autonomy and territorial governance, mechanisms of direct democracy (legislative initiative, revocation procedures, referendums), and having a vice-minister for coordination with the social movements.

This chapter has made apparent the functioning of Aboy Carlés's (2005) concept of 'foundationalism' in Morales's discourse, because it establishes sharp political frontiers between the 'neoliberal' past and a positive future when all the changes proposed by the constitution will be operational. This is intended to leave behind the problems associated with the past system. Morales's discourse has contributed to the weakening of existing institutions by constructing an antagonism between his imagined 'real' democracy and the unrepresentative system prior to the introduction of the new constitution. Yet his vision of a 'refounding the state' is more than a simple rejection of the status quo. It contains the utopian 'promise of plenitude' (Howarth, 2000) of a political system that includes a large variety of cultural practices. This has resulted in the drafting and introduction of a constitution that has rendered Bolivia's political system complex to the point of disfunctionality, since it seeks to combine what might prove irreconcilable in practice – communitarian politics and representative democracy. What may ultimately count, however, is that Morales and the MAS are the only important political actors with a vision that gives a large sector of the Bolivian people a sense of direction and meaning as a collectivity. At a time when the threat of the country's disintegration has been real, a major factor in Morales's success in becoming president has been the positive imaginary of a new social order. More mundane factors such as the distribution of increased state revenues from natural gas and a divided opposition are certainly important factors in Morales's electoral successes. Be that as it may, the belief that under Morales Bolivia will be refounded and become a better place has remained powerful during his presidency. This is because Morales, like no other contemporary politician, invokes a sense of dignity and destiny for a large part of the population who previously felt marginalized.

The difficult road ahead
for President Morales and the MAS

How was it possible for a former coca grower to be elected to Bolivia's highest office? An account of the rise of Morales and the MAS must go beyond the usual explanations that look at the multiple problems Bolivia faces and the dissatisfaction of the population with mainstream parties. Many such explanations are linked to a rather simplistic characterization of Morales as a 'populist' in the mould of Hugo Chávez, due to his appeals to 'the people', state intervention and defence of national sovereignty. However, Morales does not fit conventional theories of populism, because his political organization, MAS, is not just 'his' but is deeply rooted in social movements, and therefore does not serve only to promote Morales's political career, as a populist party would. In that aspect, MAS is quite distinct from the electoral vehicles of his predecessors, such as Hugo Bánzer's ADN and Jorge Quiroga's PODEMOS. Furthermore, we cannot characterize Morales as a populist based on the characteristics of his leadership. He does make some decisions alone and in a top-down fashion, but in general he consults widely both within official institutions and outside. Contrary to the practice of his predecessor Carlos Mesa, Morales does not communicate with the population only through mass media, but makes direct appeals to 'the people'.

Morales's success is based on his creation of a new political identity, which has positioned 'the people' and 'the traditional parties' in two antagonistic camps. Calling for the defence of 'natural resources' and of 'national sovereignty' enabled Morales to unify the many different demands behind MAS in a general articulation of dissatisfaction with the status quo. MAS took root among other sectors of the population because it allowed them to be equal in a common opposition to the status quo. Morales managed to win electoral support at the expense of other potential competitors because he was not trying to establish a clear hierarchy of all anti-establishment forces, as was tried for instance by Felipe Quispe, who sought to establish an Aymara leadership. Instead the message of Morales was simple: we are equal in our rejection of how things are; let us work together towards this common goal, but in a decentralized way; let each social movement and social sector have the freedom to choose its own leaders and how they support this general project. Morales was then able to win support at the expense of the opposition, because he constructed a clear frontier between 'us' (the people) and 'them' (the elites). This served to create a deep polarization within the country, whereby you belonged either to the people or to their enemies. Given the disastrous policies and at times violent repression pursued by earlier governments, it was not too difficult to communicate the message that these elites were not defending the interests of the majority of the population.

In conclusion, the rise of Morales and MAS is primarily due to a hegemonic construction of a political identity. This posed a challenge to the status quo that entailed a process of de-institutionalization and re-institutionalization of the system of representation with the aim of moving the new identity to the centre of the polis. Morales executed a clear break with existing institutions, calling into question the adequateness of their functioning, and promising to build a new institutional order in a new, 'refounded' state. Yet, initiating such a process brings with it the danger of producing a downward spiral of de-institutionalization and democratic de-consolidation were Morales not able to realize at least some aspects of the 'new state'. He has already achieved a significant step in this direction through the adoption of a new constitution. However, the great challenge for the coming years is to translate this bold, complex and ambiguous document into concrete policies that have a positive effect on the lives of ordinary people.

Bolivia is entering a crucial and delicate phase, since many contentious aspects of the new constitution require clarification and subsequent implementation through secondary legislation. The scale of the task of developing legal instruments for the proper functioning of the constitution represents a significant challenge to institutional capacities and resources, which is compounded by the existence of conflicting interpretations of the text. However, if these issues are not addressed within a short period of time, the credibility of the whole process and the legitimacy of central political institutions will be put at risk. The controversy in April 2009 around the electoral law will probably prove to be only the first of a number of conflicts related to the new CPE. The possibility of land expropriations and the ambiguous social control mechanisms in entities receiving state funding (including some private companies) open the door to further conflicts, especially with the *media luna* departments.

One of the central aims of MAS is to reform the institutional complexion of the first level of governance and to institutionalize the second by means of a new constitution, and specific decisions such as the appointment of a vice-minister for coordination with social movements. At the time of writing (late 2010), it is still too early to say to what extent the new constitution will be able to contribute to this. This is because its provisions are so complex and multilayered. It will not only be a huge challenge to make sense of the at times contradictory principles, but their implementation will face stiff resistance from the opposition. Morales would therefore be well advised to consult widely on the changes so as not to be accused of refashioning the institutions for the sake of his own personal power.

The search for and experimentation with alternatives to the existing forms of political action within the official institutions has been
one of the defining elements of the first Morales presidency. His
attempt to institutionalize a more direct democracy and to open up
space for indigenous political practices through the new constitution
has been a continuous source of conflict with the opposition. While
the latter is of course concerned with protecting its own power niches,
it quite rightly criticizes the over-representation (by almost 200 per
cent) of smaller indigenous groups relative to their population size, as
envisaged by the 2009 draft electoral law. This is less about making
room for indigenous practices, and more a calculation to increase the
number of votes for Morales. There has been a problematic tendency
during Morales's first presidency for power to become increasingly
centralized around him, García Linera and a dozen key advisers.
This is of course nothing new in Bolivia, but the country is now
at a historic juncture. For his second term, Morales has a majority
unprecedented since the return to democracy, and enjoys continuing
popularity and almost uncritical support from some (though not all)
powerful social movements. In October 2010, Morales stated that he
will run for president again in 2014 and that this is in line with Bolivia's constitution. Technically, this is correct, since his first presidency
was under a different constitution, but Morales conveniently forgets
that he accepted the demand of the opposition not to run twice under
the new constitution. The dispute about his candidature seems likely
to end up in court, where he might have a chance of winning the case
on account of the potential for political interference by pro-Morales
judges, despite the fact that the case itself seems unfavourable to him.
There is of course the danger that one side will not accept defeat and
call into question or even boycott the entire electoral process, opening
the way to a new period of institutional instability.

In any case, Morales's popularity remains in a different league to
that of any candidate in the splintered opposition. In addition, the
government now has deep pockets, filled with the increased income
from natural gas. This means that Morales has important leverage in

implementing the new constitution through the required secondary legislation. For better or for worse, he will be able to enact fundamental political and economic change. Regarding the latter, nowadays dubbed 'Evonomics' to denote that Bolivia's economic policy follows a different path to that of Venezuela, Bolivia has earned praise from the IMF for 'continued sound macroeconomic management', resulting in sustained growth rates that are among the highest in Latin America, close to an optimal level of foreign reserves, low inflation and fiscal surplus (IMF, 2010). However, a number of decisions remain pending, such as creating a medium-term fiscal framework, reducing vulnerability to hydrocarbon revenue fluctuations through the creation of a national savings fund, and increasing the currently low levels of private investment. Luis Arce, the finance minister, and one of the architects of the nationalization schemes, began touring the world in 2010 to encourage foreign private investment, arguing that the core of 'Evonomics' is to create a sound macroeconomic foundation upon which a responsible revolution can be built (*La Nacion – Argentina*, 26 September 2010).

Regarding political change, any reform of institutions would be futile, according to the logic of Morales's proposals, unless accompanied by measures that give to civil society organizations regular structural access to national decision-making. In the end, this comes down to finding ways of establishing new functional links between society and the state, in addition to those provided by political parties. This is an immensely complicated task, but at least until now there have been few signs that Morales has begun believing that he personally can provide such a link alone – as, for instance, is the case with Venezuela's Hugo Chávez.

The dangerous path towards re-institutionalization

Evo Morales's project of institutionalizing social movement tactics and traditional indigenous practices as official mechanisms of Bolivia's democratic system raises two issues. The first is that Morales fuels (and subsequently benefits from) the perception that the old institutions were not inclusive and responsive to all social interests. Thus his discourse further weakens the institutions and contributes to the process of de-institutionalization, because the equivalential articulation of demands challenges the particularistic, differential treatment of demands by previous governments. Yet the argument here is that, although he fuels such a perception, Morales did not create it from scratch, since feelings of disenchantment with the functioning of political institutions, especially political parties, already existed in society (see Latinobarómetro data in Mainwaring et al., 2006). Nevertheless, Morales further destabilizes the existing institutions by way of his unification of differing demands, which have hitherto been separated by internal frontiers (e.g. between coca producers and highland peasants, and between rural and urban social movements). Morales very successfully gives the impression that the most important frontier is that separating a small elite within the official institutions (after his election in the regions) from the rest of the population. This discursive logic is deeply disturbing to those groups used to political and economic power, which find themselves now in opposition.

The second issue is that the mobilizing of extra-institutional political forces in order to gain political momentum within the existing institutions – even if the aim is to reform them – is playing with fire. While splitting political action between two forms of governance might have been the only way to achieve the adoption of a new constitution, there are serious issues in the background. Although there is relative unity among popular organizations in support of Morales, they remain vulnerable to centrifugal tendencies and to fragmentation. Even for social leaders as experienced as Morales, keeping the dynamic of social movements within more or less moderate boundaries is a difficult task. Once they are mobilized, their decentralized and bottom-up organizational culture sets in motion a chain reaction of demands and mobilizations which is hard to contain. When Morales used social movements to press for a Constituent

Assembly and for the realization of certain reforms, he ran the risk that the movements might overtake him and become unwilling to agree to certain moderate reforms achieved through negotiation and compromise within the limits imposed by the framework of formal political institutions. Indeed, his recourse to hunger strike in April 2009 indicates that he had to take a drastic step in order to contain the mobilizations and channel their energy towards moderation and constructive positions. This is to argue that Morales's discursive logic has the potential to set in motion a dialectic of de-institutionalization and re-institutionalization, which implies the ability to build enough political pressure to realize essential institutional reforms. Yet the balance of this dialectic is precarious, and there is a danger that the discourse produces instead a downward spiral of de-institutionalization. This may happen in particular if a stalemate arises over the content of the secondary legislation implementing the constitution, and Morales is not able to exert moderating control over the mobilizations demanding its implementation.

Another outstanding issue is that Morales needs to determine how far MAS can maintain an internal structure that thrives on spontaneity, the absence of formalization and partial rejection of the logic of institutional politics. The nature of state intervention produces formalization, and this could endanger the internal functioning of MAS if no channels for the participation of its grassroots are institutionalized. In other words, President Morales has chosen to get his support from popular mobilizations. This has the consequence of generating resistance in more conservative sectors of society, and all the potential risks such a strategy entails. In order to maintain the support of grassroots social movements, Morales needs to translate his broad political vision into realistic targets without giving the impression of diluting it. When implementing policies to achieve these targets, Morales faces the challenge of avoiding the impression among the movements that he does decide on these policies in a top-down fashion.

Analysing the rise of Morales and MAS gives us a picture of the state of democracy in Bolivia, thus helping us understand the challenges and opportunities democracy faces in the region. I have highlighted the tension between inclusion and exclusion as a central feature of the discourse of MAS. Bolivia's political conflicts (2005–07) over the new constitution and the autonomy of the regions are a reflection of this tension. They are part of the question as to how the diversity of interests can be included under the same roof, and to what extent the general (i.e. the central state) can be excluded from the affairs of the particular (i.e. the regions). Morales struggles to combine these two logics by creating empty signifiers behind which diversity can be united, and by constructing new political frontiers and identities. In the same way, the challenge for democracy is for it to become a new imaginary that can unite the diversity of the Bolivian population and overcome the crisis of representation. This requires redrawing political frontiers and redefining political identities. The temptation will always remain to draw a frontier at the heart of the political community. The great challenge is to define what binds Bolivians, and accordingly to draw the frontier between Bolivia and the world around it.

Notes

Preface

1. Three observations are in order. First, use of the term *sindicato* is imprecise here, since not all members necessarily grow coca. Second, although the term may seem to connote 'union', the status of the Bolivian *sindicatos* is that of a social movement. Third, *sindicatos* are a very common form of organization in Bolivia, but the use of the term is here strictly limited to those *sindicatos* in the Tropic of Cochabamba.

Chapter 1

1. However, I will use the more precise terms 'patrimonialism' and 'clientelism'.
2. Although this top-down labelling of an identity may appear questionable today, it should not be forgotten that it was a very progressive idea at the time and to some extent a form of liberation.
3. State capitalism is an interventionist and protectionist policy whereby the state fixes prices, regulates imports and exports, and monopolizes key economic sectors. During the 1970s this led to an increase in public jobs from 60,000 to 150,000, distributed to MNR's supporters.
4. Central documents in which this ideology was articulated are: *Nacionalismo y Coloniaje* (Montenegro, 1990; first published 1943); W. Guevara, *A Teoria, Medios y Fines de la Revolucion Nacional – Tesis de Ayopaya* (1947); José Cuadros Quiroga, *Bases y Principios del MNR* (1942); Augusto Céspedes, *El Dictador Suicida* (1956).
5. Nowadays, the imposition of a *campesino* identity does not appear in positive light, but one should not forget that it occurred as an attempt to include indigenous people in the 1950s, at a time when more developed countries than Bolivia displayed less inclusive official discourses regarding subaltern ethnic groups.

6. Historical studies of Bolivia commonly point to the lack of connections between the various parts of the country (Klein, 1969; Malloy, 1970; Zavaletta, 1986)

7. Mismanagement, international debt and falling export prices, as well as policy blunders, combined to produce hyperinflation of 24,000 per cent, at its worst, and a devaluation of the national currency against the dollar from 25:1 to 1,000,000:1.

8. A complication in discussion about coca is that most figures have been produced for political purposes, either to eliminate coca production or to support it. This holds with respect to the existing surface area of cultivation, the quantity of coca necessary to satisfy legal consumption, and calculations of how much coca would cost if there was no demand from cocaine producers.

9. See *Le Monde Diplomatique*, 9 May 2008.

10. Vandiola is a small area in the Tropic of Cochabamba.

11. On 25 April 2007, the Office of National Drug Control Policy (ONDCP) released US estimates of coca cultivation and cocaine production in Bolivia for 2006. It reported that coca cultivation in 2006 was 'statistically unchanged as compared to the 2005 estimate' and that '[c]ocaine potential production remained unchanged … from 2005 to 2006' (see Red Andina de Información, 23 May 2007).

12. In Colombia, coca is not a traditional holy plant and was introduced principally for the production of cocaine.

13. Laserna (1996: 53) argues that in none of the relevant governmental policy papers is there an estimate of the number of traditional users. One is can deduce from other data (daily use, hectares cultivated, annual legal production in tons) that this number would be some 400,000 people.

14. The harvest of 25,000 hectares amounts to 36,500 tons of coca leaves per year according to Oomen (2003: 33).

15. www.unodc.org/documents/crop-monitoring/Bolivia/bolivia-coca-survey-2010-ES-WEB.pdf.

16. I am not aware of any reliable data on whether or not the price is kept high, or what the difference would be for the individual producer if it were higher. Calculations have usually been produced for a political purpose, either to support eradication by showing an enormous price difference or to support coca cultivation by showing that there would actually be no difference. I therefore tend to think that there is an influence on the price, but that this should not be overstated. More reliable data on the low standards of living in the coca-producing areas confirm this interpretation (see n. 17 below).

17. In 1976, the coca-producing provinces in the department of Cochabamba occupied in a ranking of poverty 34th, 49th and 55th places out of a total 99 provinces (1 being the richest and 99 the poorest province). In 1990, after the coca boom, the same provinces ranked 85th, 55th and 66th on the poverty index (Morales, 1984, 1990).

18. Informal conversation with Oscar C. Antezana, MAS minister for public works.

19. The war on drugs is of course being fought also in other countries, most notably Colombia and Peru.

20. In the Andes, a mere 14 per cent of coca plantations were destroyed between 1992 and 2001. What was destroyed in one area was compensated for in another area. The extension of coca production to Colombia is one of the consequences (Vargas Meza, 1997: 19–20; Rensselaer, 2001: 2–3).
21. Impunity is based upon the 'doctrine of national security' (2000) and the Military Penal Code (Article 138). Between September 2000 and January 2001, 7 people were killed by the armed forces and 200 wounded. In January 2003, 13 peasants were killed during protests and hundreds wounded. Not a single case was subject to official investigation.

Chapter 2

1. See www.evomorales.net/paginasCas/perfil_Cas_infan.aspx; last consulted 21 February 2010.
2. See *Opinión*, 15 April 2001.
3. See *La Razón*, 22 January 2006.
4. See www.evomorales.net/paginasCas/perfil_Cas_cocal.aspx; last consulted 21 February 2010.
5. See Blommaert, 2003 for a comprehensive analysis of the livelihood of the coca producers.
6. Located near the centre of Cochabamba, CEDIB is one of Bolivia's best sources for socio-economic and political analysis.
7. Evo Morales indicated during all the meetings what and how individuals have contributed; for instance, some *compañeros* donated 100,000 small plastic flags to the six *federaciónes*, while others worked for several days to open a local MAS office. Smaller contributions – a few bottles of beer, some maize – are also reported. Similarly, the offices of the movement were built by volunteers, who are also responsible for their maintenance.
8. Hegemonism refers to a mode of articulation that makes the claim of radically including all political differences within a community, so that the space for differences closes. This is untenable since identities are relational and need to be limited by external antagonisms. Attempting a unitary representation of the political community, hegemonism is a particular form of hegemony, the logic of which constitutes any space of political solidarity through the generalization of a particularity that comes to represent this wider political space.
9. We find an 'equivalential chain' when 'all the demands, in spite of their differential character, tend to re-aggregate themselves forming what we will call an equivalential chain. This means that each individual demand is constitutively split: on the one hand it is its own particularised self; on the other it points, through equivalential links, to the totality of the other demands…. each demand is, actually, the tip of an iceberg because although it only shows itself in its own particularity, it presents its own manifest claim as only one among a larger set of social claims' (Laclau, 2005: 37)
    The 'logic of equivalence' is the logic of simplification of the political space through, for instance, the transformation of political identities at the expense of their particularistic content (Laclau and Mouffe, 1985: 128–31).

This discursive logic, which is central to a symptomatic reading of populism, entails the construction of a common, simplified signifier that represents the various particularistic, unmet demands as a totality and as opposed to a power beyond the equivalential chain, which is held responsible for not fulfilling any of the demands. From a very particularistic demand (such as the economic demand to produce coca) a broader political demand arises ('defending natural resources'), which becomes increasingly 'empty', so that it is able to absorb, integrate and include other demands within the 'chain of equivalence'.

10. Alternative Development is the term used to describe the largely failed efforts, partly funded by the international community, to provide the coca growers with alternative means of livelihood. See Blommaert (2003) for an in-depth analysis of this issue.

11. This is not to argue that the *sindicatos* are fundamentally opposed to trying to cultivate other crops, but their experience has shown them that in the great majority of cases these crops bring the individual producer no economic benefit. It should also be noted that this antagonism between the *sindicatos* and alternative development projects significantly decreased after Evo Morales invited them in 2004 to work together on a sustainable strategy without demanding the eradication of coca. Since 2006 these projects have been run by the Mancomunidad de Municipios of the Tropic, which is staffed by members of the *sindicatos* or people sympathetic to them. This presents the chance to search for sustainable livelihood strategies without the hidden agenda of foreign donors.

12. In small *sindicatos* leaders can be as young as 17 years old.

13. The *Kataristas* were a small group of Aymara intellectuals and students formed in the late 1960s, who – based on their experience in La Paz – sought to protect indigenous identities from the threat of an assimilationist *mestizo* culture (see below).

14. The name is inspired by Tupac Katari, the nom de guerre of Aymara leader Julian Apaza, who led the indigenous rebellion and siege of La Paz in 1781. A core document of *Katarista* ideology is the 1973 *Tihuanacu Manifesto*.

15. Outright *Katarista* parties were unsuccessful politically on their own. Arguably the biggest success was the vice presidency of Hugo Cárdenas, but his participation in the government's unpopular reforms led to accusations of a political sell-out and the disappearance of *Katarista* parties.

Chapter 3

1. It was uninhabited except for settlements of small indigenous groups such as the Yuki, which the settlers of the *sindicatos* displaced further into remote areas of the Tropic (Blanes, 1983).

2. Torota was the nearest settlement. It had already established its *sindicato*, which extended its jurisdiction into all uninhabited neighbouring areas.

3. The statements from lower-level leaders and activists from the coca growers' movement stem from my research among them between 2002 and 2007. Names starting with 'Don' signifies that the individual has requested anonymity.

4. These are long-distance marches to the capital La Paz protesting about a given issue. The marches attract a great deal of attention, particularly when the thousands of peasants arrive in La Paz. Therefore governments have usually tried to negotiate and thus avoid their arrival in the capital.

5. The movement initially took places on the lists of IU, before it participated with its own party (first ASP, later MAS–IPSP).

6. Every member pays per month 1 boliviano (approx. $0.14) for each organization (*sindicato, central* and *federación*) and 1 boliviano for the expenses of the leaders on each level (*dirigente, central* and *ejecutivo*). This means that they currently pay every month a minimum of 6 bolivianos (approx. $0.85). This is a significant amount for individual members considering both their low income and the purchasing power of this sum in Bolivia, where 6 bolivianos is sufficient to buy breakfast for six days for a four-person household.

7. During the height of eradication campaigns, the item 'Coca and Territory' was first or second in importance on the agenda.

8. Usually men participate in the *sindicatos* owing to their status as head of their family. However, female heads of household can also take part in the organization and become leaders. In addition, women have begun to set up their own organizations as part of the general movement of the coca producers.

9. When leaders travelled (in 2002) they received the following compensation: La Paz, 150 bolivianos ($21); Cochabamba, 80 bolivianos ($11); Villa Tunari or Chimoré, 20 bolivianos ($1.4).

10. However, one informant told me that he had abstained from attending the meeting to elect a new leader. But the other members called him to attend. During the meeting he had to present his opinion, which resulted in his election as a leader although he had explicitly stated that he did not want to be elected (interview with Don Ernesto).

11. Concurrent with the above-mentioned changing tasks of the movement, a new type of leadership has emerged recently and the ideal of a leader has become defined more in political terms. This type of leader tends to be younger and with more formal education, in order to be able to negotiate with the authorities and conduct bureaucratic procedures for the movement. Changes in the opportunity structure, such as the requirement for collective actions and negotiations to defend their interests, were echoed in a gradual process, through which the movement adapted – for instance, by producing a new type of leader.

12. However, it should be noted that many members of a *sindicato* take part in meetings of the *central* or the *federación*. They help to find a consensus, which means that they will also explain the decision at the local level and defend the leader.

13. According to this principle, as many tasks of the organization as possible should be fulfilled at grassroots level.

14. Including demonstrations, road blocks or *marchas* (long-distance marches to La Paz).

15. One of the most frequent complaints of the coca producers was that the military destroyed during eradication campaigns not only coca but any other plantation or animals that they encountered. Even in cases where they did

not find coca, it was reported, they destroyed other crops, on account of their unaccountable power and as a form of retaliation against what the military saw as peasants hiding their coca.

16. NB: not *cocaleros*, which is regarded by the peasants as a pejorative term used by the authorities.

17. I should point out, however, that for analytical purposes I have presented here a condensed version of what has been a multilayered process, a dialectic not always visible to the actors; much of the redefinition of frontiers and the unifying of communities was as unintended as it was unplanned.

Chapter 4

1. Véliz subsequently became allied with the PCB and other parties in order to contest the municipal elections. Once the bases decided to support Morales over Véliz, the latter was certain that he would not achieve candidacy in the next national elections, and moved on to become a candidate for the Nueva Fuerza Republicana (NFR), leading some to accuse him of treason.

2. See for the results of the elections: www.bolivia.com/cne/.

3. During a speech in Chimoré on 26 June 2002. See, for instance, *Los Tiempos*, 27 June 2002.

Chapter 5

1. A popular Aymara intellectual and leader of the Movimiento Revolucionario Túpac Katari de Liberación (MRTKL). However, many former *Katarista* allies felt betrayed by his decision to accept the vice presidency, because there was no consultation with the grassroots.

2. 50 per cent of the 130 seats in Congress are filled by a first-past-the-post (FPTP) system in 68 newly created single-member constituencies; the other 50 per cent are filled by a proportional representation (PR) list system in multi-member constituencies (there is a 3 per cent threshold for parties to enter Congress).

3. Signed by Sánchez de Lozada two days before the end of his first term.

4. That is, making economic aid conditional upon successful attempts to combat drug production and anything connected to it (*Red Andina de Información* (n.d.), 'Certificación').

5. Following Sartori, such a situation is characterized by small ideological distinctions between parties, an inclination to form coalitions and a centripetal pattern of competition (Mayorga, 1997: 149–51).

6. According to Paz E., he left his inauguration session early and while foreign dignitaries were still present, because he preferred to attend a meeting about economic policy (Arze Cuadros, 2002: 389).

7. There seems to have been a double standard operating as to when a violation of the rules of parliamentary ethics required the expulsion of an MP. Morales was the first MP to be expelled under the rule, although Bolivia has seen a number of political scandals where the rules were broken in a more serious fashion.

8. See, for instance, international newspapers summarized by NotiSur, 17

October 2003: 'Bolivia: President Gonzales Sánchez de Lozada's concessions fail to stop protests', www.notisur.com; *La Jornada de México*, 17 October 2003; 'Marcha Multitudinaria en La Paz al Grito ¡Que se vaya Goni!', www. jornada.unam.mx.

9. The plant of Senkarta has a special symbolic value since it is a remnant of the formerly national petroleum company YPFB, the revenues of which helped stabilize Bolivia's currency during the period of hyperinflation.

10. There were (unconfirmed) rumours – denied by the military – that one soldier was shot by his superior officer after he had refused to shoot at the protesters (Albó, 2004: 50).

11. The resolution remembered that the peoples have sovereignty over their natural resources, and it expressed condolences to the victims of the repression of the popular movements. The EP further called for the release of all those detained during the protests; for the protection of the life of social leaders such as Evo Morales; for an exhaustive investigation into the events and no granting of asylum to leaders summonsed by Bolivian courts (Source: RC\510935ES.doc).

12. See also *Miami Herald* and *El Mercurio de Chile*, both 17 October 2003

13. Exceptions to this have been several populist articulations (e.g. Generals Ovando and Torres in the 1970s and CONDEPA leader Paredes in the 1990s) that saw in 'the people' the virtue of life according to collective tradition and praised their sacrifices.

Chapter 6

1. According to Blommaert (2003), they either still own plots of land in these areas and relatives help them use the land productively, or they receive crops from relatives in exchange for what they bring from the Tropic.

2. For instance, after questions were raised about how MAS was able to locate its campaign headquarters in an expensive office building in La Paz, it gave journalists access to documents showing that it had been given access to the building by the electoral court. Another example was the filming of a television campaign spot, which took place openly on the ground floor of the campaign building.

3. In 2005, the press office of MAS consisted basically of three volunteers, among them a Spanish university lecturer on sabbatical, who did an incredible amount of work, but realistically it was impossible for him to fulfil all the required tasks.

4. Felix Santos later caused one of MAS's worst corruption scandals and was expelled from the party. This was a very painful episode for Morales since Felix Santos had been a close companion since the early days of MAS.

5. *Ayllu* is an ancient concept of discontinuous social space which cannot be mapped with clearly defined boundaries. Rather, it consists of territorial journeys, a social space that moves together with the population, 'materially spreading cultural immanence' (Prada Alcoreza, 2002: 90) with its rituals, festivities, collective imaginaries, and so on. Through this network of relationships the Tropic of Cochabamba, for instance, is connected with the 'Valle Alto' of Cochabamba and the Altiplano. Summarizing this perception,

Prada Alcoreza (2002) calls the *ayllu* 'a living territory' and the principle of 'bio-territoriality'.

6. The term *ponchos rojos* refers to the traditional outer garment worn in the Andes. But red is a very unusual colour, usually worn only in war. With small black stripes, red is reserved for the (male) elders of a community.

7. Villegas was first minister of development and then minister of hydrocarbons and energy. He has a Ph.D. in Development Studies and was a university lecturer.

8. An exception to this is, to some extent, the group of urban intellectuals within MAS, because their socio-economic background is very different from that of Morales. This group finds its role model in the figure of García Linera, as my interviews with some of them indicated.

Chapter 7

1. See   www.informa-tico.com/php/expat.php?id=23-01-06031034&ed= 84&fecha=23-01-06&foro=735; last accessed 26 November 2007.

2. We should note that there were exceptions to this general statement; parties like PODEMOS tried to construct an image of MAS as an external other of Venezuelan anti-democrats and Colombian drug traffickers opposed to the interests of the Bolivian people. However, such statements were isolated instances rather than part of the general discourse, and never acquired a credibility comparable to the statements of MAS.

3. A *coordinadora* is a loose association of social movements, of a kind that developed during the Water War (2000). This means of connecting social movements and the government represents a significant institutional innovation on the part of MAS in furtherance of its aim to bridge the gap between official institutions and civil society.

4. All quotations from interviews and from MAS documents were originally in Spanish. Translations are by the author.

5. See, for instance, Assies and Salman, 2003; Crabtree, 2005; Harten, 2006, among others.

6. It should be noted that the term *pueblos originarios* was not coined by MAS or the coca growers; it was first used by the indigenous movements from the eastern lowlands.

7. 'We are MAS; we are the People'. Or 'We are MORE, we are the People'.

8. Morales was talking about how MAS expected to win the 2005 elections in the face of the professional, mass-media campaign of its adversaries Quiroga and Doria Medina.

9. See, for instance, the first chapter ('Principios Ideológicos y Políticos') of the statutes of MAS (2004b: 1-24).

10. Arguably, the attempt to avoid any amalgamation of demands by following the logic of difference, which puts every demand in a well-defined category, satisfies them selectively and sets them off against each other, is the underlying reason for the political failure of the neoliberal policies pursued by ADN, MNR and MIR. Political failure is here understood as the inability to create a common imaginary for all Bolivians that would give lasting electoral legitimacy to the main articulator of this imaginary.

Chapter 8

1. These are: Decentralized Departments, Autonomous Departments, Autonomous Provinces, Autonomous Municipalities, Autonomous *Indigenous-Originario-Campesino* (IOC) Territories, Autonomous Regions, IOC Municipalities, IOC Regions, IOC Provincial Regions. In addition, departments have their own specific institutions, such as Provincial Councils in Santa Cruz, *Suyus* in Oruro, and Development Corporations in Cochabamba.
2. One example is two arrested EU citizens who are suspected of having planned a terrorist attack in 2009, and who should, according to Vice President García Linera, be tried for treason.
3. See http://masbolivia.org/nacional/politica/transicion.htm; last consulted 23 August 2007.
4. The notion of a mosaic was first put forward by the *Kataristas* in the 1970s.
5. Half-moon refers to the combined shape of the eastern departments Santa Cruz, Tarija, Pando and Beni.
6. Foundationalism denotes the establishment of sharp political frontiers between a near or threatening past, which is demonized and considered illegitimate, and a propitious future that marks a contrast with the past that ought to have been left behind. This means that foundationalism implies an excess of hegemonic articulations and the construction of a chain of equivalence. The threat of a reversion to this past situation – through the breakdown of the frontier separating it from the present – is one of the most effective mechanisms for defending the populist movement, which had constructed these frontiers against its political opponents. Foundationalism and hegemonism are thus for Aboy Carlés the most extreme form of the tension between inclusion and exclusion that typifies populism as a mode of articulation.
7. The 'Declaration of Tiahuanacu' (1973) is one of the early documents in which the *Kataristas* expressed the need for an independent cultural development, in light of the threat posed by international agents (Materne, 1976: 19–28).
8. Lithium is the link to the future, because Bolivia has important reserves that have not yet been exploited.
9. 'Coca' is able to provide existentialist answers by symbolically linking the past, present and future, since it is presented as an ancient plant with important cultural, medical and economic value (see Chapter 5).

Chapter 9

1. Silvia De la Arcón was a member of the MAS working group that proposed the Ley Marcelo Quiroga Santa Cruz Contra La Corrupción Y La Impunidad (Law against Corruption and Impunity).

References

Aboy Carlés, G. (2005a). 'La democratización beligerante del populismo'. *Congreso de la Sociedad Argentina de Análisis Político*. Córdoba.

Aboy Carlés, G. (2005b). 'Populismo y democracia en la Argentina contemporánea. Entre el hegemonismo y la refundación'. *Estudios Sociales* 28. Santa Fe: Universidad Nacional del Litoral.

Albó, X. (1994). 'And from Kataristas to MNRistas? The Surprising and Bold Alliance between Aymaras and Neoliberals in Bolivia'. In D.Van Cott (ed.), *Indigenous Peoples and Democracy in Latin America*. London: Macmillan.

Albó, X. (2002a). 'Bolivia: From Indian and Campesino Leaders to Councillors and Parliamentary Deputies'. In R. Sieder (ed.), *Multiculturalism in Latin America: Indigenous Rights, Diversity and Democracy*. London: Macmillan.

Albó, X. (2002b). 'La nueva correlación campesino-indigena en el parlamento'. In *Articulo Primero: Revista de debate social y jurídico* 6 (11). Santa Cruz: Centro de Estudios Jurídicos e Investigación Social (CEJS).

Albó, X. (2004). '222 años después: la convulsionada Bolivia multiétnica'. In *Articulo Primero: Revista de debate social y jurídico* 8 (16). Santa Cruz: Centro de Estudios Jurídicos e Investigación Social (CEJS).

Albó, X., Ticona, E., and Rojas, G. (1995). *Votos y Whipalas. Campesinos y Pueblos Originarios en Democracia*. La Paz: Fundación Milenio and CIPCA.

Alvarez, S., Dagnino, E., and Escobar, A. (1998). *Cultures of Politics/Politics of Cultures: Revisioning Latin American Social Movements*. Boulder CO: Westview Press.

Amnesty International (2004). *BOLIVIA: Crisis and Justice – Days of Violence in February and October 2003*. AI Index: AMR 18/006/2004.

Anderson, B. (1983). *Imagined Communities: Reflections on the Origins and Spread of Nationalism*. London: Verso.

Arditi, B. (2004). 'Populism as a Spectre of Democracy: A Response to Canovan'. *Political Studies* 52, pp. 135–43.

Armand Ugon, M., and Loza Machicado, G. (1989). *Movimientos Populares y Neoliberalismo en Bolivia: El caso de los productores de coca del Chapare Tropical. 1985–1989*. Master's thesis, Universidad Iberoamericana, Mexico DF.

Arrueta Rodriguez, J.A. (1992). *Estrechas Sendas de la Participación, La acción colectiva de los productores de coca de Cochabamba: Entre la participación real y la participación simbólica*, Cochabamba: Universiad Mayor de San Simon (UMSS).

Arze Cuadros, E. (2002). *El Programa del MNR y la Revolución Nacional*. La Paz: Plural.

Assies, W., and Salman, T. (2003). *Crisis in Bolivia: The Elections of 2002 and Their Aftermath*. London: Chartered Institute of Housing/Institute of Latin American Studies.

Barros, S. (2002). *Orden, democracia y estabilidad. Discurso y política en la Argentina entre 1976 y 1991*. Córdoba: Alción.

Barros, S. (2003). 'La especificidad inclusiva del populismo'. Paper presented at VIth Congreso Nacional de Ciencia Política. Rosario, Argentina.

Barros, S. (2005). 'Espectralidad e inestabilidad institucional. Acerca de la ruptura populista'. Paper presented at VII Congreso Nacional de Ciencia Política, 15–18 November. Córdoba, Argentina.

Barros, S. (2006). 'Inclusión radical y conflicto en la constitución del pueblo populista'. *Confines* 2 (3), pp. 65–73.

Bayart, J.F. (1999). *The Criminalisation of the State in Africa*. Oxford: James Currey.

Blanes, J. (1983). *De los Valles Al Chapare. Estrategías familiares en un contexto de cambios*. Cochabamba: CERES.

Blanes, J., and Flores, G. (1984). *Donde va el Chapare?* Cochabamba: CERES.

Blommaert, E. (2003). *Geweld, verzet en onzekerheid: De invloed van de drugsoorlog op de rurale bestaansstrategieën in een dorp in de tropen van Cochabamba, Bolivia*. M.Sc. dissertation, Department of Anthropology, Utrecht University.

Böhrt Irahola, C., and Chávez Reyes, S. (2002). *Elecciones 2002: Resultados y Transformaciones*. La Paz: FUNDEMOS.

BolPress (2007). *Opinión: Cartas: Enrevista on-line a Raul Prada (MAS)*. www.bolpress.com/art.php?Cod=2007061111; accessed 15 September 2007.

Brechner, J. (2006). *Bolivia hacia el totalitarismo*. http://brechner.typepad.com/jose_brechner/2006/03/bolivia_hacia_e.html; accessed 20 March 2008.

Calderón, F. (1988). *Busquedas y Bloqueos*. La Paz: CERES.

Calderón, F., and Dandler, J. (eds) (1983). *Bolivia: La Fuerza Histórica del Campesinado*. Mexico: UNRISD.

Calderón, F., and Jelin, E. (1987). *Clases y movimientos sociales en América Latina*. Buenos Aires: CEDES.

Canovan, M. (2005). *The People*. Cambridge: Polity Press.

Carter, W., and Mamani, M. (1986). *La Coca en Bolivia*. La Paz: Editorial Juventud.

Castoriadis, C. (1987). *The Imaginary Institution of Society*. Cambridge: Polity.

CEDIB (1990). *Coca por Desarrollo? Sobre la Fuerza Social del Chapare*. Cochabamba: CEDIB.

Céspedes, A. (1956). *El Dictador Suicida*. Santiago de Chile: Editorial Universitaria.

Chávez, W. (2002). 'La persecución de Rocha. ¿Favoreció o perjudicó al MAS?'. *El Juguete Rabioso*, 21 July, p. 8.

Chávez, W. (2005). MAS avanza en la conformación de un frente social. *El Juguete Rabioso*, 24 July, p. 8.

Coca Antezana, O., et al. (1999). *Cifras y Datos del Desarrollo Alternativo en Bolivia*. Cochabamba: CEDIB.

Cohen, J. (1985). 'Strategy or Identity: New Theoretical Paradigms and Contemporary Social Movements'. *Social Research* 52 (4), pp. 663–716.

Conaghan, C.M. (1992). 'Capitalists, Technocrats and Politicians: Economic Policy Making and Democracy in the Central Andes.' In S. Mainwaring, G. O'Donnell and J. Valenzuela (eds), *Issues in Democratic Consolidation: The New South American Democracies in Comparative Perspective*, pp. 199–242. South Bend IN: University of Notre Dame Press.

Contreras Baspineiro, A. (2005). *Evo – una historia de dignidad*. Cochabamba: Editora JV.

Crabtree, J. (2005). *Patterns of Protest. Politics and Social Movements in Bolivia*. London: Latin America Bureau.

Cuadros Quiroga, J. (1942). 'Bases y Principios de Acción Inmediate del MNR'. Reprinted in E. Arze Cuadros (2002), *El Programa del MNR y la Revolución Nacional*, pp. 605–43. La Paz: Plural.

Dalton, R., and Wattenberg, M. (eds) (2000). *Parties without Partisans: Political Change in Advanced Industrial Democracies*. Oxford: Oxford University Press.

D'Anieri, P., et al. (1990). 'New Social Movements in Historical Perspective'. *Comparative Politics* 22 (4), pp. 445–58.

Dangle, B. (2003). *Bolivian Government Falling Apart: The Autumn of 'El Gringo' Lozada?* Cochabamba: Andean Information Network. www.counterpunch.org/dangl10182003.html; accessed 5 March 2005.

Davis, G. (ed.) (2005). *Social Movements and Organization Theory*. Cambridge: Cambridge University Press.

Della Porta, D. (1995). *Social Movements, Political Violence and the State*. Cambridge: Cambridge University Press.

Dix, R. (1992). 'Democratisation and the Institutionalisation of Latin American Political Parties'. *Comparative Political Studies* 24 (4), pp. 488–511.

Domingo, P. (2003). 'Revolution and the Unfinished Business of Nation – and State-Building'. In M. Grindle and P. Domingo, *Proclaiming Revolution: Bolivia in Comparative Perspective*, pp. 364–380. London: Institute of Latin American Studies.

Domingo, P. (2005). 'Democracy and New Social Forces in Bolivia'. *Social Forces* 83 (4), pp. 1727–44.

Economist (2007). 'Drug Trafficking in Peru', 3 May, p. 61.

El Mercurio de Chile (2003). 'Goni Descarta Gobierno De Transición', 17 October 2003. In D. Velásquez Espejo, *Noticias del Mar Boliviano*. http://elmarboliviano.blogspot.com/2003_10_17_elmarboliviano_archive.html; accessed 5 March 2003.

El Sol (2002). 'El MAS es anti-neoliberal', July, p. 7.

Escobar, A., and Alvarez, S. (eds) (1992). *The Making of Social Movements in Latin America: Identity, Strategy and Democracy*. Boulder CO: Westview Press.

Estellano, W., and Nava-Ragazzi, K. (1994). 'From Populism to Coca Economy in Bolivia'. *Latin American Perspectives* 21 (4), pp. 34–45.

Galeano, E. (2004). 'El país que quiere existir'. *Articulo Primero* 16, April, Santa Cruz: CEIJS.

Gamarra, E. (1996). 'Bolivia: Managing Democracy in the 1990s'. In J. Domínguez and A. Lowenthal, *Constructing Democratic Governance: Latin America and the Caribbean in the 1990s*, pp. 72–95. Baltimore: Johns Hopkins University Press.

Gamarra, E. (2001). 'Has Bolivia Won the War? Lessons from Plan Dignidad'. Paper presented at the workshop 'Political Economy of the Drug Industry', 14 June, Utrecht University.

Gamarra, E. (2002). 'Cuando la innovación no es suficiente: ruptura democrática en Bolivia'. In C. Freres and K. Pacheco (eds), *Nuevos Horizontes Andinos*, pp. 11–37. Caracas: Nueva Sociedad.

Gamarra, E. (2003). 'Political Parties Since 1964: The Construction of Bolivia's Multiparty System'. In M. Grindle and P. Domingo (eds), *Proclaiming Revolution: Bolivia in Comparative Perspective*, pp. 289–317. London: Institute of Latin American Studies.

Gamarra, E., and Malloy, J. (1995). 'The Patrimonial Dynamics of Party Politics in Bolivia.' In S. Mainwaring and T. Scully (eds), *Building Democratic Institutions: Party Systems in Latin America*, pp. 399–432. Stanford CA: Stanford University Press.

García Arganas, F. (1997). 'The Drug War at the Supply End'. *Latin American Perspectives* 24 (5), pp. 59–80.

García Linera, A. (2002). 'El ocaso de un ciclo estatal'. In R. Gutiérrez, A. García Linera, R. Prada and L. Tapía, *Democratizaciones Plebeyas*, pp. 9–22. La Paz: Muela del Diablo.

García Linera, A. (2004). 'Como lograr la hegemonía indígena-popular en la constituyente?' *Jugete Rabioso*, 12 December, pp. 8–9.

García Linera, A. (2005). 'La lucha por el poder en Bolivia'. In A. García Linera, L. Tapia, O. Vega Camacho and R. Prada, *Horizontes y limites del estado y el poder*, pp. 11–76. La Paz: Muela del Diablo.

García Linera, A., Tapia, L., Vega Camacho, O., and Prada, R. (2005). *Horizontes y límites del estado y el poder*. La Paz: Muela del Diablo.

García Orellana, A., García Yapur, F., and Quitón H., L. (2003). *La 'Guerra del Agua'. Abril de 2000, la crisis de la política en Bolivia*. La Paz: PIEB.

Gramsci, A. (1971). *Selections From the Prison Notebooks*, trans. Q. Hoare and G. Nowell Smith. London: Lawrence & Wishart.

Grindle, M. (2003a). '1952 and All That: The Bolivian Revolution in Comparative Perspective'. In M. Grindle and P. Domingo, *Proclaiming Revolution: Bolivia in Comparative Perspective*, pp. 1–24. London: Institute of Latin American Studies.

Grindle, M. (2003b). 'Shadowing the Past? Policy reform in Bolivia, 1985–2002'. In M. Grindle and P. Domingo, *Proclaiming Revolution: Bolivia in Comparative Perspective*, pp. 318–44. London: Institute of Latin American Studies.

Groppo, A. (2003). 'The Two Princes. Discourse Analysis and Comparative Populism: A Study of the Political Emergence of Peronism in Argentina and Varguism in Brazil'. Paper presented at the VI Congreso Nacional de Ciencia Política, 5–8 November.

Guevara Arze, W. (1947). 'Teoria, Medios y Fines de la Revolucion Nacional – Tesis de Ayopaya'. Reprinted in W. Guevara Arze, *Bases para replantear la Revolución Nacional*. La Paz: Editorial Juventud, 1988.

Gutiérrez, R., Tapia, L., Prada Alcoreza, R., and García Linera, A. (2002). *Democratizaciones Plebeyas*. La Paz: Muela del Diablo.

Hahn, D. (1996). 'The Use and Abuse of Ethnicity: The Case of the Bolivian CSUTCB'. *Latin American Perspectives* 23 (2), pp. 91–106.

Harten, S. (2006). 'The Convergence of Social Movements: Hope for Democracy?'. *Bolivian Studies Journal* 13.

Harten, S. (2007). '¿Hacia un partido "tradicional"? Un análisis del cambio organizativo interno en el Movimiento Al Socialismo (MAS) en Bolivia', *Nuevo Mundo Mundos Nuevos*, Coloquios, http://nuevomundo.revues.org//index4468.html.

Healy, K. (1991). 'Political Ascent of Bolivia's Peasant Coca Leaf Producers'. *Journal of Interamerican Studies and World Affairs* 33 (1), pp. 87–121.

Healy, K. (2001). *Llamas, Weavings, and Organic Chocolate. Multicultural Grassroot Development in the Andes and the Amazon of Bolivia*. South Bend IN: University of Notre Dame Press.

Horowitz, D. (2000). *Ethnic Groups in Conflict*. Berkeley: University of California Press.

Howarth, D. (2000). *Discourse*. Buckingham and Philadelphia: Open University Press.

Howarth, D., Norval, A., and Stavrakakis, Y. (2000). *Discourse Theory and Political Analysis*. Manchester: Manchester University Press.

Howarth, D., and Torfing, J. (eds). (2005). *Discourse Theory in European Politics: Identity, Policy, and Governance*. New York: Palgrave Macmillan.

Ibáñez Rojo, E. (2000). 'The UDP Government and the Crisis of the Bolivian Left, 1982–1985'. *Journal of Latin American Studies* 32, pp. 175–205.

IMF (International Monetary Fund) (2010). 'IMF Executive Board Concludes 2009 Article IV Consultation with Bolivia'. Public Information Notice (PIN) No. 10/09, 21 January.

Indymedia Bolivia (2007). 'Entrevista: Carlos Sánchez de Berzaín', 23 September, http://bolivia.indymedia.org/node/1393; accessed 1 October 2007.

Informa-tico (2006). 'Bolivia: Ama quella, ama llulla, ama sua'. *Informa-tico.com* 4 (84), 23 January, www.informa-tico.com/php/expat.php?id=23-01-06031034&ed=84&fecha=23-01-06&foro=735; accessed 26 November 2007.

Iriate, G. (2004). *Análisis Crítico de la Realidad*, 15th edn. Cochabamba: Grupo Editorial Kipus.

Janssen, J., Melis, V., Nootens, G., Oomen, J., Rijnhout, L., and Ríos, T., (2003). *De Wereld van Kook. Over coca en een 500 jaar oud mis(ver)stand*. Antwerp: Boliviacentrum.

Katz, R., and Mair, P. (1997). 'Party Organization, Party Democracy, and the Emergence of the Cartel Party'. In P. Mair, *Party System Change. Approaches and Interpretations*, pp. 93–119. Oxford: Clarendon Press.

Klein, H. (1969). *Parties and Political Change in Bolivia, 1880–1952*. Cambridge: Cambrige University Press.

Kohl, B. (2002). 'Stabilising Neo-liberalism in Bolivia: Popular Participation and Privatisation'. *Political Geography* 21: 449–72.

Laclau, E. (1990). *New Reflections on the Revolution of Our Time*. London: Verso.

Laclau, E. (1996). 'Why Do Empty Signifiers Matter in Politics?' In E. Laclau, *Emancipation(s)*. London: Verso.

Laclau, E. (2005). 'Populism: What's in a Name?'. In F. Panizza (ed.), *Populism and the Mirror of Democracy*, pp. 32–49. London: Verso.

Laclau, E., and Mouffe, C. (1985). *Hegemony and Socialist Strategy*. London: Verso.

Lagos, M. (1996). 'The Latinobarómetro: Media and Political Attitudes in South America'. Paper presented at the meeting of the American Political Science Association (APSA), 29 August–1 September, San Francisco.

Lagos, M. (1997). 'Latin America's Smiling Mask'. *Journal of Democracy* 8 (3), pp. 125–38.

La Nación – Argentina (2010). 'Evonomics, la ortodoxia a la boliviana'. *La Nación*, 26 September, www.lanacion.com.ar/nota.asp?nota_id=1308098.

La Prensa (2007). 'Evo defiende a Fidel, critica a Bush y pide a la ONU otra sede'. *La Prensa*, 27 September, www.cedib.org/pcedib/?module= displaystory&story_ id=20236&format=html; accessed 28 September 2007.

La Razón (2003). 'En 20 años hubo 148 muertos en conflictos y ninguna se aclaró'. *La Razón*, 31 January, p. 2.

La Razón (2007). 'El Gobierno tiene 3 frentes de conflicto'. *La Razón*, 12 June, www.la-razon.com/versiones/20070612_005935/nota_247_438959.htm.

Laserna, R. (1996). *Veinte juicios y prejuicios sobre coca-cocaina*. La Paz: CLAVE.

Laserna, R., Cortés, J., Ledo, C., Ramírez, A., and Valdevieso, R. (1995). *Sostenibilidad y Desarrollo Humano. Calidad de Vida en Cochabamba*. Cochabamba: Los Amigos del Libro.

La Voz (2005). 'Exige Diculpa Pública'. *La Voz*, 12 November, p. 3.

Lazar, S. (2004). 'Personalist Politics, Clientelism and Citizenship: Local Elections in El Alto, Bolivia'. *Bulletin of Latin American Research* 23 (2), pp. 228–43.

Levy, J. (2008). 'Koka ist nicht Kokain. Plädoyer für eine vielseitige Nutzpflanze'. *Le Monde Diplomatique*, 9 May, pp. 8–9.

Linz, J., and Stepan, A. (1996). *Problems of Democratic Transition and Consolidation*. Baltimore MD: Johns Hopkins University Press.

Los Tiempos (2002). 'Embajador Rocha advirtió los Bolivianos de no votar por Evo Morales'. *Los Tiempos*, 27 June, p. 1.

Los Tiempos (2005). 'Obispos escuchan a las preocupaciones de Evo'. *Los Tiempos – Usted Elige*, 16 November, p. A3.

Loyaza C. (2001). *Tierra Territorio. Instrumento Político*. Cochabamba: Chajra Runaj Masis.

Luckham, R., Goetz, A.-M., and Kaldor, M. (2003). 'Democratic Institutions and Democratic Politics'. In S. Bastian and R. Luckham. *Can Democracy be Designed?*, pp. 14–59. London: Zed Books.

Luxemburg, R. (1940). *The Russian Revolution*. New York: Workers Age Publishers. www.marxists.org/archive/luxemburg/1918/russian-revolution/index.htm.

Mainwaring, S. (1988). 'Political Parties in Brazil and the Southern Cone'. *Comparative Politics* 21 (1): 91–120.

Mainwaring, S., O'Donnell, G., and Valenzuela, J.S. (eds) (1992). *Issues in Democratic Consolidation: The New South American Democracies in Comparative Perspective*. South Bend IN: University of Notre Dame Press.

Mainwaring, S., Bejarano, A., and Pizzaro Leongómez, E. (2006). *The Crisis of Democratic Representation in the Andes*. Palo Alto CA: Stanford University Press.

Malloy, J. (1970). *Bolivia: The Uncompleted Revolution*. Pittsburg: University of Pittsburg Press.

Massal, J., and Bonilla, M. (2000). *Los Movimientos Sociales en las democracias Andinas*. Quito: FLASCO Ecuador – IFEA.

Materne, Y. (1976). *The Indian Awakening in Latin America*. New York: Friendship Press.

Mayorga, R. (ed.) (1987). *Democracia a la Deriva. Dilemas de la participación y concertación social en Bolivia*. La Paz: CLACSO and CERES.

Mayorga, R. (1997). 'Bolivia's Silent Revolution'. *Journal of Democracy* 8 (1), pp.142–56.

Mayorga, R. (2006). 'Outsiders and Neopopulism: The Road to Plebiscary Democracy'. In S. Mainwaring, A. Bejerano and E. Pizzaro Leongómez, *The Crisis of Representation in the Andes*, pp. 132–69. Palo Alto CA: Stanford University Press.

Mayorga, R., and Gorman, S. (1978). 'National-Popular State, State Capitalism and Military Dictatorship in Bolivia: 1952–1975'. *Latin American Perspectives* 5 (2), pp. 89–119.

McAdam, D. (1982). *Political Process and the Development of Black Insurgency, 1930–1970*. Chicago: University of Chicago Press.

McAdam, D., McCarthy, J., and Zald, M. (eds) (1996). *Comparative Perspectives on Social Movements*. Cambridge: Cambridge University Press.

Montenegro, C. (1990). *Nacionalismo y Coloniaje*. La Paz: Juventud (1943).

Morales, A. (2003). 'The National Revolution and its Legacy'. In M. Grindle and P. Domingo (eds), *Proclaiming Revolution: Bolivia in Comparative Perspective*, pp. 213–31. London: Institute of Latin American Studies.

Morales, R. (1984). *Desarrollo y Pobreza en Bolivia*. La Paz: UNICEF.

Morales, R. (1990). *Áreas de Pobreza en Bolivia*. La Paz: Caritas Boliviana.

Morales Peña, C. (2007). *Jorge Tuto Quiroga: 'Vamos a apoyar las autonomías por los pueblos indígenas'*, 2 March. www.podemosbolivia.com/n20070302.htm; accessed 26 September 2007.

Mouffe, C. (1993). *The Return of the Political*. London: Verso.

MAS (Movimiento Al Socialismo) (2004a). *Estatuto Orgánico*. La Paz: GRAFIVAL.

MAS (Movimiento Al Socialismo) (2004b). 'Principios Ideológicos y Políticos'. In MAS, *Estatuto Orgánico. Poder. Territorio. Sabiduría*, pp. 1–24. La Paz: GRAFIVAL.

MAS (Movimiento Al Socialismo) (2005a). *Elecciones Nacionales 2005. Plan de gobierno y propuesta del MAS*. Pamphlet.

MAS (Movimiento Al Socialismo) (2005b). *Propuesta intergral para el poder y el bienestar comunitario. Informe final sobre programa de gobierno*, 4 July. Cochabamba: Internal document of MAS, Comisión IV: Soberanía e identidad nacional.

O'Donnell, G. (1992). 'Transitions, Continuities and Paradoxes'. In S. Mainwaring, G. O'Donnell and J. Valenzuela (eds), *Issues in Democratic Consolidation: The New South American Democracies in Comparative Perspective*. South Bend IN: University of Notre Dame Press

Olson, M. (1992). *La Lógica de la Acción Colectiva, Bienes Públicos y la Teoría de Grupos*. Mexico City: Limusa Noriega Editores.

Oomen, J. (2003). *Coca – Geschenk van de Goden*. Antwerp: Boliviacentrum

Oporto, H. (1998). *La descentralización en Bolivia*. La Paz: ILDIS.

Orgáz García, M. (2004). *La guerra del gas*, 3rd edn. La Paz: C&C Editores.

Painter, J. (1994). *Bolivia and Coca: A Study in Dependency*. Boulder CO and London: Lynne Rienner.

Panizza, F. (2005a). 'Unarmed Utopia Revisited: The resurgence of Left of Centre Politics in Latin America'. *Political Studies* 53, pp. 716–34.

Panizza, F. (ed.) (2005b). *Populism and the Mirror of Democracy*. London: Verso.

Panizza, F. (2007). 'The Fault Lines of Populism and Democracy in Latin America'. Congress of the Latin American Studies Association, Montreal, 5–8 September.

PASOC – Equipo de Análisis de Conyuntura de la Pastoral Sociál Caritas (2004). 'Una nueva irrupción de los movimientos sociales en el siglo XXI'. In *Articulo Primero* 8 (16). Santa Cruz: Centro de Estudios Jurídicos e Investigación Social (CEJS).

Paz Estenssorro, V. (1955). *Discursos Parlamentarios*. La Paz: Editorial Canata.

Pendergrast, M. (1993). *God, Country and Coca-Cola*. London: Macmillan.

Peralta García, M. (2005). 'Bolivia: Democracia en Transición'. *Foro de Análisis Político* 2 (7), pp. 59–78.

Pérez, P. (2007). *'Yo Soy Un Refugiado Político'. Eentrevista con Carlos Sánchez de Berzaín*, 19 September. www.radiofides.com/entrevistas_proc.asp?ID=3; accessed 30 September 2007.

Pettersson, B., and MacKay, L. (1993). *Human Rights Violations from the 'War on Drugs' in Bolivia*. Cochabamba: RAI.

Plamenatz, J. (1976). 'Two Types of Nationalism'. In E. Kamenka, *Nationalism: The Nature and Evolution of an Idea*, pp. 22–36. London: Edward Arnold.

PODEMOS (Poder Democrático y Social) (2005a). *Programa de Gobierno 2006–2010*. La Paz: PODEMOS.

PODEMOS (Poder Democrático y Social) (2005b). *Constituyente Para La Gente. Proyecto de Constitución Política del Estado*. La Paz: PODEMOS.

Prada Alcoreza, R. (2002). 'Multitud y Contrapoder. Estudio del presente: movimientos sociales contemporáneos.' In R. Gutiérrez et. al., *Democratizaciones Plebeyas*, pp. 73–146. La Paz: Muela del Diablo Editores.

Prada Alcoreza, R. (2004). *Largo Octubre*. La Paz: Plural.

Quijano, A. (2000). 'Los movimientos campesinos contemporáneos en América Latina'. *Observatorio Social de América Latina*, September, pp. 171–80.

Quispe, J. (2007). *La Trasición del Estado Nación hacía un Estado Plurinacional*, 29 June. http://masbolivia.org/nacional/politica/transicion.htm; accessed 23 August 2007.

Ramos Cachi, V. (2001). 'La militarización de la erradicación de cultivos de coca. Institucionalización y encubrimiento de las violaciones de los Derechos Humanos'. *Acción Andina* 4, pp. 125–36.

Red Andina de Información (2001). 'Coca no es cocaína'. www.scbbs-bo.com/ain/coca; accessed 12 March 2001.

Red Andina de Información (2007a). 'US Influence and Impact in Bolivia. Certification Process Conditions Economic Assistance', 30 January. http://ain-bolivia. org/index.php?option=com_content&task=view&id=62&Itemid=32; accessed 3 September 2007.

Red Andina de Información (2007b). 'Human Rights and the War on Drugs', 30 January. http://ain-bolivia.org/index.php?option=com_content&task=view&id= 63&Itemid=28; accessed 3 September 2007.

Red Andina de Información (2007c). 'ONDCP Reports No Increase in Coca Cultivation in Bolivia in 2007', 23 May. http://ain-bolivia.org/index.php?option= com_content&task=view&id=88&Itemid=28; accessed 20 July 2008.

Red Andina de Información (2007d). *Political Analysis: Bolivia's Constitutional Assembly*

Temporarily Suspended, 24 August. http://ain-bolivia.org/index.php?option=com_content&task=view&id=95&Itemid=32; accessed 3 September 2007.

Rensselaer, L. (2001). 'Perversely Harmful Effects of Counter Narcotics Policies in the Andes'. Paper presented at the workshop 'Political Economy of the Drug Industry', Utrecht University, 14 June.

Rivera Cusocanqui, S. (1987). 'Autonomía y dependencia en el movimiento campesino contemporáneo'. In R. Mayorga (ed.), *Democracia a la Deriva. Dilemas de la participación y concertación social en Bolivia*, pp. 243–80. La Paz: CLACSO and CERES.

Rivera Pizarro, A. (1991). *Que Sabemos Del Chapare?*. Cochabamba: CERES.

Rolón Anaya, M. (1999). *Politica y partidos en Bolivia*, 3rd edn. La Paz: Libreria Editorial Juventud.

Romero Bonifaz, C. (2004). 'Las jornadas de octubre: levantamiento popular en Bolivia'. *Articulo Primero* 8 (16). La Paz: CEJS.

Rubín de Celis, P. (2000). *Del Nacionalismo Revolucionary Al Desierto Neoliberal*. La Paz: Fondo Editorial de los Diputados.

Sanabria, H. (1993). *The Coca Boom and Rural Change in Bolivia*. Michigan: University of Michigan Press.

Sandoval Rodriguez, I. (1970). *Nacionalismo en Bolivia*. La Paz: E. Burillo.

Sanjinés C.J. (2002). 'Mestizaje Upside Down: Subaltern Knowledges and the Known'. *Nepantla: Views from South* 3 (1), pp. 39–60.

Scully, M., and Creed, D. (2005). 'Subverting Our Stories of Subversion'. In G. Davis et al. (eds), *Social Movements and Organization Theory*. Cambridge: Cambridge University Press.

Smith, A. (1986). *The Ethnic Origins of Nations*. Oxford: Blackwell.

Snow, D., Burke Rochford, E., Worden, S., and Benford, R. (1986). 'Frame Alignment Processes, Micromobilization, and Movement Participation'. *American Sociological Review* 51, pp. 464–81.

Soberanía (2002a). 'Causachun coca, Wañuchun yanquis'. *Soberanía – Movimiento al Socialismo MAS-IPSP* 2 (7), 9 June, p. 3.

Soberanía (2002b). 'El Alto nos recibió.' *Soberanía – Movimiento al Socialismo MAS-IPSP* 2 (7), 9 June, p. 6.

Soberanía.org. (2003). 'Goni, una empresa transnacional', 15 October. *Soberanía.org*. online magazine (Carácas, Venezuela). www.soberania.org/Articulos/articulo_531.htm; accessed 9 June 2008.

Ströbele-Gregor, J. (1997). 'Ley de Participación Popular y movimiento popular in Bolivia'. Paper presented at the Congreso de la Asociación Alemana de Investigación sobre América Latina (ADLAF), October.

Suárez, J. (2003). *Una Semana Fundamental. 10–18 Octubre 2003*. La Paz: Muela del Diablo.

Tapia, L. (2005). 'El Presidente Colonial'. In A. García Linera, L. Tapia, O. Vega Camacho and R. Prada Alcoreza, *Horizontes y límites del estado y el poder*, pp. 77–112. La Paz: Muela del Diablo.

UN (Unidad Nacional) (2005). *Dar la cara por Bolivia. Soluciones. Acciones de Gobierno 2006-2010*. La Paz: Unidad Nacional.

UNODC (2002). *Bolivia coca cultivation survey for 2001*. New York: United Nations

Office On Drugs and Crime. www.unodc.org/unodc/en/crop-monitoring/previous-surveys.html; accessed 17 March 2003.

Urioste, M. (1987). 'Concertación o hegemonía? La gestión del gobierno de la UDP'. In R. Mayorga (ed.), *Democracia a la derriva. Dilemas de la participación y concertación social en Bolivia*, pp. 281–96. La Paz: CLASCO and CERES.

Van Cott, D.L. (2000). *The Friendly Liquidation of the Past: The Politics of Diversity in Latin America*. Pittsburgh: Pittsburgh University Press.

Van Cott, D.L. (2005). *From Movements to Parties in Latin America: The Evolution of Ethnic Politics*. Cambridge: Cambridge University Press.

Van Lindert, P., and Nijenhuis, G. (2002). 'Popular Participation and the Participatory Planning Practice in Latin America: Some Evidence from Bolivia and Brazil'. In I. Baud and J. Post (eds), *Re-aligning Actors in an Urbanizing World. Government and Institutions from a Development Perspective*, pp. 175–96. Farnham: Ashgate.

Vargas Meza, R. (1997). 'Colombia: The Heresy of the Mancheans'. In M. Jelsma (ed.), *Democracy, Human Rights, and Militarism in The War on Drugs in Latin America*. Guatemala City: TNI, Cedib and Inforpress Centroamericana.

Viteri, A. (2004). 'Tierra y territorio como derechos'. *Pueblos* 14, pp. 30–31.

Whitehead, L. (2003). 'The Bolivian National Revolution: A Comparison'. In M. Grindle and P. Domingo (eds), *Proclaiming Revolution: Bolivia in Comparative Perspective*, pp. 25–53. London: Institute of Latin American Studies.

Yañez, C.E. (2002). 'Cultura y Migración Campesina.' In A. Argandoña and C. Ascarrunz (eds), *Futuro del Trópico de Cochabamba: Escenarios para el Desarrollo Sostenible*, pp. 5–55. Cochabamba: Universidad Mayor de San Simón.

Zambrana V., J. (2005). *Dimensiones socioculturales andinas en las transformaciones del sistema educativo boliviano*. Doctoral thesis, Université Catholique de Louvain, Louvain la Neuve.

Zavaletta Mercado, R. (1986). *Lo nacional-popular en Bolivia*. Mexico City: Siglo XXI.

Zunes, S. (2001). 'The United States and Bolivia. The Taming of a Revolution, 1952–1957'. *Latin American Perspectives* 120, 28 (5): 33–49.

Index